JOSTEIN SAETHER was bor: studied Waldorf education, painting and art theory and has worked as an artist, an exhibition designer and colour consultant. He also co-founded the Skilleby Atelier artists' community in Järna, Sweden, and has painted many murals in public and private buildings. More recently he has taught colour theory, painting, aesthetics and stage design at the Rudolf Steiner Seminar in Järna. He is now involved in research, seminar and counselling work in the field of spiritual development. He lives in Saarland, Germany.

LIVING WITH INVISIBLE PEOPLE

A KARMIC AUTOBIOGRAPHY

JOSTEIN SAETHER

CLAIRVIEW

For Sigrid Mørch-Reiersen (1895–1986) in spirit unity,
For my life's friends in love,
For my contemporaries in gratitude,
For my children in hope.

Clairview Books
An imprint of Temple Lodge Publishing
Hillside House, The Square
Forest Row, East Sussex
RH18 5ES

www.clairviewbooks.com

First published in English by Clairview 2001

Translated from German by J. Collis

Originally published in German under the title *Wandeln unter unsichtbaren Menschen, Eine karmische Autobiographie* by Verlag Urachhaus, Stuttgart 1999. This edition has been substantially restructured and reedited by Clairview Books

A catalogue record for this book is available from the British Library

ISBN 1 902636 26 0

Cover by Andrew Morgan Design
Typeset by DP Photosetting, Aylesbury, Bucks.
Printed and bound by Cromwell Press Limited, Trowbridge, Wilts.

Contents

Publisher's Foreword

In recent years many people have claimed to have had memories of previous incarnations on earth, and the subject of past lives has become much more common within the general culture, but the work of Jostein Saether represents a new departure in the field. Saether is pioneering a new method, at once spiritual and scientific, of gathering such information. Whereas many in the field of past-life studies use regression techniques, guided meditations, mediumship, channelling, dreams, etc., Saether gained his insights through a programme of specific mental exercises and personal meditation. These practices eventually led him to be able to 'see clearly'—to genuine 'clairvoyance' in the technical sense of the term. By developing this ability and directing it, Saether was able actively, and in full consciousness, to 'research' his past lives. (In older esoteric texts this is referred to as 'reading the Akashic Record'.) The important distinction in relation to other methods is that here the individual is always fully awake and aware, and is extending and accentuating his or her senses rather than dimming them.

The methods Saether used to research past lives derive from those formulated by the Austrian-born philosopher and spiritual scientist Rudolf Steiner. Towards the end of his life, during the year 1924, Steiner spoke at great length about his spiritual research into various incarnations and karmic relationships of a number of well-known individuals.* In the same lectures he also gave suggestions as to how others could replicate and develop his

---

* *Karmic Relationships*, Vols. I–VIII, London: Rudolf Steiner Press.

research. Jostein Saether has adapted these methods for his own use. In this book he publishes his preliminary results.

As this is a new, pioneering method of historical and spiritual research, it is suggested that the reader treat the results presented here in a discerning way. Neither publisher nor author are asking readers to 'believe' the contents. Although some details of Saether's results may be compared and checked with external historical records, ultimately they can only be judged through spiritual methods of research. Theoretically, each of us has the ability to develop our own capacity to do such investigation, and thereby we would be able to corroborate or disprove the author's results. But whatever stage may have been reached in our personal spiritual training, there is one quality we can all bring to bear immediately: our instinctive, intuitive sense for truth. Personally, I believe one should not rush to make judgements about Saether's experiences, but rather allow the thoughts and pictures in this book simply to 'live' inwardly. Eventually, a sense for the truth will arise.

Although the editors have endeavoured to make the contents accessible to the general reader, it should be noted that this work has been written within the context of a particular discipline of spiritual philosophy—what Rudolf Steiner called 'anthroposophy'. Notes have been added to explain specialist terminology etc., and material which is specifically addressed to those within the movement built up around Steiner's work—the 'anthroposophic movement'—has been moved to the final chapter. Nevertheless, the reader should bear in mind that the author did have a specific audience in mind.

In the first chapter he describes aspects of his life in some detail, in particular those relating to his spiritual path and his work within the anthroposophic movement. Those who wish to read immediately about Saether's initiation and karmic research can just as well begin with chapters 2 or 3. In fact, this volume is not composed as a conventional book, and in many places is presented as a series of 'episodes' and aphoristic thoughts. For the English edition we have—with the author's agreement—rearranged some of the text and sorted the contents to fit more cleanly into seven thematic chapters. But the book still retains the quality of a journal—the narration of individual episodes on the path of one person's spiritual development. The reader should bear this in mind and not judge it primarily as a literary or artistic composition.

Although the author is Norwegian, the original edition of this work appeared in Germany, where the anthroposophic movement is most established. The publication received some stinging criticism, and the author was personally vilified and attacked by certain reviewers. Despite this, we have taken the decision to make it available in English in the spirit of facilitating the distribution of research material. The book is not published as a finished and polished masterpiece, but as work in progress. Essentially, the author is presenting research to his peers for review and constructive comment. It is our hope that this publication will encourage others to step forward and speak openly of their considered spiritual experiences.

SG, May 2001

I bow in reverence before the many souls
who in my present time
now shape again their human destinies.

Many perhaps were once among the great,
yet do I fail to fathom former ages,
guessing only how in restless sway

modern with ancient wisely they conjoin.

Christian Morgenstern

Introduction

In this book I endeavour to describe my spiritual experiences, and in doing so my purpose is to bring alive the idea of reincarnation and karma by giving examples of what I have met with in life and in my own meditative research. In this sense the book is a report on one individual's spiritual insights and bears the stamp of my own personal path of knowledge.

From my youth the work of Rudolf Steiner (1861–1925) has formed an integral part of my life. I have studied it and worked with it not only in art and education but also meditatively and through his karma exercises.* For 28 years his philosophy has been one of the motifs in my life and at the same time the source from which I derive its meaning, and I regard my book as the outcome of work which could not have been carried through without his insights, especially in the field of karma research.

This book is not a scientific essay but a descriptive account in which I include some indications as to my methods and the steps I have taken on the path of spiritual schooling. Some of the themes have been dealt with in a degree of detail that will allow them to stand, I hope, as a point of departure for the reader's own inner work. A number of Steiner's exercises are described according to how I have understood and practised them. But this is not a book of exercises as such, and sight must not be lost of the fact that what I recount in it are my own individual experiences.

---

* Steiner described exercises for experiencing past lives and personal karmic connnections. The principal such exercise is given in *Karmic Relationships, Vol.II*, London: Rudolf Steiner Press 1974, lecture of 9 May 1924.

Since this book describes my path through earlier incarnations discovered by means of meditative work, I have called it a 'karmic autobiography'. I have received no direct help from other people such as regression therapists or clairvoyants. Only in one instance, which I shall describe, did a 'fellow wanderer' make a specific suggestion as to how I might proceed.

A good many books already exist in which the authors use the form of the novel to tell of earlier lives and the karmic connections between several incarnations, for example *And the Wolves Howled* by Barbro Karlén from Sweden, and *Einweihung* by Elisabeth Haich (1879–1989). Telling these stories in the form of a novel probably helps to distance readers in a way that enables them to accept the events described and form their own judgements regarding them. On the other hand, the books by Jenny Cockell are not novels. She describes quite frankly and directly the events that happened in her last incarnation exactly as she remembers them. In his 'readings' Edgar Cayce, the American known as the 'sleeping prophet', also gave direct indications about many former incarnations. I have similarly decided to write quite directly about all the former incarnations I know I have been through. In later chapters I shall try to make it as clear as possible why I am being so frank.

Chapter 1 of this book gives a general summary of my present incarnation, including many incidents from my childhood and youth as well as descriptions of and anecdotes about people who have played an important part in my development. I wanted to give readers a more personal impression of my life: like a brightly coloured mosaic consisting not only of miniature portraits of friends, fellow students, teachers and art colleagues but also containing details, happenings, games, projects and different locations. I wanted to show by this that many motifs from my childhood and youth which may appear merely incidental at first are in fact quite significant when seen as part of the larger picture, so I have described them in detail. If readers bear these 'miniatures' in mind when reading my descriptions of earlier incarnations in Chapter 3 they might discover a number of karmic threads and connections. Dealing with this multi-layered wealth of detail in memory and biography work is an important aspect of the methods applied in karma research. Rudolf Steiner pointed out that seeming trifles are sometimes the very items through which revealing knowledge can be gleaned. I shall describe a few examples of this in more detail in Chapter 5.

This karmic autobiography includes, in Chapter 1, my present life up to the existential crisis that developed in 1995. A number of the people who have played a part in shaping my biography up till now are mentioned by name if they have died or are very old. Many others who have played parts in my life are described but not named. I have endeavoured to depict events that led to painful social conflicts in a way that does not involve interpreting people's behaviour but merely sets down the external facts. I hope that the friends involved, who in some cases are mentioned by name, will recognize themselves without feeling I have judged them incorrectly.

In Chapter 2 I have portrayed my work with Rudolf Steiner's karma exercises coupled with the further results I attained during my meditative endeavours in the autumn of 1996. The activity for which Steiner employed the ancient term of 'building a hut' is a focal point of that chapter in that I have dwelt on how I brought this spiritual exercise into play meditatively.

Chapter 3 contains my accounts of 12 former incarnations of my own which I have so far discovered: a first one in Lemuria, three subsequent ones in Atlantis,* and eight others in various post-Atlantean cultural epochs.† The descriptions of events—which I have seen for myself—in those incarnations are supplemented by some necessary cultural and esoteric explanations.

I have gone more deeply in Chapters 4 to 7 into certain initiation experiences which the spiritual world has vouchsafed me since November 1996. I have endeavoured to show that I have also been through stages of spiritual knowledge higher than that known as Imagination.‡

My research up to Easter 1997 brought me many answers to questions concerning individuals I have met again in my present life. In fact in my various karmic circles in different countries I have discovered persons corresponding to nearly all the men and women described or mentioned in Chapter 3. I have been able to follow our progress through several incarnations and have thus reached an understanding of why one circumstance or another has arisen in our karmic relat-ionships. In order to help readers recognize the links between one life and the next and prevent possible speculation I decided—in the cases of a few individuals who are now in the spiritual world of the dead—to reveal these links as I understand them today. In other cases, where individuals are still on the earth in their present incarnation, I have uncovered some connections but not brought these right up to the present.

---

* According to Steiner and other spiritual teachers, the four great epochs now past are known as Polaris, Hyperborea, Lemuria and Atlantis. These are followed by the post-Atlantean (present) and the sixth and seventh epochs (future).

† The post-Atlantean epoch is sub-divided into seven cultural epochs, each lasting a little more than 2,000 years: Ancient India, Ancient Persia, Egypt-Chaldea, Greece-Rome, the fifth (present) and the sixth and seventh (future).

‡ 'Imagination', 'Inspiration' and 'Intuition' are used in a technical sense to denote levels of spiritual experience. See further in Rudolf Steiner, *An Outline of Esoteric Science*, New York: Anthroposophic Press 1997.

I regard making these karmic connections public as a way of assisting spiritual seekers who want to develop their own karma research. The grave and serious nature of all the spiritual experiences and karmic facts revealed in this book leads me to hope that suitable tact will be applied by those wanting to use them or communicate them to others. It has been no small challenge for me to risk bringing these motifs out into the open and stand before the world so spiritually naked.

Another purpose I had in writing the book was to confirm from my own point of view certain results of Rudolf Steiner's spiritual research, namely in the first instance his descriptions of Atlantean cultures in the books *Cosmic Memory* and *An Outline of Esoteric Science*. In addition I wanted to confirm a number of aspects of spiritual-scientific karma research. By putting forward examples from my own sequence of incarnations I hoped to show up several aspects of general karmic laws but also certain exceptions. To follow these matters calls for a great deal of one's own work. I hope that this description of my incarnation sequence is comprehensive enough to encourage other researchers to examine and check it using Steiner's methods.

In conclusion, I am absolutely not interested in gaining anything for my present life by describing my earlier incarnations or my status in the world in those times. Far be it from me to want to make a public name for myself in this incarnation or gain any advantage whatsoever. I realize, though, that this book might generate vehement indignation specifically on account of the historically known persons I have depicted, for in addition to the unknown lives I have also described three which are linked to known names. There was a historically documented life as a woman in Roman times, the life of a man in the Middle Ages, and another as a very well-known woman at the time of the Counter-Reformation. To count just two of these personalities as part of one's 'karmic property' might in itself strike many readers as arrogant. How much more, then, must my mention of that third famous figure appear as an expression of mental instability! An accusation of hallucination suggests itself, or at least the suspicion that I must be a fantasist.

According to various witnesses, even in Rudolf Steiner's day there were said to be 18 re-born 'Mary Magdalenes' amongst his circle. I am well aware that by claiming the life of the well-known woman of the sixteenth century I might be bringing a form of 'soul decapitation' upon myself, for it could be interpreted as the act of a kind of usurper. However, I am sure that many thousands of historically well-known figures are, at present, incarnated on the earth. We should not be afraid of meeting such people one day, or of discovering that we ourselves once lived in the lime-light of history. What an interesting challenge it would be if numbers of these personalities were to come forward and intro-duce themselves: perhaps we might even get used to the idea! Another reason for publishing my account—and this is one of my main concerns—is to show that our present knowledge of historical events can and indeed should in many cases be corrected and even revised in the light of karmic understanding.

It goes without saying that all those past human lives lacking well-known names to make them stand out in historical source material or records are of course links in the chain of human evolution equal in importance to those of historical individuals. Unknown lives still wait to become a part of history. In the Akashic Record* there are no qualitative differences between one human life and another; so we should learn to regard earthly

---

* The history and evolution of the earth and all its inhabitants is retained in the earth's 'etheric' or life body and can be 'read' by someone who has acquired the necessary faculties. This 'record' is known in esoteric terms as the 'Akashic Record'. See Rudolf Steiner *Cosmic Memory*, Garber Communications, New York 1990.

differences as an expression of changing social circumstances and points of view which it is up to us to transform as time goes on. This is the sense in which one can speak of 'karmic evolution'.

Another thing I want to stress is that my primary concern is not with stating *who* I was in earlier lives but rather with finding out *what* I was like, and showing that this 'what' appears again in 'what-I-am-like' now. My reason for combining this more general question with definite statements about my former personalities within their historical environments is that I think it important to show others who know me, or who move in the same circles, where they might look in history to find their own karmic past.

Over the coming decades the concept of reincarnation and karma will, in my opinion, be capable of leading to one of the greatest transformations in social life if people can find and apply it as a genuine impulse in the concrete situations of their lives. Knowledge of karma would then enable us to develop new moral impulses in the way we relate to one another, impulses which would to a large extent challenge established tradition. In this book I can unfortunately only hint at the way this has transformed my own life, but I hope that the general drift of my argument will show that it has to do with freeing the capacity for love in a way that can lead to an expansion of our sense of responsibility for the earth and for our fellow human beings.

If someone following the path described here, or another similar path, were to reach results that contradict mine, I should have to embark on a re-examination. At present, however, I stand by what is published in this book because I regard it as having been drawn from the truth. All are invited to investigate and test my results with all the methods of science and spiritual science at their disposal.

The most important aim of this book derives from my great hope that I can provide a point of orientation for others when they set out on the search for former incarnations and are looking for relevant experience in spiritual matters. I do not regard myself as a spiritual teacher in the traditional sense—and I hope the simple style I have adopted makes this clear. What I would like to do together with other pupils of the spirit is create ways of developing a future culture of the spirit. In this sense this book is intended for all individuals or groups who want to experience reincarnation and karma as an impulse for their lives.

I hope that this karmic autobiography will help me find more conversation partners and fellow travellers in these endeavours.

The title *Living with Invisible People* has several meanings for me. It hints at a search in everyday life for the reality of the spiritual world which also encompasses human beings who are not yet born as well as those who have already died. Secondly it refers to the need to look for the other person's higher self instead of turning away from him or her because of external traits visible to the senses. A third meaning involves our endeavour to carry experiences from earlier lives consciously in our present personality; this enables us to think, feel and act in ways we would be incapable of if we lacked a knowledge of karma.

I would like this book to demonstrate that it is perfectly possible to come 'straight off the street' and still be taken seriously by the divine world of spirit for one's honest quest and endeavour. In a sense it is a way of actively solemnizing the new mysteries. No doubt I shall find out whether it is possible today to speak about this subject not only indirectly and in general terms but also directly and individually, quoting one's own experiences.

My hope is that by writing in greatest inner honesty, I shall touch the hearts of readers without impinging on their individual freedom, so that at the dawn of a new millennium I can share a little in the creation of a genuine modern spirituality which can arise between human heart and human heart out of love for the truth.

While I was writing the book a great many people assisted and confirmed my work by their attitude and understanding, by friendly, moral and financial support, and also by conducting their own research into karma. A list of all these friends would be very long indeed, so I have confined myself to naming only a few. But I have not forgotten the others, and I thank all of them from the bottom of my heart!

I thank the eurythmist Gudrun D. Gundersen for many intimate conversations about spiritual schooling and questions of karma, for her constant encouragement and for the warmth of soul I experienced in her welcoming house while I gave lectures and seminars in Norway. I thank the author and religious historian Hans-Jørgen Høins (died 2001) in Denmark for his friendly companionship and public support, and for the many historical and literary sources he suggested, especially concerning the Middle Ages. I thank the independent researcher and scholar Lothar Foos for fruitful discussions and informative talks and for his interest in wanting to follow up and check my Imaginations—especially of the oracles in Atlantis—on the basis of his profound knowledge of Rudolf Steiner's works. My wife Constanze and the many new friends I have found over the last two years in many European countries I thank for having the confidence to regard my endeavours and my counselling efforts as a stimulus in their lives.

I also mention here the pain and sorrow I feel in connection with my dear children and their mother and all my former friends and colleagues in Sweden from whom I have separated in consequence of the circumstances surrounding this uncommon project.

The following words from a lecture Rudolf Steiner gave at

Torquay, England, on 22 August 1924 are quoted here as a bridge across which I send this book out into the world:*

> It is essential that the following point of view should find wider acceptance: that investigations into the spiritual world must be undertaken by those who, in their present life on earth, are able to call upon forces from earlier incarnations, for it is these forces which release the necessary powers for spiritual investigation; and further, that the results of these investigations shall be accepted by increasing numbers of people and incorporated into ideas which are comprehensible; and that, when the results of spiritual research are accepted by sound comprehension, a way is prepared for those people, by virtue of this comprehension, to have real experience of the spiritual world. For I have often said that the soundest way to enter the spiritual world is first of all to read about it or to assimilate what we are told about it. If we accept these ideas, they become inwardly quickened, and we attain not only to understanding, but also to clairvoyant vision to whatever degree our karma permits. In this respect we must give serious thought to the idea of karma.

---

* *True and False Paths of Spiritual Investigation*, London: Rudolf Steiner Press 1985.

Prologue

One afternoon in September 1996, seated on a simple green wooden chair in the guest room I lived in at Umeå, I was following my biography backwards to my earliest memory and trying to concentrate the inner impetus of my own self to push further back towards birth. After making this effort I endeavoured to float without any thoughts or feelings in a mood of nothingness. Suddenly there was a gentle jolt in my soul and I thought I was about to wake up in everyday consciousness. Instead there followed a waking-up in a vivid world of moving pictures.

I found myself in the midst of events which I immediately knew were in the past and belonged to me. I experienced myself thinking in the self of my present life while at the same time participating in those past events with the thoughts, feelings and actions of that time. I had woken up in a new dimension of consciousness in which two time sequences were co-temporal or ran parallel with one another.

Here I will attempt to describe in words this experience: I was lying in a kind of cart which shortly before that moment had been a small boat but now had wheels. The cart was being propelled by four men, one at each corner, who soon made it travel quite fast. My present self recognized the front man on the right as a woman I know in my present life. This recognition entered my consciousness with an intuitive jolt. At the moment of experiencing it I was perfectly sure it was true. My self as it was when this was happening knew what was going on. Here were the Mystery Dramas of Eleusis in ancient Greece which were celebrated annually at the beginning of February as a public festival with processions moving from Athens towards Eleusis. At that time—around the fifth pre-Christian century, as my present self calculated—I had been accepted as a candidate for the second, closed part of the Eleusinian Mysteries. This was why I was lying in the cart.

Something was going on between me and the front man on the right at the moment when he wanted to get the cart moving fast. We suddenly recognized one another. I thought, 'Is this you?' And I knew he was thinking the same. First his expression was one of astonishment, but then anger rose up in him. As soon as the cart had gathered speed I entered a dark tunnel in which various spiritual apparitions were made to appear by means of mechanisms, masks and actors. Then the picture slowly receded and I closed the meditation in deepest gratitude.

This was my major spiritual breakthrough. Over the ensuing months and years I was, through my active meditation and research, able to receive many more pictures and insights of previous lives on earth, which I recount in this book.

But first, let us go back to the beginning of my present life...

1

Episodes from my present life

Everything we do must surely have
a purpose and a prototype.
Seneca 'De tranquillitate animi'

I was born at Sunndal, Norway, on 3 February 1954. Sun, Moon,
Mercury and Venus were in the constellation of Aquarius, Jupiter
was in Gemini, Mars and Saturn in Scorpio, Uranus in Cancer,
Neptune in Libra, and Pluto in Leo.

The birth took place at 9 o'clock on a Wednesday morning just
when the midwife had nodded off after a long night of waiting.
My parents told me I arrived in the world quickly and without
complications. My father Ingar was eating breakfast in the
adjoining kitchen while my brother Georg, older by two years,
played on the floor. My mother Turid wanted to follow her
family's custom and call me Mikal, but my godmother, who was
also present at the birth, objected and said: 'His name should be
Jostein.' So that is what happened.

My earliest memory goes back to the time shortly before my
third birthday. My father had lifted me up into the loft through a
trap-door in the bedroom ceiling. There was a chest with all his
many tools and he wanted me to get him a screwdriver. I can see
myself standing there with the screwdriver in my right hand,
screaming because I didn't want to go back down to my parents
who were both waiting for me down below with outstretched arms.
I wanted to stay up there to investigate the chest more thoroughly
and watch the light streaming in through a little window.

In my second memory I am three years old. I am playing out-side with Georg and two other boys. We are jumping down from a bank into the snow piled up at the side of the road by the snow-plough. A car comes and stops level with us. We run home and that is the first time I see my newborn brother Torbjørn. I have a sense of being in the middle between two brothers, an older and a younger one.

There are more memories of the following summer. We spent several months living in my father's carpentry workshop, which had been suitably adapted, because our house in the style of a woodcutter's hut was to have another storey added. The day is sunny and my mother lets me wear my new boots. I stride proudly down the carpentry workshop steps and make my way to the strawberry beds. With my mouth full of 'strawberry delight' I stand there in the sun for a long while in my new boots.

My father was a carpenter by trade, and he had built our house himself. He needed the help of a relative only for especially tricky jobs. Many of my childhood memories are connected with his work. One day he took me in a lorry from where he was working to the sand quarry. It was a new experience for me to see the huge cranes and bulldozers, and all those many people at work.

Father made little wooden boats for us. We played with them on a small stream that ran past our house, a tributary of the river Harema, where we—that is Georg, the neighbour's son Odd, Arnfinn, who lived a bit further away, and myself—built landing stages for the boats and bridges for our toy cars. We also played together a lot on a leftover heap of sand in the corner of the garden. Georg later told me I never liked getting my hands dirty and kept wiping them on my clothes. Even so I became a specialist in the building of little houses in the sand, which always had to have a balcony constructed with the help of nails.

Photos show me with a large wooden horse on wheels, but I have no memories of this because on a spring day when I was two

Odd threw it into the Harema. A few kilometres away from our house the Harema flowed into the Driva, a bigger river. The resulting sandbanks caused the Harema to form a quiet pool where we bathed in summer, and built large cities in the sand. In winter we went skating there.

When I was five we went out on the thin ice. There was a crack and I suddenly fell over and slid into the freezing water, ending up underneath the edge of the ice. Only Georg's quick reaction combined with the help of Odd and Arnfinn saved me. I remember walking home across the snow-covered furrows of a ploughed field with my clothes frozen stiff. This was a decisive happening. Prior to it I can remember only isolated incidents and situations. But after this experience in the water it is as though my memory began to retain everything. Even today I can still remember all kinds of situations in detail, not only external circumstances but also my inner reactions.

The extra storey on our house was roofed with small tiles, and a pile of broken tiles had been dumped in a corner. Our vegetable garden between the house and the carpentry shop sloped down to the Harema where there was a path leading to a neighbour's house. Georg wanted to show me how good he was at spinning the little tiles through the air and how far he could throw them. I stood there trying to see where they landed. Suddenly something hit the back of my head and I saw blood running down. After that I remember my mother looking after me and being very strict about keeping me lying on the sofa all day long. As I was lying there the door suddenly opened and Georg came in with all the neighbours' children. I had never seen so many people in our house all at once and thought it was terrific.

We were still living in the carpentry workshop when I once followed my mother over to the house where she wanted to do something. Because of the building works we had to leave via the cellar stairs. There was a laundry room down there and while my mother was busy in it I played around with something in the semi-darkness. At first I was absorbed in what I was doing, but then I suddenly noticed that I was all alone in the dark cellar.

I went to the door but found it locked. The door at the top of the stairs was of course also locked. I started screaming 'Mama'. She didn't come. Only after I had been crying for what seemed like ages and wet myself did she come back and ask what I was doing all alone in the cellar. She thought I had run over to Odd's with Georg.

On another occasion, when I was five, I returned home to find no one there. The front door was even locked. I remember walking up and down the road crying. Odd's three-year-old sister Gerd came and comforted me and suggested we might go off together to look for my parents. The next moment they arrived back from shopping.

A little later I see myself standing at the living-room window eating a banana and watching a thunderstorm. I was happy then, and never again have I been afraid of thunder and lightning because I saw a rainbow after I had been so lonely.

I have many memories of my mother who was always at home while we were children. She was a quiet person and was constantly aware of what we were up to. We were allowed to play wherever we liked, and if we didn't come home at the proper time she used to come and fetch us.

She was born on the Helgeland coast of northern Norway and had grown up as the only sister amongst three brothers. Her parents had a smallholding near Ullvangen in the Leirfjord parish. Her father, Johannes Mikalsen, was a fisherman and carpenter. We spent many holidays up there in the north, travelling there by train in my early childhood and later by car. I remember a grand experience in Trondheim when we were looking for our night train: we had to cross over the rails in front of a huge locomotive with its engine running.

We were allowed to carve wooden boats and trains in the large carpentry workshop which was equipped with a lot of modern machinery where my grandfather manufactured window frames during the winter months. We three brothers spent many hours building railway landscapes in a play area on the side of a hill behind the house. The ground here was different from that at home; the soil was red and the rocks in many places were slate-like and crumbly, which meant that we were able to dig the pit we needed for our railway lay-out.

One of my earliest memories takes me back to my mother's home district. I am playing with Georg and two older girls, one of whom is a relation. We run into a birch wood where there is a small clearing. The pale green branches form a transparent roof over our heads through which the sun sparkles. A mood arising from the girls' happy laughter, my delight in life and in being here in this bright wood together with my brother awakens in me a longing for a sublime, divine secret which, as I suddenly realize, exists in an invisible world. This was when a sense of something spiritual first arose in me, though of course I only found concepts with which to describe it later on.

When staying with our grandparents in Helgeland we always joined in the July hay harvest. The grass was cut with a mower drawn by a white Norwegian horse. Hilly parts or sections where the rocks broke through, preventing the horse from getting past with the mower, were mown by scythe. The men—my grand-father, three uncles and my father—moved with their well-sharpened scythes in diagonal formation, side by side or one behind the other. The women followed, raking up the hay with wooden rakes and stacking it on drying racks. We children were allowed to practise with smaller scythes at the edge of the field.

But if we wanted juice and cake at coffee-time, grandfather said, we must also help with putting the hay on the racks.

Our grandmother Dagny took us with her when she went to milk her single cow or feed the hens or sheep. In her scullery next to the carpentry shop she put the milk through a separator. She baked all the bread needed every day for the many summer visitors. In her large kitchen there was an oven heated with dried peat. Grandfather once took us to see the peat bog. It was a communal peat bog on which many farmers had built their own peat sheds, including our grandfather. We had never seen such a thing where we lived. Deep ditches where the peat had been cut criss-crossed the bog, and the black clods were then laid out on stands in the sheds to dry.

My mother often stood in the kitchen with her mother preparing lunch or washing the dishes. We followed grand-mother to the vegetable cellar to fetch potatoes and carrots. The air in that subterranean room was excitingly cool and acrid. We came down the steep stairs to breakfast to the sound of grand-mother happily turning the coffee grinder. After the midday meal we had to be very quiet for an hour while the men slept. We could play in the house but were expected to be absolutely quiet if we stayed in the same room. We read, drew pictures at the table or played cards.

The weather was usually good, and we brothers used to go to a nearby fiord with our two cousins, Finn and Rune. There we played in and under the many fish-drying huts that stood on the cliffs on wooden stilts. The smell of the drying nets, the calls of the seabirds and the reflection on the water encouraged us to bathe. It was thrilling to watch the salt water flow up with the incoming tide.

We often went fishing with our parents in grandfather's rowing boat, or we accompanied grandfather or Uncle Einar to clean the nets and fetch the fish that had been caught. At home we then watched as grandfather put certain kinds of fish in brine to pickle and hung up others in the chimney to smoke. He stuffed the little stove with sawdust from the carpentry workshop and the smoke wafted around our railway playground like wisps of mist.

The most interesting place to play in at our grandparents' house was, though, the huge storeroom above the carpentry workshop, and we spent a lot of time there in rainy weather. The festoons of dried fish served almost as well as real chewing gum. There were old pieces of furniture, clothes, shoes and toys from our mother's childhood. We were allowed to play with anything so long as we put it back in the same place. We tried on the old clothes and performed scenes for one another, or we played hide-and-seek. The roof sloped right down to the floor, so there were many places to hide, and the seeker counting to 50 down in the workshop had a great deal of trouble finding the others. By listening to the scrambling feet above your head you did your best to guess where they might be hiding. At rest time we lay on the floor in a corner where there were piles of old magazines, looking at the adventure pictures and, when we were older, reading the stories.

Sundays were proper Sundays at our grandparents'. People wore their best clothes, with men and boys in white shirt and tie. This is where I began to comb my hair back like my uncle (my father having gone bald at quite a young age). Standing on the veranda we were allowed to peer into the distance through the binoculars while Uncle Per told tales of his journeys to far countries. He and Uncle Einar were sailors. For Christmas they always sent us a tin of English toffees. Our third uncle, Roald, was a carpenter. In the room we slept in we admired a model sailing ship he had built as a boy. Later we enjoyed the magazines we found in Einar's room which had helpful hints we could copy in our hobbies and showed all sorts of new inventions from around the world.

One summer when I was five we were to go home by train with our mother because father had already travelled ahead to do some work. Uncle Per and Uncle Einar came with us on the bus to Mosjoen where we had to wait until midnight for our train. Torbjørn was still too young, but Georg and I received presents from the uncles. Georg got an oval box which lurched across the floor on account of a loose ball inside it. I got a small accordion that I kept by me for a long time.

As there weren't many buses in those days we had a long wait in the local hotel for a train. Georg and I got bored and started messing around. Uncle Einar wanted us to be quiet and threatened to throw us down into the cellar. He was sitting on a chest and for a split second he let us peer into its dark interior, saying that it was the way down into the cellar. We didn't know whether to believe him or not.

Back home we were happy to see the familiar scenes once more— the flowers in front of the house, the places where we played in the garden and by the stream, and how the strawberries and carrots had grown. We ran over to Odd to tell him our summer news and play with him in his grandparents' farmyard. They were my godparents. His grandfather Ola had a bicycle repair workshop in his garage and we used to watch him mending the bikes. He called me 'Steinjo', but I couldn't make out why.

When we were a bit older Ola gave us used bicycle spokes which we bent to form revolvers. Round the handles we wove coloured detonator wire given us by Arnfinn's father who worked as a roadbuilder. He collected it up for us after blasting operations and we had all kinds of uses for this many-coloured wire. Our revolvers were not harmless. We 'loaded' the chambers with sulphur from matches mixed with saltpetre. Using a match to fire them we learnt our first lessons in how chemistry and mechanics work in the world. On the whole we had no serious accidents, but my cousin Rune lost three fingers on one hand through being careless with dynamite.

Ola also grew potatoes and kept pigs. Of course we watched when the pigs were slaughtered, and blood pancakes were standard fare on autumn days. He used to row people from Oslo or Germany to places on the Driva river where they could fish for salmon. There were many spots where you couldn't fish without a license, but since salmon fishing was Odd's father's trade we always knew where people could fish without being caught by the professionals.

The Driva river meanders from side to side across the two kilometre wide Sunndal valley making space for farms and settlements alternately on one bank and then the other. In our part there were seven farms scattered one behind the other along the gravel road that ran for about two kilometres down the side of the arable land enclosed by the river bend. There were also 13 houses. On the other side of the river, along the main road, were two villages, the larger of which boasted the village shop, the school and the youth club.

The Sunndal mountains on either side of the valley, which is oriented towards the south-east, rise to a height of almost 6,000 feet. The highest peak on the other side of the river is called Furunebba and is surrounded by several summits that together resemble an embalmed pharaoh, as we children discovered. The land on our side of the Driva, east of the Harema, is called Hoven after the oldest and largest farm. Here there are grave mounds dating back to the Vikings. Until a few hundred years ago there was a church on Hoven which fell victim to a flood. The new church was then built in Sunndalsøra, about four kilometres to the west of our house. We children called the whole district Mæle.

The Harema is fed by two rivers that meet in the valley at the foot of the mountain. The summits on our side are rounded, like

bald heads. Along one of the paths we discovered a spot where you could see a Red Indian in profile with a fir tree growing on his hooked nose. We often used to go up those paths, sometimes even twice in one day. Running down again as fast as we could was a sport for us boys. One path ended in a ravine which you had to clamber up. This was the path followed by the hunters, i.e. our fathers, every autumn when they went to shoot reindeer, stags and wild birds. Once we saw a herd of reindeer quite close by on a patch of snow. It was an impressive moment when we found ourselves breathing the same air as these proud, shy creatures.

During the war the Germans had done a lot of good work in the Sunndal valley. They had made the main road through Sunndalsøra the widest in all Norway, of course so that it could also be used as a runway for military aeroplanes. At a spot where the road was being repaired and a new bridge built over the Harema there was a plaque bearing the date 1941. We practised climbing up the stone walls underneath that bridge, and we also spent a lot of time in the trees alongside the river where we built a good many tree-houses.

There was an abandoned chaise at a place near our home. We used to sit for hours on the leather-covered wooden seats telling each other imaginary tales of where we were going across the high mountains.

For years during the summer months we enjoyed playing Cowboys and Indians. I loved the Indians. Later on I discovered a series of books about people who had emigrated to America, in which the Indians played the main part. I found a nearly new hat on the rubbish heap of a close-by farm 'Østigar' which I always wore for the game.

However, it wasn't a good idea to play it in the part of the farm where Lars 'Østigar' kept his bullocks. Once, when I was five and the youngest in the group, we were playing there when the young bullocks came running after us, led by an enormous bull. The other boys vaulted over the stone wall, and at the last moment one of Odd's uncles, who was about seven years older than me, hoisted me up as well. The angry bull's pointed horns swished by just below me, but I was saved.

We didn't like Lars 'Østigar' much because he was so strict and always shouted at us. He had a milk stand down by the road where the churns of fresh milk were collected by the dairy lorry. My family put an empty five-litre can there which we collected full in the afternoon and placed in a small well to keep cool before the days of fridges. The empty churns were returned to the farmer together with butter and cheese. One day that same summer Georg, Odd, Arnfinn and I saw a number of brown parcels there. Thinking there would be plenty left for the farmer we picked one up and ran to hide in an old ruin. We had hardly unwrapped the parcel and tasted the stale cheese it contained, which was nasty, when we found ourselves looking up into the farmer's angry eyes. Such experiences taught me what grown-ups called 'conscience'.

During that same summer when I was five we went along a public footpath to pick wild strawberries. Lars 'Østigar' came up and chased us away shouting, 'I haven't given you permission to pick berries on my land.' My mother tried to reason with him but failed to calm his bad temper. She began to cry and we went home. I tried to comfort her, and it was awful seeing her crying because of a nasty grown-up. Now I knew what 'injustice' was.

On another occasion he came and accused us of letting his calves and horse out of their paddock. He had found one of the gates open. We said we hadn't been there and I reminded him that the public footpath to Haremdal passed over his land and was often used by strangers. Later I came to realize that this Lars 'Østigar' had given me a great deal that helped develop my self-confidence as a child.

Odd's uncles had strung a rope from the branch of a tree for us to swing on. This was tremendous fun but could also be quite dangerous. Georg once had a fall that winded him for several minutes. I don't remember ever falling off it, but I got winded a number of times doing other things, for example while tobogganing on a piece of roofing felt, or falling while skijumping, something we often did after school.

The winters were always full of snow in my childhood. We ski'd a lot, but our favourite spot was the smaller ski-jump which allowed jumps of up to 24 metres. My personal best was 22 metres. On the big jump, which allowed up to 40 metres, I did 28. I liked skating even better than skiing. In earlier years we did this on various frozen ponds or the ice on the Driva river. Later I went by bike with Odd to the skating rink three kilometres away at Grøa, or to the main sports ground at Sunndalsøra. As teenagers

Odd and I joined the Grøa football club, which meant that I also got to Møre and Romsdal for boys' league matches.

From October to March the sun remained hidden from our house by the high mountains. On 3 March we children celebrated its return after its slow approach over several days across neighbouring fields. The transition from winter to spring meant avalanches. The suspension bridge we had to cross to get to school was often buried under masses of snow. When my friend Arnfinn was one year old his family house was entirely filled with snow by an avalanche. In April the river ice began to melt, which tempted us to engage in dangerous games on the floes.

At home I drew a good deal. My mother—who made beautiful portrait drawings, did Norwegian 'rose-painting' and collected pebbles for artistic picture frames along the river bank—supported this activity. One favourite theme my brothers and I shared was that of complicated houses perched on outcrops of rock, in which all the houses had turrets and balconies and were linked to one another by pathways or wooden ladders.

Another subject I enjoyed and carried on alone once we had started school was to draw maps of strange countries and islands with secret places, cities, caves and railway lines. Every detail of woods, lakes, settlements and mountains was minutely drawn. I loved studying the atlas and thoroughly getting to know the geography of the whole world. As a small child I drew buses with the driver shown in characteristic profile with his peaked cap.

I also liked copying the play of light and shade on mountainsides, and the faces of old people with all those wrinkles around the mouth and eyes. From about nine I began to specialize in drawing portraits of actors whose photos I found in magazines, a favourite being 'The Saint', the English actor Roger Moore with his characteristic smile and the little mole on the left side of his nose. Encouraged by a friend of mine, the editor of the local newspaper had a look at one of my portraits, but because it wasn't done in Indian ink he couldn't publish it. When I was twelve I took a correspondence course in drawing, and this was also when my love of watercolours first dawned.

Of course we also did jigsaw puzzles and played Monopoly. One puzzle I remember showed a Central European town with black and white houses joined across a street by a humped bridge. In the kitchen at Odd's house, where I always felt at home, I played cards with his mother and grandmother, my godmother. I heard gramophone music for the first time in Odd's house. They had records of the famous Swedish musician Karl Jularbo. Encouraged by Odd I bought my first tape recorder as a teenager.

I taught myself to read at five. After Georg had started school, my parents helped him with his homework while I watched from the opposite side of the table, so I first learnt the letters upside down, but I soon got the hang of reading properly. I remember going to fetch eggs from a farm one day and proudly telling the farmer's wife I could read. Reading opened up a new world to me, the world of books. Often I sat at home reading rather than going out to play with friends.

A book I borrowed more than once in my schooldays was about bird-watching and how to survive in nature without modern equipment. I read the Norwegian folk-tales about the three brothers, but my favourites were the stories of Hans Christian Andersen.

On my first day at school my father took me the two kilometres on his red motorbike, a Czech 'Jawa'. After that I always had to walk or cycle with the other children. For the first three years we went to school every other day and from the fourth class onwards daily, although we always had one day off, frequently in mid-week. In school I found new friends, the first of whom was Atle who lived on our side of the Driva near the suspension bridge. He and his brothers and sisters were being brought up as 'Christians'. In our house religion was hardly touched on in my childhood. My mother even recounted how she had thrown the New Testament into the stove at her boarding school in protest against its antiquated rules.

Later I also got to know Arnstein who lived next door to my cousins in the village of Hoelsand on the other side of the Driva. With Atle, Arnstein and others I played in different farms on that side of the river. When we had no school we cycled to Sunndalsøra where we went to the library or the café, or sometimes to the banks of the river beside the aluminium factory which covered a huge area at the end of the valley. Both my brothers now work there.

Really the whole of my childhood and youth were influenced by the interaction between peasant tradition and modern civilization. An interesting sign of this was the deformed sheep's skull kept for years by Lars 'Østigar' nailed to a beam underneath his stable. The deformation was caused by the fluoride emissions from the aluminium works. In the 1970s the farmers stopped keeping milking cows and sheep in the lower part of the Sunndal valley because of the pollution, which also caused the soft fruits in our garden to grow an extra skin. In adulthood a doctor detected aluminium poisoning in my brain, which probably accounts for my bad short-term memory.

I liked a number of subjects in school. Being hungry for knowledge I was conscientious about my homework. I often learned the reading passages in religion, history and geography almost off by heart, so the teachers always got the right answer from me. My right hand spent a lot of time waving in the air. I can still remember the stories from the Old Testament, my favourites being the ones about Joseph and his brothers in Egypt and Pharaoh's dreams. From the fourth class onwards we spent two days a week in a larger school where we did gym, handcrafts, cooking in the school kitchen, and English. My favourite subject at the time was artistic writing, which unfortunately we only had once a week.

On one occasion my mother had given me new black rubber boots lined with felt. We were having orienteering lessons with some classes from other schools and had to leave our outdoor shoes in the entrance hall. After the lesson I found an old pair of similar boots where my beautiful new ones had stood. I immediately told the teacher and even thought I knew who the thief was. But she wouldn't follow the matter up, so I was left with the old boots. There was no way of proving that of the two boys I was the one speaking the truth!

Our own local school had only two classrooms plus a room for the teacher and a library. Usually we behaved quite well, but sometimes I did get into fights, usually with Arnfinn. Because of some little thing I would start teasing him about his red hair, whereupon he would attack me. Usually the school bell or the teacher separated us.

In classes four to six I had a teacher called Ingolf Saether—no relation—who always used apples in various ways in the lessons. For arithmetic he would divide up apples with his penknife. When he set us tasks he sat at his desk cutting the apples into even smaller pieces and eating them while also scraping his ears clean with the same knife. Many years after he died Torbjørn told me that this teacher had been given a penknife by his grandfather which he later lost. As an adult he was always looking for a similar knife to buy.

We were allowed to help ourselves from a cupboard in the classroom if we needed new pencils, books or other things. One day, just before the bell went, the teacher had to go and answer the telephone. We boys sneaked to the cupboard and filled our pockets with new fountain-pen cartridges. At the bus stop by the suspension bridge later on we laid out the cartridges on the road in nice long rows and went to hide behind the balustrade to wait for our older brothers and sisters who came from the other school by the following bus. We hadn't reckoned with our teacher being on the same bus, which duly arrived and ran over the cartridges with its front wheels. He got out first to let the youngsters off and of course saw all the ink and burst cartridges, as well as us watching in surprise from behind the wall. Next day he gave us a severe ticking off.

We usually played ball games in break-times. I also liked the long-jump and sprinting. Once I did the 60 metres in wellington boots in 9.1 seconds. Winter sports-days involved all the schools of the neighbourhood. My best achievement was fifth in ski-jumping, and since I was in the fifth class at the time I thought this rather fitting.

Something new burst into my life in my ninth year: television. Until then we had only had the radio which we had listened to with bated breath every Saturday from 3 to 4 o'clock when the weekly radio play for children was broadcast. But now I began to discover more and more about the world: sport, politics, debates, plays and later all those thriller serials. From the age of seven I had seen a good many Westerns in the cinema. In winter we often had to queue for an hour in the cold for tickets.

I experienced the murder of President Kennedy as something terrible, and began to discover that many things were wrong with the world. I sympathized with the independent socialists. Later, at grammar school, I subscribed to a socialist paper and was a member of the Young Socialists for two years. We used to debate against the Marxist-Leninists. From then onwards I was against any kind of weapon and of course refused military service. I hardly ever joined in when my brothers and their friends went hunting game birds with bows and arrows, and later with shotguns. When Georg and the others used the stuffed owl that had sat in our living room during my childhood as a decoy and forgot it in the woods, where wind and weather spoilt it, I got very angry with him.

There was a period when we searched the woods and fiord cliffs for birds' eggs. You were only allowed to take one egg from a nest. We poked holes in each end and carefully blew out the eggwhite and yolk. It wasn't always easy to carry home the delicate eggs with their many-coloured patterns.

The beautiful landscapes of my homeland provided all kinds of opportunities for games and occupations. On dark autumn evenings we sometimes stole apples from farmers' gardens. We built tree-houses and constructed canoes with which to shoot the rapids of the Driva. We explored the caves at the edge of the mountains and built wooden structures round the entrances. We climbed up the cliffs and rolled stones over the edges. Once a farmer came to find out whether we had killed one of his calves by doing this. We had not done so, but had seen unfamiliar bicycles near his yard that morning.

Our family also enjoyed another, somewhat less precipitous landscape at Valsøyfjord, my father's home. The journey there involved about two hours by car, then a ferry across a fiord, and then a road that passed by seven or eight more fiords. The farm my father came from had been in his family since the seventeenth century. When I was a child my Uncle Sverre, the current owner, put up a monolith with a long list of all the names engraved on a copper plaque.

My father had three sisters who lived near us at Sunndal with their families. Another brother, whom I never met, suffered from schizophrenia and lived in an institution. My grandfather, Gullik Sivertsen Saether, was a short, strong-willed man who spent his whole life modernizing and extending the farm at Valsøyfjord. He transformed even the steeper hillsides into strips of arable land and loved planting fir trees in his woods. His grandson is now building a new forest track to open up these large woodlands for harvesting.

When he was very old—he died aged over 90—my grandfather once told me how he had lost a boundary dispute with a local minister. This had turned him against the church. He said I should become a schoolteacher because I would then be employed by the state and have long holidays. He stressed the long holidays, for he and my grandmother, Jonetta, never had a holiday throughout their long working lives.

The atmosphere at Valsøyfjord was always cheerful and cosy even during the frequent political discussions that went on. This was thanks mainly to two people, firstly my Uncle Sverre, who was even shorter than his father, though his hands were larger, and who loved children, and secondly my grandmother. I remember her in her flowered frock standing in the kitchen after milking the cows, making pancakes or waffles for us children. When she died I inherited her waffle-irons.

Of all the games we played there with our cousins, our favourite was one summer when we bought toy gliders. For days on end we ran endlessly up the hillsides to fly them and down to collect them. I asked myself whether one day human beings would be able to fly.

I had various dreams about flying. There was one in which I flew low above the ground round our house. I had a propeller like the one in a picture-book we had, only it was fixed to my back and therefore invisible. In another dream I soared high above the mountain tops and was able to swoop down the waterfalls, sliding into the water and out again into the air. When I finally landed in the valley I could no longer fly and encountered many difficulties on the long walk home.

I also had a good many dreams about falling. There was a recurring one in which I fell into a deep well with skis on my feet. The skis made a frightful noise scraping down the walls of the well. Then the well suddenly came to an end and I continued to fall in pure air, but I always awoke without reaching the ground.

My lion dream was especially dramatic. First I was crossing a fiord with my family in a rowing boat. Then we walked a long way across a landscape in which I finally found myself alone. I came to a large building which I entered by a side-door on the right. Having passed through several small rooms I reached a great hall. On entering I noticed there was no floor in the centre, and when I looked down there were lots of wild and hungry lions. Suddenly there was no way back, and I had to muster all my strength to leap across the lion-abyss, which to my surprise I succeeded in doing. Luckily the door to the outside was not locked; I had saved myself and the lions stayed inside.

My grandfather Johannes died when I was nine. I felt my mother's sorrow more strongly than my own. She travelled to his funeral alone, and on her return I wanted to know exactly how he had died and why such a thing has to happen.

By then I was already familiar with the idea of reincarnation through weekly journals my mother read. Although it was an idea I could immediately relate to, I could not at first see any connection with my grandfather's death. Later I talked with my mother a lot about these things, and we developed a close bond that lasted until her early death in 1987.

In the summer of my twelfth year we once again went to northern Norway. There I made a new friend, the son of my mother's childhood friend. Our families met on a number of occasions, and my new friend and I talked about all kinds of vital questions such as our experiences with girls, what male and female sexual organs looked like, and other 'secret' subjects. One evening we heard that his father had gone missing. He had set out in his motor-boat to check his fishing nets, but another fisherman had found the boat empty. My friend and I went out in that boat to search for his father. We talked little, but didn't want to give up hope of finding him.

A few days later divers found the body on the bottom of the fiord. The news troubled me a great deal, but my friend was quite calm about his father's sudden death. I was greatly impressed.

In 1967 my father acquired permission to build in Grødalen, a mountain valley adjoining Sunndal. The spot lay about 800 metres above sea level and a number of neighbours and acquaintances had already built holiday cabins there. My father prepared all the woodwork at home in his workshop, so it took only a few days to construct our's on a hillock, surrounded by birches and fir trees. We brothers helped as much as we could. We named it 'Hausin'.

Prior to this we had gone there on day trips during the shorter holidays, but now we spent many holidays up there, especially at Easter. My mother only missed the first Easter festival at 'Hausin' because at 38 she was expecting her fourth child. We had always longed for a sister, and Dagny Helen was born on 18 May, one day after Norway's national holiday. I was in the seventh class at school.

Apart from when we were at home, my brothers and I began to spend less and less time together. We had different friends and were developing our own interests. On the one hand I continued to do sport and spend time with Odd, Arn-stein and other mates, including girls. We would meet in the evenings to listen to pop music (Jim Reeves, the Beatles, Bob Dylan) and talk about ghosts, films and anything else that was topical. On the other hand I spent a good deal of time at home looking after our little sister and thus experiencing her early achievements from close up; I also immersed myself in my many book projects.

One day on the way home from school with Arnstein and Atle I invented a new game. We rode on our bikes across the ditch by the road and into a field of stubble. There we dropped to the ground and pretended to be dead. We swooped about in wide curves with outstretched arms. I tried to imagine what things must look like beyond the threshold of death. We talked about someone who had found death by suicide.

Twice a year everyone from Mæle met for a dance in the open air at the festivals of Whitsun and St John. During the preceding weeks we collected dry twigs and branches blown off the trees by storms with which we built huge bonfires. The Whitsun fire was usually at the bottom of a high cliff from the top of which we threw down the branches for burning. The St John's fire was usually beside the Driva because of the danger of forest fires. The children brought fizzy drinks and biscuits. The adults drank beer or home-brewed schnapps. I got to know about this home-brewing, forbidden in Norway by strict laws, very early on in life. We youngsters used to do it ourselves when someone's parents were away, or in one of the huts Georg and his friends had built in the woods.

The dancing was what I was most interested in. Fathers played the accordion, or we danced to recorded pop music. I fell in love with various girls and experienced all kinds of feelings in my soul. Later the Saturday night dances in various community halls formed the social highlight of the week. For several years I followed these pursuits in a youth club with my friends from school.

For some subjects in school we were divided into three groups according to ability. I was amongst the best in the class which was, however, by no means only positive because a number of boys teased me on account of my being a 'know-all'. In fact for about two years I was seriously bullied. I was quite capable of defending myself, so no bad fights developed in my case, but it was not nice to notice that the teachers on duty during break-times took hardly any notice of such mobbings.

I wore glasses from the third class onwards. My astigmatism had been discovered when I found it difficult to read the sub-titles on TV. I had the glasses until I reached twenty-one when I stopped because my sight had improved. I remember when I was five standing at the top of the steps feeling cross with the other children playing in the snow, I can't remember why. Erik, Odd's uncle, threw a snowball with a stone hidden in it and hit my left eye, which was my worst one. It wasn't funny being called 'Specs-Jesus' by boys who had no trouble seeing properly.

One way of earning money as a youngster was to work at the shooting range at Furu. We were a group of boys and girls who took cover in the ditch behind the targets and held up long sticks to show what numbers the shooters had hit. After every round of shooting, the holes in the cardboard targets had to be closed up with sticky tape.

We communicated with the range manager via an old-fashioned walkie-talkie. There were usually two of us at each target, one to hold up the sticks while the other stuck the holes shut. It was a long day and by the evening we felt our money had been well earned.

We cycled straight to the kiosk where we bought sweets or wild-west comics and illustrated tales of Jules Verne. Those over 16 sometimes also bought an erotic magazine for men. There was a phase during which the walls in every male teenager's bedroom were covered from floor to ceiling with photos of pretty women.

A new phase in my life began after my confirmation. With some of the money I had been given I bought Ola's old motor bike. With Georg's help—he already had one—I restored it and resprayed it bright blue and bright red. A bicycle dealer still had an old box full of Villiers spare parts (luckily—since the make had long since ceased production). As soon as I was old enough I took my motor-cycle test.

My schoolwork suffered as a result of spending so much time on this new hobby. By the end of the ninth class my marks were too low to guarantee a place at the grammar school where I wanted to go because of the science it offered. Earlier I had wanted to become either a vet or an architect, but when I got accepted for the language stream of the grammar school on the basis of my English I had to begin thinking of a different kind of future, and art was another of my interests. I decided to leave matters to fate.

As a child and youngster I suffered no very remarkable illnesses or injuries, but like all children I did go through some episodes which helped me experience the mysteries of the body. Visits to the optician meant going to Molde, a city that later became famous for its roses and its jazz festivals. When I was 12 a large mole growing on my right hand had to be removed, and at 17 I had my tonsils out, both in the Molde hospital. Recompense for the second operation was making the acquaintance of a charming young female patient there.

Tingvoll was about 50 kilometres away from Sunndalsøra towards the regional capital Kristiansund. Here I found a room in a house shared with 7 other students amongst whom I immediately made new friends. Our house 'Holan' had a bad name in the village because of the drinking bouts its inhabitants indulged in. During my first term I, like the others, spent my grant money on rhubarb wine. But I also followed up my real interests in the company of Jostein D., Einar Bjørn (whose father owned 'Holan') and Jo: we bought UFO-magazines and esoteric literature from Sweden.

I had discovered philosophy for myself and was thus already familiar with Socrates, Plato and the neo-Platonist Plotinus. In our small circle we discussed Erich von Däniken's theories and decided to re-write the Bible in accordance with our ideas. We ordered books on reincarnation and parapsychological phenomena and investigated Christianity as practised in the local mission church. I especially looked forward to the religion lessons at the school because I enjoyed asking the teacher, whom we knew to be a confessing Christian, polemical questions. For a term I was also editor of the school magazine (which was stuck on a wall) for which I wrote essays on the same subjects.

I read a lot of literature in addition to my homework. Writing essays was important to me. At the age of 12 I had begun to write a long thriller which, however, never got finished. At the grammar school I put a great deal of effort into my essays. Henrik Ibsen spoke directly to my heart with his dramas *Peer Gynt*, *The Wild Duck*, and *When We Dead Awaken*. I discovered the Norwegian poet Sigbjørn Obstfelder and the German poets Goethe, Schiller and Heinrich Heine. I also began to write poetry myself, in a symbolistic style.

I grew my hair long and liked listening to music by Bob Dylan, Simon and Garfunkel, the Rolling Stones and Creedence Clearwater Revival. Our house had neither a bath nor a shower, so the local swimming baths were much frequented by us at weekends.

At 17, in the spring of 1971, some of my mates and I decided to get rid of our shoulder-length hair. First we shaved the tops of our heads and then I decided to cut it all off. This did not meet with any approval at home, nor with my former companions with whom I went dancing at Grøa. I felt excluded by my old friends and walked the long way home through the light summer night staring at the ground. I experienced this loneliness like awakening from a dream.

Pensive yet contented I arrived at our house and went to bed, but could not sleep. I lay awake for several hours thinking about various episodes in my life. Suddenly I was overwhelmed by a strong and unfamiliar feeling. I felt as though I was going to die soon and thought to myself that if this was to be my fate, so be it, let death come. I was not afraid, and immediately the death-feeling went away.

A world of pictures unfolded before my eyes, pictures I recognized as belonging to a former life as a man in nineteenth-century America. The name Ronald B. Dixon was associated with this man whom I saw as myself on my death-bed in that life. The sequence of pictures finally formed into a remarkable archway of time which merged into a date: 3 May 1953. Later I realized this date was exactly nine months before my birth, so perhaps it was the moment of my conception.

I was wide awake during this experience and fully aware that I was lying in the bed in the room I had slept in since my child-hood. On trying to capture the happening in my diary next morning I found it very difficult to get a grip on the memories.

In the days that followed I tried to tell some members of my family and also some friends about this shocking and yet also sublime experience. Very few of them showed any ability to understand it at all or to help me by confirming that such things were possible. I therefore resolved to remain silent. Meanwhile I had lost all the fear and doubt I had hitherto felt regarding the supersensible world and death, for I had personally experienced the spiritual world as true.

In the following autumn, in my second year at grammar school, I intensified my efforts in two directions. On the one hand I bought an American exercise machine to get my body into good condition and over several months put on five kilos by taking protein supplements. On the other hand, following indications published by an author who had lived in India, I began to meditate.

Then, in the late autumn of that year, a far-reaching encounter led me to Rudolf Steiner's spiritual philosophy 'anthroposophy'.

A suggestion by Einar Bjørn's father drew our attention to Arnold Wangsmo. He was well-known publicly on account of his newspaper articles, and he had expressed his views in a number of controversies, in 'the manner of a free-thinker', as Einar's father put it. He himself regarded Wangsmo as too 'way-out', but he thought our generation might like him. We, a group of five young men and one girl, contacted him straight away and went to visit him one Saturday. We realized immediately that here was *the* 'philosopher of Nordmøre', as he had been called in a newspaper interview.

Wangsmo smoked the whole time we were with him. After listening to our questions he began to tell us about Rudolf Steiner. He also told us about his years with members of the Riksmål Association, Riksmål being a specific branch of the Norwegian language. (Since the nineteenth century there have been several versions of written Norwegian which are still at loggerheads today.)

Arnold Wangsmo told us about his correspondence with the poet Alf Larsen. In the 1930s and 40s he had been well-known as a critic of culture through his writings in the monthly journal *Janus* which he published between 1933 and 1941. He had spoken publicly in favour of Rudolf Steiner's thoughts on social issues, thoughts that had enabled him to see and criticize what was developing as the National Socialism being spread in Norway by Vidkun Quisling.

Wangsmo spoke about the poet Olav Aukrust who had also been a student of Steiner. He recited long passages from Aukrust's main work 'Himmelvarden' which describes his spiritual schooling using images of soul and nature. Wangsmo spoke about reincarnation and karma and described how the stars and planets impress themselves in the brain of a child at the moment of birth as an expression of that cosmic moment. He talked of Christianity and of Christ as a cosmic being whom he called 'Logos'.

I knew that in this night I had found the motif of my destiny. Anthroposophy was an expression in the world for something I had always carried in my heart. This man, who never spoke about himself but always pointed to others, gave me the answer to my deepest existential question: What is the purpose of a life on earth? We visited Wangsmo several times, but the little group gradually shrank until I was the only one still setting out on the two-kilometre walk. Of that group of young students I am the only one who is still in contact with him. Later I also met his wife, Margot, and their two sons, all of whom are connected with anthroposophy.

Wangsmo came to visit us in Sunndal and both my parents were interested in getting to know him. They began to read Rudolf Steiner's work. My mother and I had always exchanged books with one another, and we continued to do so. She became closely linked with anthroposophy, whereas my father was initially only interested in Steiner's social ideas.

Arnold Wangsmo lent me anthroposophical literature and back numbers of Norwegian journals. I began to order books by Steiner, Friedrich Rittelmeyer, Emil Bock, Hermann Poppelbaum and others from the publishers Vidar in Oslo. The first parcel arrived around Christmas 1971, containing Steiner's lectures on the Gospel of John,* *Reincarnation and Karma*, and other works. Over the next year and a half I regularly received parcels from

---

* *The Gospel of St John*, New York: Anthroposophic Press 1962, and *The Gospel of St John and its Relation to the Other Gospels*, New York: Anthroposophic Press 1982.

Oslo which I unpacked at my desk in the classroom. Without desisting from my study of anthroposophy, henceforth as important to me as eating and sleeping, I passed my school-leaving exams with good marks.

In addition to English, which I kept up, and French, which I unfortunately forgot entirely as the years went by, I now also began to lay the foundations for German. From then on the German romantics, especially Goethe, Schiller and Novalis, were among my poetic companions for many years.

Wangsmo encouraged me to get involved in a newspaper debate in which, among other things, anthroposophy was being criticized. With his help I wrote my first essay intended for publication. In the summer of 1972, while I was helping two elderly sisters on their farm, I wrote another essay in two parts, on 'Logos, or the Creative Word'.

During my second and third year at grammar school I followed the set work with much enthusiasm. My studies of Steiner and other authors influenced even my school essays, which I especially enjoyed writing on literary or philosophical subjects. My final exam essay was a study of Socrates and Plato with reference to Steiner's descriptions in *Goethe's World View* and *Christianity as Mystical Fact*. I was especially taken with Plato's theme of the world soul crucified, and with the demeanour of Socrates at his death.

As with Wangsmo, further poetic companions for many years were Aukrust, Larsen and Bjerke. One poem by Alf Larsen about the effects of the Risen One in the realm of nature generated quite specific feelings in my soul. Later, at the end of the 1970s, his humorous poems encouraged me to start writing poetry myself once again.

One of Larsen's essays led me to the novels of Olav Slåtto. I read the series on the history of the Røgnald people, and identified with the main character through my own similar painful experiences such as those in Ibsen's poem *Brand*.

In my personal life I went through troubles in love and lapses of behaviour in my social life. One episode, which changed my attitude to alcohol, was as follows. I was an enthusiastic participant in school dances and carnival celebrations. One evening I hid a bottle of wine in my coat-pocket and crept in at the back entrance of the school, only to be confronted by my class teacher in the dark corridor. He saw through me immediately and said: 'Well, Jostein, I would never have expected you to do such a thing.' Ashamed, I said I would go home. On the way I threw the unopened bottle in the ditch, and since then alcohol has never played any special part in my life.

Arnold Wangsmo told me of a Scandinavian youth seminar for anthroposophy in Sweden. I got the address and wrote off for a prospectus. In the winter of 1973 I decided to attend a youth conference there the following summer and then, beginning in the autumn, an 'introductory year'. So, after those undramatic final exams and a holiday job planting one thousand fir saplings which earned me the same number of Norwegian kroner, I set off by train via Oslo on my first trip abroad.

I broke the journey in Oslo to visit Sigrid Mørch-Reiersen, a very old anthroposophist (born 1895) with whom the librarian of the Vidar branch had put me in touch a year earlier. I subsequently remained in contact with her almost until her death in 1986, and called on her whenever I was passing through Oslo. She answered my questions concerning anthroposophy and told me Rudolf Steiner had said that you are likely to have been connected in some way in a former life with the people you dream about.

Sigrid spoke about Steiner Waldorf education and said I ought to become a teacher in one of the schools. She had been a teacher of domestic science during her working life, and for some years also a literature teacher in a school for the blind. I discovered later that she was immensely kind to all those she knew or met.

She presented me with several years' worth of back numbers of a Norwegian journal about Steiner Waldorf education. The special link between us, however, was the subject of those who have died, and she also gave me the four booklets *Bridge over the River* which contain accounts received from a musician called Siegwart who had been killed in the First World War. Through his sisters who still lived on the earth he passed on many things about his life in the spiritual world after death. I was impressed to hear that Rudolf Steiner had confirmed these reports as being true spiritual documentations. Ten years after Sigrid's death our conversations on this subject were to lead to an unexpected soul experience for me.

As I got into the shuttle train in Södertälje I met my first Swedish anthroposophists. It was a hot summer's day and I dumped my heavy rucksack beside an elderly lady and two men, one older and one younger. They were Rut Nilson, Arne Klingborg and Urban Forsén, with whom I was to be much in contact over the following decades.

Encouraged by Rut Nilson I began to study the story of the Grail. Even when she was very old she still gave lectures on Parsifal's path and on her research into the Rosicrucian movement in England in the seventeenth century. These lectures made me feel that she belonged to those spiritual streams. She told of her own meetings with Rudolf Steiner at Dornach, Switzerland, and of the conflagration that destroyed the first Goetheanum,* which she had witnessed. In prophetic images she described a

---

* Steiner's architectural masterpiece and centre for the General Anthroposophical Society at Dornach near Basle, Switzerland.

future when such double-domed buildings would stand on every hill in the world wherever communities formed islands of culture. The group which she founded brought together those who felt attracted by her gentle, humorous and heart-warming personality.

Urban Forsén was a man whose moral example I strove to follow. His modest, kindly and yet self-assured manner encouraged me to observe what my own effect on other people was. To earn myself some pocket-money I worked every afternoon in his shop Robygge. I bought the plant-dyed yarns he sold, and crocheted hats and waistcoats. For years my personal style derived from there: light-coloured cotton clothes, beard and shoulder-length hair. Through Urban I discovered the Christian Community's 'Act of Consecration of Man'* which thus far I had only read about.

My meeting with Arne Klingborg marked the beginning of one of the main karmic motifs of my life. Many years were to pass before this could unfold fully, but it was the way he had of inspiring enthusiasm that revived the artistic streak in my soul. Through him I discovered the world of colour and began to paint once more.

The fourth important encounter for me was with Jørgen Smit. My first contact with him had been by letter in the winter of 1973 when I wrote to ask for a place at the Järna Seminar. His friendly and sober way of expressing himself, and also his somehow crumpled yet delicate handwriting attracted me immediately. When I then met this human giant, in both the physical and spiritual sense, it became clear to me that I definitely wanted to become a member of the Anthroposophical Society.

During our first private talk I wanted to tell him about the

---

* The Communion service of the Christian Community church.

reincarnation experience I had had as a seventeen-year-old. I was very content to hear him say that it appeared to him to have been an experience of Imagination rather than something visionary. This showed me that he knew about spiritual experiences, and I straight away joined the Anthroposophical Society. Later during another conversation he helped me clarify questions I had about the avatars.

While I was working at Robygge he often used to come into the shop to see whether there were any new books, or perhaps to buy a bar of soap. I was always able to ask him spiritual questions on those occasions. Once I said to him: 'Jørgen, when you write a book, what will it be about?' With a friendly and happy glance that was also serious he said: 'It will be a book about Tycho Brahe.' When I asked the reason he gave me a quick answer and hurriedly left the shop. From reading Rudolf Steiner's lectures on karma I already knew what he had said about the importance of the individuality of Julian the Apostate-Herzeloyde-Tycho Brahe for the development of anthroposophy in our time, and I was not disappointed by Jørgen's reply.

There were three things that I found particularly inspiring about the courses he gave as a part of the teacher training course I attended up to 1975. Firstly there were his announcements telling us of the position of the planets each morning. His connection to the significance of the planets also showed in the way he helped produce a planetary calendar for sale in the above-mentioned shop. Secondly there were his efforts to practise with us Rudolf Steiner's exercises for artistic speech. This made such an impression on me that I continued to do the exercises for several years. Thirdly there was his relationship with time, of which I here give a few examples.

At lunch Jørgen Smit was always surrounded by happy young people who wanted to hear something from him, and he also often asked us questions. On one occasion we were talking about shift-work, and when I mentioned that my father had worked in an aluminium factory for several years he wanted to know all about it, including whether my father's health had suffered. Several years later he gave a series of lectures on the importance of rhythm in nature and in human life, and I recognized a number of examples from our talks round the table at lunch, now integrated into a larger picture.

In my experience Jørgen Smit always remained objective and maintained a certain distance towards others. I remember one situation in which he did this with some good humour. The festival of St Lucia is celebrated in Sweden during Advent as the high point of the year. In my early student times at Järna I used to join in the fun first thing in the morning when we went from house to house with candles and special biscuits in order to sing to people as they still lay in bed. But Jørgen disappointed us, for at an hour which we considered to be in the middle of the night he was already up and dressed, sitting in his living room reading a book. Either he didn't want to receive us in bed, or he always rose so early. The following year we crept up to his house, but there he was, once again sitting fully dressed in his living room. He enjoyed our singing, though. Jørgen was musical. He played the bass recorder to accompany the Seminar choir. And when he sang he had a good ear and you could always rely on his powerful bass voice.

People who have had to arrange a meeting with him will surely remember how he got out his diary and scanned the days and weeks ahead to find a free hour. I rarely took such an opportunity myself. After he had been called to Dornach (to join the central council of the Anthroposophical Society) in 1975 he always wanted to catch up with the life and work of specific persons on his return to Järna during his winter lecture tour. Once in the mid-80s we were drinking coffee together. We had been having a good chat for half an hour about human relationships, but just as

I began to ask him a question he got up and walked away without saying a word. I was taken by surprise and thought perhaps I had said something tactless. But it couldn't have been that, for I had not even finished putting my question. Then I looked at my watch and saw that it was exactly 3 o'clock. Perhaps he had another appointment!

For teaching practice during my student years I used to go to the Rudolf Steiner School in Bergen where Jørgen Smit had taught for over 20 years. Later I worked in special needs education near Bergen where I also met many people who had been a part of his karmic circle. Much later I heard many anecdotes, reports and stories about his work at Dornach from people who had experienced him on specific occasions. So when he died in 1991 I was able to form an overall picture of his biography both from my own memory and from what I had heard from others.

How I was able to renew my contact with Jørgen Smit after he died is something that will be told in a later chapter.

Another encounter I had was with Walter Liebendörfer. His lectures at the Seminar and his essays on biology, zoology and embryology in the educational journal *På väg* encouraged me to get involved once again in the debate about Darwinism and the theory of evolution in our local newspaper at home in Norway. I submitted an essay setting out the Goetheanist view of the human being existing first in spirit before entering into the stream of earthly evolution as a physical entity. I was rather disappointed to find that the readership did not react at all to my spiritual thoughts.

Amongst my fellow students at the Seminar I made several new friends in these first two years at Järna, one of whom I shall mention here. His name was Terje, and he was nine years older than me. In the early 1960s he had been the youth champion of the Norwegian skating team in Oslo. He played the guitar and sang lovely songs by Swedish songwriters. I lodged with him and his wife Pia in their house at Järna village while attending the one-year education course in which he also participated. They asked me to be their marriage witness. At home I used to have fun with Pia's children and often found myself lying on the floor with five-year-old Tobias, as much absorbed as he was in playing with his wooden railway.

Uwe Lemke, a priest in the Christian Community, used to attend a study group in their home. He was known as the writer of a book about Gotland and its art treasures. In a group I participated in with Terje and other friends we read Rudolf Steiner's lectures *Egyptian Myths and Mysteries*. One of the female participants even had an Egyptian profile, which gave us the opportunity to joke about our possible former incarnations. I owned a moped at the time, which enabled me to discover the beautiful coastline of the Baltic sea. I read Rudolf Steiner's lectures on karma and began regular work with the karma exercises as well as the 'subsidiary' exercises recommended by him. I also did a lot of drawing and painting.

A highlight in 1974 was a student performance of August Strindberg's *Lammet och vilddjuret* (The lamb and the wild beast), a little known, rarely-performed play about early Christianity. Terje played the part of Emperor Nero, and I was a Roman who gave a speech about the changing times while Joseph, Mary and the Jesus Child passed across the stage. After the event of Golgotha this Roman became a Christian in the catacombs. Arne Klingborg, who directed the production, thought my performance 'too melodramatic'.

That summer in August I travelled around Europe on an InterRail ticket, visiting Dornach in Switzerland for the first time, where a taxi dropped me in the middle of the night: my first experience in real life of the second Goetheanum.* It was too late to find any-where to sleep, so I spread my sleeping bag under a tree in the meadow on the hill above the building.

Next morning a friendly Waldorf teacher from Fulda in Ger-many arranged for me to have a bed for a week in the Heating House. He also had access to a key for the room where Rudolf Steiner's great sculpture is housed, the 'group' with the Repre-sentative of Mankind standing between the opposing powers of Lucifer and Ahriman.† I was familiar with it from photographs and from art courses with Arne Klingborg, and it was very impressive.

I saw several scenes from Goethe's *Faust*, and after a con-ference also worked as a cleaner in the large auditorium. The summer weather was very hot, and I was puzzled as to why we were not allowed to strip to the waist while cleaning in there.

This was at a time when I was studying Rudolf Steiner's bio-graphy and planning to write an essay for a Norwegian journal in connection with the fiftieth anniversary of his death. However, pressure of other work meant that this was never finished.

Back at Järna I worked in the library, not to earn money but to get to know the many books and also because there was such a pleasant atmosphere in that beautiful building designed by the

---

* The first Goetheanum was destroyed in an arson attack at the turn of the year 1922/23.

† This refers to two specific spiritual beings who, in Steiner's terminology, have particular tasks as 'spirits of hindrance'. Lucifer has an expansive, inspiring effect on people and strives to entice them into grandiose visions, causing them to lose touch with earthly reality. Literally 'light-bringer', he is known as Loki in the Norse tradition. Ahriman, from Persian 'the father of lies', seeks to harden, materialize and ultimately trap humanity within the earthly realm. Both are necessary for human development—within their rightful spheres of influence. See Rudolf Steiner, *The Influences of Lucifer and Ahriman*, New York: Anthro-posophic Press 1993.

Danish architect Erik Asmussen. Young people met there in a group that read the novels of Walter Ljungquist.

I now became very interested in this Swedish writer on whose novels a number of films had been based during the 1940s. After a few trips to antiquarian bookshops in Stockholm I had a complete set of his works. His novel 'The Storm' had an important effect on my development. A man's life-crisis is described in the first person singular just as the same man later saw it and re-experienced it with hindsight. In Ljungquist's novels I felt the special soul quality of the way a self works and takes initiatives through the feeling qualities as characterized by Rudolf Steiner for the Swedish folk soul. This helped me to understand that the many years I later spent in Sweden were something I myself had sought out for karmic reasons.

From 1975 to 1978 I lived at Garnes, a village near Bergen situated between two fiords. After finishing my studies at Järna I had intended to study literature and art history at Bergen University, but was not allowed to postpone my statutory community service period any longer. Two musicians I had got to know at Järna were now working at Rostadheimen, a home for special needs children, and they suggested I apply for a place there.

This home had been founded in the 1960s by Åslaug and Edvin Nysæther. In the 50s they had worked at Saltå, a similar establishment at Järna, and were very good friends with the special needs teacher Hans Glaser. Åslaug and I shared an interest in painting. As well as painting she also ran the weaving workshop, and I was taken on as one of her helpers. We bought ourselves two new sewing machines because this meant we could get them for a lower price, and I began to sew my own clothes. My very close friendship with her was to gain an entirely new dimension many years after her early death in 1980.

With Edvin and those in his care I worked in the garden, where we continued to cultivate the rhubarb and chives grown commercially by an old farmer's wife. Later the whole estate was turned over to biodynamic cultivation.*

Encouraged by the two musician colleagues I tried to cultivate the fallow region of my soul, my lack of musical talent, playing Choroi recorder and beginning to learn the lyre. I also took on the religion lessons for the younger residents and carried some responsibility for the Sunday services.

On the basis of my youthful enthusiasm and my training at Järna I was immediately included in the circle of those responsible for the home. During the meetings we studied Rudolf Steiner's *Education for Special Needs* with the anthroposophical doctor Egil Tynæss, while Edvin's brother Ingmann, a physiotherapist, worked with us on Steiner's teachings about the senses.

For the next two years I worked as a teacher at Rostadheimen, thus briefly becoming an employee of the state. This was my first educational contact with children and young people with special needs.

The home was also in the process of creating a foundation 'Verdandi' for the adults in its care, and in working on the statutes for this foundation I came into contact with Professor Leif Holbæk-Hansen at Bergen's commercial university. In his three-volume standard work on economics he discusses Rudolf Steiner's social ideas in connection with global economics. For our contacts with the authorities I worked out a diagram showing how our organization was modelled on the 'threefold' social principle.

My years at Rostadheimen gave me a sense of having finally

---

* A specific form of organic farming which uses special preparations to enliven soil and plants.

reached adulthood. The vibrant social atmosphere of the place, which I have never again experienced with such intimacy, showed me how anthroposophy can indeed be incorporated into practical and social life. Words by Rudolf Steiner which we read during our weekly study evenings became a reality in our everyday lives: 'When people seek the spirit with heartfelt honesty, then will they also find their way towards one another, from soul to soul.'

In the winter of 1977 I met Mette who, in the 1980s, was to take on the management of Rostadheimen after completing her training as a special needs teacher. For almost two years we had a very close relationship. She helped me emerge from my loneliness of soul which until then I had not wanted to let anyone discover.

Another new friend was Jan through whom I came into contact with different groups of young people in Bergen. In meetings with his friends we discussed not only anthroposophy but also the role of anarchy in history and in present-day society. It was under his influence that I made my one and only experiment with hashish. This taught me to understand how easily people who are searching for the spirit can be led down blind alleys by this and other even stronger drugs.

Every Tuesday our small group of anthroposophists from Garnes took the train through the tunnel to Bergen to attend lectures organized by the group there. The high point of these years was a series of lectures on the forces working behind the scenes of history given by Karl Milton Hartveit, Nils-Gustav Hertzberg, Hans-Jørgen Høins and Bjørn Moen. Hartveit became well-known in Scandinavia through his books on the New Age and freemasonry. I soon became good friends with the other three, and we founded 'Kolumbus', a youth forum intended as an alternative to the work of the anthroposophical group, which met every Thursday evening in the vegetarian restaurant run by Moen.

During this period I gave two lectures in which I endeavoured to describe my on-going work on reincarnation and karma. Using stories told by Australian aborigines and by the so-called 'sleeping prophet' Edgar Cayce and also by discussing modern methods of regression by hypnosis I tried to describe the idea of reincarnation as something we must make it our task to study. I also gave a painting course with simple experiments on Goethe's theory of colours.

In my free time I began to read Jens Bjørneboe. I couldn't get over his plays (I saw one later in Stockholm) or his novels about the history of brutality in Europe. I read the novels 'Silence' and 'Moment of Freedom' almost without putting them down. Enthused by his sense of social responsibility I joined KROM, an organization concerned with the rights of prisoners.

On a visit to Järna in the summer of 1977 I was able to ask Arne Klingborg in person about a new initiative of his, the art course 'Konstnärliga linjen'. My experiences with the people I had been caring for and the realization that art has intrinsic value in education and therapy led me to join the course. Mette helped me financially.

Thus I returned to Järna in the autumn of 1978. For my first term I lived in a student flat in 'Almandinen', the music house with a domed roof in which Rut Nilson, now very old, was living. I helped her in the garden and wrote letters for her on my typewriter. We had a number of wonderful conversations, so that in what was one of the last years of her life our relationship with one another grew deeper. I clearly remember her in the early 1980s standing at the dining room window waiting for her meal. She no longer spoke very much, but a mysterious smile played about her lips as though the things she saw were quite different from our disputes amongst various factions.

I visited Karin Ruths-Hoffman, also now very old, in her flat and helped her do the ironing, a good occupation to engage in while listening to her stories. She was busy editing her memoirs and told me many anecdotes.

After carrying out the artistic tasks set us in the 'Magasinet', our course studio, I spent a good deal of time working at my poetry. Over the following years I completed a number of collections, but whenever I sent one to a publisher it invariably came back. On a few occasions I read some poems in public, which I found sufficiently satisfying.

I came to appreciate many of the artists and architects who were our teachers, and learnt much from all of them, but to describe each one would be going too far in the present context.

For the second term I moved to 'Trompeten' as I was beginning to find Rut Nilson's house a little too quiet. I wanted to be with other students with whom I could talk about art, poetry and existential questions. Falling in love with another woman led to the ending of my relationship with Mette. Although this new situation did not in fact lead to a firm commitment, circumstances now arose which meant that I did not return to Rostadheimen as planned but instead decided to stay at Järna where I remained for the next 19 years, until 1997, albeit at various different addresses.

I got involved with the work of setting up the large exhibitions on architecture and horticultural art which Arne Klingborg initiated and arranged in 1980 and 1983 in Stockholm's art venue 'Liljevalchs'. There were a number of young artists from my year at Järna who wanted to join in this work. We looked for a suitable studio and finally established the 'Skilleby Atelier' with the support of a big donation from the Agape Foundation. On the

Skilleby estate we renovated a nineteenth-century barn where we took part in painting the hundreds of pictures needed for the exhibitions.

Those two exhibitions put on by Arne Klingborg were much appreciated by the general public and are documented in books. These include reproductions of several pictures I painted, for example of Gaudi's architecture.

I shall never forget the final two weeks in the run-up to the exhibition on 'Unfulfilled Functionalism' in May 1980. Humanly, socially, artistically and practically there sat, wrote, composed, walked, painted, ran, climbed, harkened, directed, taught, spoke and listened amongst us an invisible being in human form who brought into what was being created only what he himself had experienced in horticulture and architecture, sculpture, painting, music, poetry and drama, eurythmy and spiritual humanity. This was Arne Klingborg. To us—over 60 participants from more than 10 countries around the world—he was not only a helpful teacher but also a friend when we made a mess of things.

At about the same time I began an apprenticeship under Fritz Fuchs. He had been a colour designer much appreciated in Germany and Scandinavia and had also worked with Arne Klingborg for many years. He took up and developed Klingborg's suggestions regarding the impulse and technique of translucent lazure painting. I worked for three years in his firm Färgbygge (colourful buildings) which he had founded to manufacture the German Aglaia casein and beeswax paints. I was able to talk to Fritz about many things. During breaks in the work he told me of his many journeys and encounters with people all over Europe. We also talked about the theatre. In the 1990s, after we had begun a new period of working together, he followed with interest my initiatives and efforts at Järna.

All this meant that from 1979 the work I was doing involved applying layers of lazure paint to many thousands of square metres of architectural surfaces in several countries. I got to know new people and other ways of working in many places, not only within Scandinavia.

In 1982 Skilleby Atelier became an independent firm, which a year later we made into a commercial foundation that would support the possible building of a hall/auditorium on Seminar land with any profits it might make. Initially there was quite a turnover of participants in the Atelier. I brought in a young artist with whom I worked closely for several years on many projects in Norway. During a trip to a project in Cornwall we decided to embark on life as a couple. She taught me important things about developing one's sense for the aesthetic. She also helped me be more conscientious and responsible in connection with the projects we undertook and which others expected us to finish at the time agreed. The problems I had with my short-term memory often led to difficult situations from which she frequently saved me at the last moment.

For several years during the winter months my life partner and I ran a sewing workshop within the Atelier, making lampshades. It gave us artistic satisfaction to see the perfectly sewn white cotton pieces attached to the frames in various coloured surroundings.

In 1984 we bought an old house in Hölö, a village near Järna, which we did up. In 1988 our daughter Elona Maria was born, followed in 1991 by our son David Johannes. In 1989 we built a house on a piece of land near Skilleby which we had bought together with several other colleagues who also built houses for their families.

In its early years the Atelier became a social meeting place with poetry evenings and gatherings of artists. A number of artistic communities and architects' offices came into being at Järna at that time, all of which were connected with the goals of the Rudolf Steiner Seminar.

My meditative research in recent years has shown me how important these prior experiences in artistic work were for some of the steps I have achieved in the spiritual realm. I shall unfortunately not be able to give chapter and verse here as to why this is the case, but it is something Rudolf Steiner worked out very thoroughly in many lectures. However, some sketches of experiences and projects will help elucidate how I have proceeded on my path.

For many of the exhibitions and trade-fair projects I was involved in or organized I had to make copies or very accurately reproduce things like photographs or my own sketches of buildings or landscapes. In other situations, for example art courses, works of art had to be copied in every detail. These copies were often done from reproductions, backed up by my own observation in museums or on study trips when I was able to find the originals. The value of entering in a living way into pictures and then reproducing them oneself is an educational effort that has long been recognized at Steiner Waldorf schools. I think that in doing this I practised an ability to enter objectively into the living world of Imagination.

Lazure painting as a way of colouring especially indoor spaces is both a social and an artistic exercise. While small walls can be painted by a single person, large expanses call for collaboration between two or more colleagues. This schools a specific sense of space and a capability of adapting one's own body and hand movements to harmonize with those of others. In really successful cases this engenders a 'social ear'.

From 1982 onwards—in projects with various architects, e.g. Erik Asmussen, Thomas Broman, Lars Danielsson, Hasse Nejdeman, Espen Tharaldsen and Håkan Zetterström, for whom

I did the colour design—I had many opportunities to paint murals and other pictures. These murals, on which I worked with other artists in some cases, had to harmonize with the overall concept of architecture and colour. In a number of projects I endeavoured to incorporate the colour plan into often abstract paintings. Frequently proposals for the murals had to be presented to the client, the co-workers at the establishment concerned and the architect in the form of sketches. In other situations I was given a free hand, which meant that I could allow the design of the murals to arise spontaneously.

In 1985 I was asked by the congregation of a church near Stockholm to paint a representational depiction of the Baptism in the River Jordan. This picture, measuring 5 × 8 metres, was not an altarpiece. It was painted on to one of the side-walls in the octagonal church. I was at the time deeply occupied with Christology themes in anthroposophy, but I also had to endeavour to satisfy the priest and congregation of Baptists who did not want any 'symbols' but simply a straightforward picture of the Baptism.

In south-west Sweden at the beginning of the 90s I painted a number of murals in homes for the elderly and establishments for old people with memory loss. Here I did many representational depictions of rural life in appropriate colours to try and bring back the old people's forgotten memories.

For many years I worked with other artists on sketches for educational murals in the classrooms of Steiner Waldorf schools. This is an artistic field which Rudolf Steiner considered very important; in fact his suggestions and indications for the overall picture element in the schools are still extant. I only once had the opportunity to do the actual painting, in the Steiner Waldorf school in Gjøvik, Norway. In another school in Norway I twice painted murals in staircases and corridors together with pupils of the twelfth class.

For a long time I was also concerned with tasks arising in connection with painting altarpieces for the Christian Community. Together with a group of colleagues we made sketches, talked with priests and older artists and tried through eurythmy exercises to approach the problems involved in experiencing the Risen Christ. Although I was never given a commission in this field, the work I did in connection with it was very important to me. To the realization that I was incapable of making a true representation of Christ another feeling was added during the Communion service, namely that the surface of a picture borders very closely on the spiritual world.

Together with other artists I took part in several group exhibitions in anthroposophical places and also in public galleries. As well as working as a teacher and lazure painter I did a lot of work in tempera on canvas. I developed my own style both in very large and very small abstract works. By building up a composition of clearly-defined surfaces I sought to create 'imaginative' colour spaces in which dramatic figures appeared in a smaller scale. For a while I experimented with pointillistic dots and dashes as a way of breaking up the surface. With my sanguine temperament I felt very at home using egg-tempera which has to be applied to the canvas very rapidly to achieve a lively expression.

In the autumn of 1988 a group in Stockholm invited me to put on a one-man exhibition. For this I painted a number of pictures in which I attempted to link my thoughts and feelings in combinations of colours which were connected with the threshold to the spiritual world. In one series of pictures I tried to progress from clear, prismatic colours, chiefly red and green, to dark combinations. While I was painting one of these pictures I had a sensation of standing on the brink of an abyss. With every brush-stroke I had to feel my way in a world invisible to the naked eye. For a brief moment my soul felt as though it was standing before the door to its real home—a sublime experience that was gone in a flash. I had to put down my brush and look at the picture objectively before concluding that it was finished.

One of the older painters who had taught art history at the Seminar was Kurt Wegner. He gave lectures illustrated by slides, speaking with special sensitivity on the art treasures of Chartres and on oriental art. He was a first-rate watercolourist and liked coming to us at the Atelier to see our work. Often he invited us to visit him in his own studio where he showed us his paintings and chatted for hours about his excursions through Norwegian and Swedish landscapes on the lookout for atmospheric scenes and moods to paint.

Kurt Wegner drew my attention to what he termed 'the free and easy brush-stroke' that ought to be visible in a painting. This was entirely new to me, for hitherto I had only paid attention to the freshness of the colours as Arne Klingborg had taught me. When Wegner died in the mid-1980s I watched beside his bier in his flower-filled studio. His face was much changed and had lost all its wrinkles. A pure, youthful light shone from his forehead, and the impression this gave me was of an old soul rejuvenated through death.

In my first year studying art at the Seminar I had made friends with Didrik. After growing up in the village in Östergötland where the writer Walther Ljungquist had lived he had studied aesthetics in Uppsala. Didrik was struggling with incipient blindness, but meanwhile, until he had to retrain as a masseur, he worked in our Atelier for many years and later with Färgbygge. He was on the staff of the monthly journal *Antropos* which was published by the Anthroposophical Society at that time.

He introduced me to the editor, Ingrid Sahlberg. I had already met her in 1978 during a conference in Denmark where she had given a course on Russian literature. We soon became close collaborators and great friends. In 1980 I became a full member of the small editorial team, and when Didrik left I also took care of the journal's layout for many years.

I continued to write essays and articles until 1987. In a larger project on 'The battle against the self' I followed up various themes, finding examples in the writings of Friedrich Schiller, Jacques Lysseyran and Robert Jungk. I wrote essays on Adam Mickiewicz, Friedrich Nietzsche, Janusz Korczak, Andrei Sacharov, Joseph Beuys and Andrei Tarkovsky, and kept abreast of Scandinavian films, art and literature.

All my life I have kept up with political and cultural events in the world. While I was working for *Antropos* I subscribed for many years to a journal which carried translations of articles from reputable foreign papers, for I wanted a wider perspective than the one given by Swedish TV and Stockholm newspapers. I shall here touch only on two events which shocked me deeply on account of the questions they raised regarding their background and the social consequences they generated.

On an evening in February 1986 some friends and I were talking about different aspects of the way anthroposophy was developing in the world. One of those friends told us about his contacts with people outside anthroposophical circles. As we were wondering how we might bring about some fruitful inter-change with non-anthroposophists he said that we ought to make contact with the Social Democrats. We went on talking until midnight and among others also mentioned Olof Palme, the Swedish prime minister. His activities as a peacemaker were described in almost euphoric terms. Then, early next morning, one of those friends rang with the news that Palme had been assassinated. As it did with thousands of others, this murder engaged my thoughts for many years thereafter.

In August 1991 I was carrying out a commission for a large mural in a church of the Swedish Mission Association. The abstract motif was to arise in an encounter between various shades of red and blue. Having worked through similar motifs in a number of painting courses I had formed an idea that politicians with their penchant for subjective provocation and confrontation with opponents might be able to develop their souls through simple painting exercises. I was still busy with this project when the television news reported on the coup d'état in Moscow and the imprisonment of Mikhail Gorbachev leading to his downfall. Despite my strong sympathy and involvement with his problems I had to continue with my work and finish the mural calmly. Nevertheless this topical event clamoured to be included in my brush-strokes and flooding colours. I wanted my noblest feelings and the wish that Russia and the rest of the world might find peace to become a kind of prayer in my picture, a prayer that could be perceived by the spiritual world.

In 1980 Anna Hallström, a eurythmist who worked closely with Jørgen Smit, invited me to give a painting course at the international youth conference at Järna. This led to my being invited to teach at the Seminar. Until 1995 I gave various training courses in mural painting, watercolour painting, drawing, Goethe's theory of colours, aesthetics and stage scenery design.

In the first half of the 1980s the then leader of the Art Section of the School of Spiritual Science* at Dornach, Hans Herrmann, came to Järna to talk with anthroposophical artists and tell them about others connected with the art impulse at the Goetheanum. He also visited our Skilleby Atelier where we got on well with him. A painter who had trained with Herrmann in Dornach and I then wanted to attend a Section meeting there. In the end we did not go because Herrmann had meanwhile resigned, which led to the meeting being cancelled.

---

* A modern-day esoteric school for the renewal of culture and spirituality.

Some time later an artist friend and I went to Arne Klingborg to discuss certain details connected with artistic collaboration. We in the younger generation felt it was time for a group of the Section to be founded in Sweden. However, Arne was too busy with other things, so that our conversation turned instead to practical and artistic matters in the Seminar. He asked us point blank whether we would take on some of his courses. This is how it came about that my friend took on responsibility for the artistic training course while I took over certain courses for first-year students. Both of us became Arne's assistants in the course on Goethe's theory of colours.

From 1990, after Christian Hitsch had become the new leader of the Art Section and been invited to Järna, we continued to work on founding a Swedish branch of that Section. I now did the section work with architects, sculptors and painters of the younger generation. In the summer of 1991 Christian Hitsch confirmed our work during an international conference at Järna. We did not want to appoint a single Section leader from amongst our circle because we thought it better to tackle tasks out of the situation itself. Several artists, especially from the older genera-tion, did not want to support our free style, and during the ensuing disputes our circle of Section members, initially over 20 in number, dwindled more and more. Despite these to my mind tragic though necessary developments we invited Inger Hädelin to practise themes from the Class Lessons in eurythmy with us at the beginning of each meeting.

In this circle I once made a contribution on the early Lessons of the First Class of the School of Spiritual Science in which I sketched the trials of the soul at the threshold of the spiritual world using as examples paintings by Edvard Munch with whom I had always felt closely connected. In the last meeting of the Section circle I attended shortly before my departure from Sweden I described my meditative work and karma research.

From 1979 onwards I participated in an open group that had been set up to work on the possibility of building a hall in the grounds of the Seminar. The idea had been cultivated since the 1960s and it took shape over several years. The many stimulating conversations always focussed on eurythmy and Rudolf Steiner's mystery dramas.

The plans were worked on during international meetings of architects at Järna in several of which I participated. In 1984 a foundation for the northern countries was founded to promote the building project. This is how the 'House for Anthroposophy in Scandinavia' came into being. It was not quite finished in time for its inauguration in 1992, after which it acquired the name Kulturhuset i Ytterjärna. This is the name by which this northern embodiment of the Goetheanum idea became known to, and appreciated by, the general public.

Many of the artists who had experienced the early communal atmosphere and therefore wanted to participate in the project found that this would no longer be possible because the foundation's executive committee had appointed Arne Klingborg as the artistic director. This was to be expected since in Järna's long history it had always been small groups of pioneers who had started projects. Nevertheless many people had hoped that no such appointment would be made. From my angle as a spectator I tried to mediate between the various parties, but soon discovered that an open way of working in which many artists could participate would no longer be possible.

In a letter to Arne Klingborg I proposed that other surfaces in the building might be made available for artists who would not be working with him on the main ceiling. I said that the members of the Section circle felt co-responsible for the hall and would therefore appreciate being able to work on it artistically. I also told him that the situation as it stood was causing unease amongst the artists.

In the meeting of artists and architects that resulted from this letter Klingborg made another suggestion, namely that there could be an art exhibition in the building during the inauguration celebrations. This exhibition was arranged and over 30 artists participated.

During the spring of 1991 circumstances led to my being allowed to work with Arne Klingborg on his great ceiling painting. It was wonderful to see our beloved teacher, now very old, appearing so young and well as he tackled this large task in his own way. However, after the inauguration other artists who had not been permitted to join in the work expressed much criticism and little praise about this painting, the main theme of which depicted Rudolf Steiner's Imaginations for the four seasons. Since I had participated in the project and thus been able to follow its development I had to concede that under the given circumstances it could not have been any different. It bears the enchantment of many good forces which will shine out like the sun long into the future.

The 1993 Michaelmas conference at Dornach brought me to an inner turning point. This did not result from the content of the lectures, the dramatic plenary sessions or the conversation groups, but from conversations with a number of individuals about news of an earthquake in India that had killed over 40,000 people. I spoke briefly about this earthquake to several hundred people having lunch in the Carpentry Workshop canteen. Gearing myself up to do this and the effort needed to raise the necessary courage led me to a question: How can I find a method in everyday life by means of which I might make contact with those who have died? This question was accompanied for several days by a feeling that Jørgen Smit, who had by then died, was expecting something of me.

I was trying at the time to be very conscious of the annual

themes which the Executive Council at Dornach had suggested to members of the Anthroposophical Society for their inner work leading up to the turn of the century. Parallel with this I was contemplating my own biography from the viewpoint of all the initiative situations I had found myself in with other people which, for whatever reason, had not worked out. I shall mention a few of these situations.

Around 1981 I was involved with a number of artist friends connected with the Steiner Waldorf teacher and poet Hans-Jørgen Høinæs on an initiative to found an anthroposophical Seminar Centre in a beautiful estate beside a fiord near Tønsberg. We had good meetings with local politicians and authorities who were interested in our plan to renovate rather than pull down the old buildings. However, we failed to raise sufficient funds. The group dispersed across Europe and each individual became involved in other initiatives or tasks elsewhere.

The land belonging to our Skilleby Atelier had originally comprised three large farms in which a number of buildings had fallen vacant. Discussions were held stage by stage with several anthroposophical firms in the hope of establishing a community of craftspeople and artists in which each would remain economically independent. I got very involved in this, making architectural sketches and layout maps. After many attempts with different participants it transpired that our ideas as how best to proceed were too divergent. Then, in 1986, I myself thought of training to be an architect, but for various reasons I never actually applied for a place.

In the early 1990s discussions about how to continue with the Atelier led to internal conflicts that appeared externally to be the consequence of our poor financial situation. Several of us had frequently worked as lecturers at the Järna Seminar and this was financially regulated via the firm. However, the Seminar itself was in economic difficulties, so for quite some time we had been giving our fees back in the form of loans. In consequence our own situation became very tight, and for me this led to my having to re-think my relationship with money and mutual trust. Several times for lack of funds I helped myself from our shared account and had to face up to the fact that I was insufficiently mature to discuss the resulting problems openly with my colleagues.

For several years we struggled to understand our relationships and solve our problems without the help of outside counsellors. In various studies and through biography work we endeavoured to find out what was behind our external behaviour patterns. Then something woke me up: One of our number announced that he felt paralysed in his creative work by my overabundance of artistic ideas.

There were other incidents at the Seminar as well, which robbed me of almost all my illusions, so that I could no longer avoid facing up to the need for some very stern self-examination. I began to work at achieving self-knowledge by various methods. Something of this I recorded in a collection of poems 'The Lion Dream' (which remained unpublished) as well as in several fragments of novels and a play. I subscribed to a theatrical magazine and tried twice to get a place in Stockholm to train as an actor and director. I also attended a course on writing film scripts. By watching myself from the inside and taking external measures I endeavoured to discover how I influenced and affected other people and circumstances.

After our firm was dissolved in the spring of 1996 we had to leave our much-loved quarters on Skilleby farm because the farmer had different interests. With some others I tried to ensure that the buildings we had occupied would continue to be available for artistic work. On my initiative an anthroposophical artists' association was set up comprising about 20 members. Nevertheless, we could not retain the use of the Atelier buildings and these are now used for biodynamic research which is, unquestionably, also very much needed.

Between 1992 and 1995 I twice worked at the Järna Seminar as director of the training course for art teachers at Steiner Waldorf schools and once as director of the course for mural painting. During this period I tried to attract new teaching staff from Finland and Norway. For example I succeeded in getting the art teacher, sculptor and painter Odd Lindbråten to join us to teach graphics. He asked me to come to the school at Moss, Norway, to paint murals with his class twelve pupils.

With my students I tried to bring about a working atmosphere which would help them recognize their individual artistic position and discover their own way of questioning art in the hope that we could then talk about these things in the group. I wanted to search for deeper knowledge connected with Rudolf Steiner's artistic impulse, knowledge that can be worked towards together when each one brings in his or her own experiences.

In 1992–93 I wrote a play 'Pneum'. Although it was not performed I was able to use it with the students as a practice piece during a scenery design course. Its subject was the situation an artist faces in creative moments when spiritual questions lead to feelings of powerlessness which can then be experienced as threshold situations which make art socially effective.

In my final year at the Seminar I found that there were few colleagues with whom I could speak in the way I could with my students. On account of certain circumstances the situation became so difficult for me that I gave in my notice in 1995 with effect from the end of the summer term.

Before moving on to events following my departure from the Järna Seminar I shall first mention two relationships which it would be inappropriate to omit since they were very important in my life, namely my friendship with Sonja Robbert and Willy Buzzi.

I first experienced Sonja Robbert in the 1970s as a strict and conscientious painting teacher in Järna. Born in Denmark in 1909, she had lived as an artist in France in the 1930s after which, towards the end of the 1950s, she painted stage panoramas in watercolours for eurythmy for Marie Savitch at Dornach. At Farum, Denmark, in the 1960s, she established her studio for painting with children as well as adults. From this 'island of culture', where music also played a part, Arne Klingborg called her to Järna when she was 59. Since then she had been a part of the artistic and cultural life there. She gave courses on subjects such as the history of dance, Goethe's 'Fairy Tale' and his theory of colours, Steiner's mystery plays and his *Nature of Colour*, the seasons of the year, and the eurythmy figures.

She always made me welcome in her comfortable studio flat. We talked about art in general as well as teaching it, and also esoteric questions in anthroposophy. She showed me the model stages she had built for teaching and exhibition purposes. Each miniature (there were seven altogether) had the proportions of the Goetheanum stage and was equipped with little transformers, lighting switches and bars of coloured torch bulbs. She set up the little 'actors' or 'eurythmists' made of painted paper in the sets she had designed for Goethe's 'Fairy Tale' or a scene in one of the mystery plays. I often helped her put on exhibitions either of her model stages or of pictures selected from among her copious works. I was allowed to use these models for my stage design courses after she had donated them to the Seminar.

Sonja Robbert's main concern is expressed in the phrase 'coloured space'. She held that the age of representational art was actually long gone. Every artist, she maintained, including the representational artist, should try to enter the realm of music.

There the spiritual in art could be grasped in consciousness of self where creation could be accomplished out of nothingness. She had painted her great stage panoramas as a way of getting away from the traditional blue backdrops. The coloured lights illuminating the panoramas were to create for the audience a living 'coloured space' in which the eurythmists could be creative in the present moment. It has to be said that Sonja Robbert's colour impulse has to date met with little understanding, which means that so far it has not been taken further.

I had read some of Willy Buzzi's books in the 1970s, but only got to know him on my return to Järna after my three years back in Norway. He was born in Trondheim, Norway, and grew up virtually next door to the great medieval cathedral of St Olaf which I had seen several times as a child. He was one of the few Goethean researchers and anthroposophical writers in Scandinavia. Research into films was one of his main themes, but he also wrote on many other subjects.

He took up Steiner's suggestions about the etheric geography of the earth and developed these to the stage of creating a new atlas which has, however, so far not been published. He worked for many years in a Weleda company at Järna, and we used to discuss all kinds of subjects. I invited him to contribute to the art teacher training with an introduction to film studies. He was very happy to oblige, and the students were delighted to listen to someone who was knowledgeable about films.

One of our topics was drama in art and life, for example the mysteries of lying, sitting, standing and walking. This led to my interest in the film work of Andrei Tarkovsky. In 1985 I participated with a number of parents, teachers and pupils from a Järna Steiner Waldorf school in a film *Sacrifice* Tarkovsky was making in Stockholm for which he needed several hundred extras. He already had cancer and it was a moving experience to see him directing the cameras in a 'street devastated by war' along which we had to walk several times in a cold spring wind, semi-naked in our torn garments, until a satisfactory version of the scene was obtained.

When Andrei Tarkovsky died I wrote an appreciation of his work in the form of a study of his film *Solaris*. By showing parallels with Rudolf Steiner's work I tried to demonstrate that Tarkovsky had a way of 'sculpting time'.

From the autumn of 1994, in addition to my work at the Seminar, I attended a course twice a week on the theory of art from Plato via Kant to the Post-Modernist theorists of the twentieth century. This course ended with a written project which I completed at an art academy in Stockholm.

My thesis, which was accepted, was entitled: 'The consonance between intuition and painting. A study of Rudolf Steiner's imaginative tale "The Spiritual Being of Art" (1909) describing the relationship between intuition and painting'. I described the historical context of this lecture and clarified various concepts he used, such as 'astral Imagination', 'seraphic being', 'light of soul', 'movement of soul', 'the inner nature of colours' and others. I tried to explain what Steiner meant by 'Intuition' and described the extent of his work on colour and painting as well as his continuation of Goethe's theory of colours in his lectures on the nature of colour. One chapter dealt with Steiner's aesthetics. Another was about intuition and artistic creativity as seen by the philosophers Vladimir Soloviev and Edmund Husserl, and also Wassily Kandinsky and Paul Klee, the latter two having been Steiner's contemporaries. Including notes and a bibliography, the thesis covered 40 A4 pages.

I wrote this thesis during the period when my destiny situation at Järna was coming to a head.

In addition to my work in education and art I have always taken a special interest in the lectures Rudolf Steiner gave on karma in 1924.* In the mid-1980s I once more began to study Platonic and Aristotelian motifs. This theme of the two streams—which, in the karma lectures that touched on the Middle Ages, Steiner linked from various angles with the anthroposophists of the twentieth century and especially with certain tasks involving the meeting of the two streams in the final years of that century—had already been a vital subject for me in the 1970s. I had a feeling that I might be karmically connected with Platonic circles, especially the Chartres stream, and I tried to characterize this in my thoughts and recognize signs of it amongst the people I knew.

Not many in my immediate circles were as interested as I was in this subject. So in the 80s I set my questions aside and turned once more to my private, social and artistic tasks. I have already mentioned that a time then began when I found myself increasingly coming up against blank walls in my immediate relationships. This led me in the winter of 1996 to look elsewhere for work. The dramatic first half of the 90s, which I had experienced inwardly as a tragedy, made me turn with renewed vigour to studies of history and modern art theory.

I read not only academic literature but also anthroposophical authors such as Sigismund von Gleich, Ernst Uehli, Renate Riemeck, Christoph Lindenberg and many others. I looked in every direction but especially at Atlantis and the cultural epochs. I spent a lot of time on Egypt and the time of Rameses II. From January 1995 I even took a correspondence course at the University of Växjö, but the situation that was developing meant that I could not finish it.

During study trips to Italy in 1993 and Greece in 1995 I had certain *déjà-vu* experiences and also remembered having similar

---

* Published as *Karmic Relationships Vols.I–VIII*, London: Rudolf Steiner Press.

experiences in England during the 1980s. Increasingly it was the Middle Ages in Europe that interested me most deeply, especially the twelfth century. My concern was no longer fixed solely on France and the schools of Paris and Chartres. The range of my interests now encompassed Duke Henry the Lion, Emperor Frederick Barbarossa and Pope Alexander III together with all the conflicts in and around the Holy Roman Empire between the Second and Third Crusade.

I studied piles of specialist literature on persons and events during the time of the Hohenstaufen emperors and for the first time charted possible karmic connections between the twelfth century and our time. I tried to work out how I might begin to work meditatively on the inklings I began to have during my studies. I was convinced that Rudolf Steiner's suggestions regarding the teachers and pupils of Chartres should be linked for our time with far wider twelfth-century circles.

In Ernst Uehli's excellent book on the three great Hohenstaufen emperors I had found hardly anything about Chartres, and in Renate Riemeck's on the Councils of the church there was no reference in connection with the Third Lateran Council (1179) of the Chartres teachers John of Salisbury or Alanus de Insulis being there. I continued to search both in the most recent literature on the Middle Ages and in older works in order to find proof of my suppositions. I even had to try and learn some Latin.

Reading the registers of Rainald von Dassel, Archbishop of Cologne and Barbarossa's Chancellor around 1160, I stumbled across the name of the French master Girard Pucelle. This close friend and colleague of John of Salisbury was, for a brief period before Rainald's death, his counsellor in the conflict with Pope Alexander III. In Girard Pucelle I had discovered an individual who acted as a bridge between the Chartres stream and the Hohenstaufen stream, a bridge for the existence of which my studies had led me to search. As my researches continued I found other such human bridges, for example Duke Hermann of Carinthia who corresponded with the Chartres teacher Thierry.

During these historical studies which took me further and further into situations of those times I had a surprising intuitive experience in my thoughts in the winter of 1995. I was able to identify with Christian von Buch (1135–1183), Rainald von Dassel's successor as Barbarossa's Chancellor and later one of the Emperor's most zealous diplomats and military leaders in Italy.

I should like to describe how my train of thought led to this identification with Christian von Buch by means of the following story which shows clearly that there are ways in which other people can contribute karmically to how one can arrive at the right question to ask.

While I was pursuing my history studies at the beginning of the 1990s a number of anthroposophists made suggestions whose relevance was not immediately obvious to me. One such was that I should read Lessing's *Nathan the Wise*. Although I became absorbed in the play I could not understand why I ought to see a connection between my search on the one hand and events at the time of Sultan Saladin and the Third Crusade on the other.

Another indication came from a woman who was convinced she could receive communications from her angel. She hinted at certain karmic relationships between us and a number of our mutual friends, saying that those relationships stemmed from a family drama which had taken place in the Middle Ages. Our friend A, she said, had probably participated in founding a city, but the century was uncertain. She reminded me of the story of Parsifal's son, Lohengrin. As I had just seen Wagner's opera, my inner picture of what had happened agreed to some extent with what she was implying. Our friend B had been the wife of A at that time. My friend herself, who had been the daughter of this pair, had been sexually abused by her mother for her own ends in a manner that was normal for the times. My friend's husband, C, at that time B's brother, and I were friends and together had rescued her from her mother's sphere of influence. In telling these karmic stories my friend kept mentioning the city of Lübeck, maintaining that these events had taken place there.

I studied the development of cities in Europe, paying particular attention to Lübeck and the influence of that Hanseatic city in the Baltic region. These studies led me to Duke Henry the Lion whom I tried to link with our friend A. Thus began my detailed research into the history of the twelfth century which I continued for some time.

From Henry the Lion I went on to study Emperor Frederick Barbarossa and followed all the complicated events of the Holy Roman Empire leading to the schism of the Church (1159–1176). I traced the relationships between individuals then and tried to discover how they related karmically to various events now. While I was reading about the assassination of Arnold von Seelenhofen, Archbishop of Mainz, the above-mentioned story told by my friend came to life. I began to feel that her tale of the family drama in the Middle Ages had something to do with this story in which Rudolf von Zähringen and Christian von Buch were rivals for the vacant See. Having assassinated their archbishop, the citizens of Mainz had begun to realize that the Emperor would make them do penance for this murder. They searched among the great families for a successor who, they hoped, would afford them protection. They elected Rudolf von Zähringen who was not only a brother of Duke Berthold of Zähringen but also a brother-in-law of Henry the Lion, as well as being related to the Emperor. However, a diet of princes headed by Rainald von Dassel, Archbishop and Chancellor, annulled the election and excommunicated the citizens of Mainz. The candidate now elected by the princes was Christian von Buch, a young cathedral provost. The Emperor, however, countered both proposals and installed instead Conrad of Wittelsbach as the new Archbishop of Mainz.

Rudolf and Berthold von Zähringen's sister Clementia was Henry the Lion's wife until 1162. Their daughter Gertrude became the wife of Friedrich von Rothenburg, Duke of Swabia, a son of the former king Conrad III. Duke Friedrich, with a number of others, died in Rome in 1167 in an outbreak of malaria. In the autumn of that year Christian von Buch, who had been Archbishop of Mainz since 1165, and Berthold von Zähringen rode to Saxony as peacemakers in the conflict between Henry the Lion and his Saxon enemies. They probably brought Gertrude news of her husband's death on their way through Swabia.

In my quest for knowledge during the winter of 1995 I tried as follows to relate the above-mentioned persons karmically to the individuals discussed with my friend. I thought of her as Gertrude, our friend A as Henry the Lion, our friend B as Clementia von Zähringen, B's husband as Berthold von Zähringen and myself as Christian von Buch. Gertrude subsequently married the pretender to the Danish throne, later King Canute VI. It is not difficult to imagine Christian von Buch being a negotiator in this connection as he had already cultivated contact with the Danes in the early 1160s in his capacity as an ambassador for the anti-Pope Victor IV.

Having read several biographies of Henry the Lion and Frederick Barbarossa, as well as of other figures of the time, and thus gained a picture of the activities and personality of Christian von Buch, the idea ripened within me that I had been Christian von Buch in an earlier incarnation. Initially this was not a pleasant thought, since the historians did not fail to stress the hard and unpleasant aspects of that military leader's character.

As I continued to study the period between the Second and Third Crusade I also realized the meaning of the suggestion that I should read Lessing's play. My karma research was to show the relationship the individual behind the figure of Saladin had with my present karmic circle. My continuing karma research from 1996 onwards also confirmed the conclusions about Christian von Buch which I had reached in 1995. In Chapter 3 I shall enter in more detail into this life of mine in the twelfth century.

I was occupied with these historical and karmic questions in the summer of 1995 when my doctor prescribed three months' rest on account of 'burn-out syndrome'. I had intended to continue my studies at Växjö in the autumn, but could not do so. My family went away on holiday while I stayed at home. I did not have the strength to be sociable and preferred to be alone and look after our angora goats. But instead of getting on with maintenance work around the house and garden I sat for hours at my desk looking out of the window.

While I was still working on the medieval figure of Christian von Buch a humorous sketch occurred to me which I wrote down in 10 days. It depicted the year from 1179 to 1180 which he spent in prison in Italy. His daydreams, which I tried to sense, shaped themselves into images of a future in which many of his contemporaries, transformed both in looks and gender, had parts to play. The result was a kind of burlesque Grail intrigue. When I later showed this drama to some of my friends they could make nothing of it.

The autumn passed and I still lacked the strength to begin anything new. There was a high level of unemployment in Sweden at the time, and after the three months I, too, joined the dole queue while applying to several state schools that were looking for art teachers. For the next three months I received neither offers of work nor any money from the employment authorities because my private firm was still registered and I couldn't prove that I had no income. It felt rather odd to find myself giving advice to a former student from the art teacher training course who had found a job in a school which had rejected my application. I stayed at home, did a few necessary chores and sat by the window for hours looking out at the trees and goats.

The doctor prescribed another month's rest. The slightest agitation brought me to tears. Everything was dreadful, yet in retrospect the experience was necessary. This 'burn-out' robbed me of any illusions I still had about life. I went to Norway, visited and talked to old friends and relatives and considered moving back there with or without my family.

During that autumn I entered into the fifth 'self-knowledge project' of my life. The first had been in 1971 shortly before I had the feeling of dying and the imaginative pictures about America. The second was in the autumn of 1978 when I decided not to return to Bergen but to stay on at Järna to work on artistic tasks there. The third was in 1985–87, the period when I was occupied with Tarkovsky and when my mother died. The fourth was from the death of Jørgen Smit in 1991 to the 1993 Michaelmas Conference, a period during which I took up my studies of history. Now, in the autumn of 1995, when for the fifth time I trawled my soul for all its illusions, habits, impatiences, interests, wishes, ideas, concepts, opinions and so on, a period began when I endeavoured to practise self-knowledge the whole time. Those inner enemies, which Goethe described in his essay 'An Attempt to Mediate between Object and Subject', became important targets of investigation. The upshot was that I began again to work with Rudolf Steiner's karma exercises and other meditations.

Many events from my present life up to the crisis at 42 have been omitted from this biographical sketch. I have tried to select matters which will help the reader understand the rest of this book, but it wasn't easy to choose from among the many memories that came flooding back as I wrote.

Other recollections important to me kept interposing themselves: encounters with people, childhood memories, teenage
problems, love affairs and illnesses, happenings in Finland and
Denmark, travels in Rome, Michelangelo's frescos in the Sistine
Chapel, a jolly encounter with a lady in a Cretan village, coming
to grips with politics and other topical issues, the black flags at
Dungannon in 1981, the step-well at Mycenae, Kurosawa's
biographical film, a course in vegetarian cookery in Vidarsen, an
anthroposophical conference on feminism in Oslo, a trip to Haus
Rüspe with Arne Klingborg, a visit to Weimar and Berlin before
the fall of the Wall, my critical essay on a novel by Kaj Skagen,
wonderful encounters with people and nature in Iceland, funny
skits with friends after our annual watercolour courses, other
humorous episodes with colleagues during trips to Hamburg,
many discussions and talks on the state of the Anthroposophical
Society, wonderful dance performances in Stockholm, much
enjoyed eurythmy courses in Bergen—how is it possible to
describe so many wonderful, beautiful, melancholy, sad, funny,
dramatic, spectacular and tragic things?

One reason there is no need to go into it all is that everyone has
had similar experiences in life, experiences that show we are all
following the same earthly path, striving to find our archetypal
self, our higher, invisible, spiritual self which can help us find
and love the higher self in others too.

Out of the many journeys my destiny has enabled me to make I
should here like to conclude with only two images which later,
when I received the karmic Imaginations, helped me understand
my life's experiences and realize that every activity we find ourselves involved in has a deeper meaning, just as Seneca said two
thousand years ago.

In 1981 I went to Cornwall on a work project with three artist
friends. On the way there we visited some of England's Celtic

sites, also Stonehenge, several cathedrals and a number of renaissance castles and gardens. Peredur Trust, who had commissioned the lazuring we were to do, was situated near Tintagel, so we had several opportunities to go there. Having completed the commission we also went to Northern Ireland. That sojourn in Cornwall gave me a strong sense of being on a continent. I submerged myself in the Grail legend and tried to understand the tasks of the knights of King Arthur. I had to admit that I felt inwardly connected with this 'continent' which, although invisible, had somehow continued to exist spiritually. The English landscape touched a layer in my soul which since then has always stirred when I find myself in similar surroundings.

Quite a different sense of being at home arose in me during an art trip to Greece in April 1995 which took me to Athens, Delphi, Eleusis, Corinth and Epidaurus. The ancient mystery centre of Eleusis is today surrounded by a modern industrial city of a kind not suited to attract many tourists. Apart from the polluted air I felt extremely well in this place. Standing and walking about amongst the few archaeological remnants of the great building I felt I had arrived at a location very familiar to me. I sat down on the steps in a number of spots in the inner part of the complex and was able to sense and almost see how I had long ago participated in rituals there.

2

The spiritual breakthrough and early experiences

Humility of spirit, eagerly enquiring mind.
Tranquillity in living, silent inner questing.
Bernard of Chartres

Biography work

Before Christmas 1995 I picked myself up by my bootstraps and contacted several old friends. This led to the beginning of a new period of mural painting and teaching, first at Järna, then at Umeå in northern Sweden, and finally at Moss in Norway. The new life situation which began for me in 1996 following the crisis meant that I lived in these different places for several months at a time. There I had the opportunity to turn once more to the inner schooling path. In addition to other meditations, I had from the 1970s onwards dwelt repeatedly on some of Rudolf Steiner's karma exercises, though with no obvious results.

In the 1980s I had focussed quite a bit on the biographies of Richard Wagner, Henrik Ibsen, August Strindberg, Vincent van Gogh, Edvard Munch, Rudolf Steiner and also other poets, playwrights and artists. I had gone thoroughly into Strindberg's dramatic life and also his plays. I had brought out a themed issue of *Antropos* in which the Swedish Waldorf teacher Hans Möller interpreted Strindberg's biography on the basis of seven-year periods. This background had been helpful when I began to take a new look at my own biography in 1991. I discovered a reflective law which other people later confirmed to me on the basis of various models.

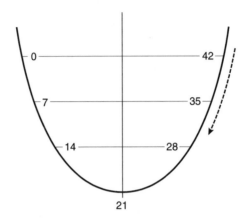

To illustrate this I had sketched an overview of my life on a parabola, with my 21st year at the lowest point of the curve. Every seven-year period was depicted by a line, so that the year of birth mirrored the 42nd year, the 7th the 35th, and the 14th the 28th. From the lowest point (21) I drew a vertical line which cut the parabola exactly in half, and I called this the 'mirror of self'. On this line I had been able to enter karmic questions that arose. I discovered that specific encounters, illnesses, crises and other experiences of the first three seven-year periods reappeared in a metamorphosed form in the corresponding seven-year periods on the other side of the line. I also discovered that for the years after 42 you have to draw the line of your life running back along the parabola. When you do this you recognize correspondences with earlier biographical facts. In my work as a counsellor for questions of spiritual schooling I have often used this parabola as a method of obtaining a quick overview of a biography.

This discovery showed me a most beautiful life pattern, a wonderful image of my life with dramatic and painful but also calm and happy 'points and stretches along the way' where the background forces of karma appeared to bubble up. I found that my experiences during childhood and youth could be seen to harmonize inwardly with experiences after the age of 21.

By the time of the dramatic events in 1995 I had forgotten about this biography parabola, but immediately after the crisis I developed a meditation out of the parabola studies which I called 'filling, drinking and refilling the Grail of life'. It was on this meditation that I based my new work with Rudolf Steiner's karma exercise described below.

Meditation and karma exercises

As I meditated I discovered a fact which I should like to describe by comparing it with painting in tempera. In order to mix oil with water you need a medium, for example egg. The egg has a specific shape which has to be smashed in order to extract the medium for painting in tempera. The paint made from the mixture of egg, oil, water and pigment enables pictures painted on a prepared base to remain visible to the eye for countless centuries. This is borne out by the many tempera paintings still visible on ceramic bases and also on wood in ancient churches.

Henceforth meditation became for me a sculpture of the soul whose uprightness is maintained by the self—reminiscent of Tarkovsky's descriptions of the way he sculpted time—an individually created medium in the truest sense, where spiritual facts could be preserved in earthly waking consciousness. I felt it was important for meditation, which is a process in time, to have an appropriate beginning and ending, and for this I used either a verse by Rudolf Steiner or a eurythmy gesture. Later I discovered that eurythmy gestures carried out inwardly in meditation can help one experience the qualities of the four ethers.

I shall not dwell here on the position of the body while

meditating except to say that I tried out lying, standing and sitting in various ways. I was even able to meditate successfully while sitting in the bath. Other positions I experimented with need not be termed yoga. Earlier on, because of my external tasks and duties, the only opportunity I had for meditating and doing karma exercises was in bed once all the other members of my family had gone to sleep. So I had learnt to meditate lying down without falling asleep. My first experiences with the 'karma exercises' (see below) came while I was meditating in the sitting position.

Both the 'subsidiary exercises'* and the backward review of the day† can help us develop specific etheric and psychological habits in meditation which, as I discovered, are needed by someone wanting to work with Rudolf Steiner's biographical karma exercise. The task of experiencing the 'reverse' etheric world accords exactly with those exercises. Over the years I have practised in various ways the following exercise described by Rudolf Steiner.

My first Imagination about Eleusis

In 1996 I began to practise the biographical karma exercise with greater stringency, choosing in advance two characteristic episodes from each seven-year period. Looking at them as though they were painted on a wall like a mural I followed these memories backwards. That is to say, I went backwards through the

---

* Basic spiritual exercises for strengthening the forces of thinking, feeling and will. For a detailed description see F. Lowndes *Enlivening the Chakra of the Heart*, London: Sophia Books 1999.

† A meditation in which the individual reviews the events of the day in backward order. See further in *Guidance in Esoteric Training*, London: Rudolf Steiner Press 1998.

sequence of memories but did not find it necessary to follow each episode itself backwards.

From the point where my own memories of childhood ceased to be accessible I endeavoured to go further back, in fact right back to conception by means of accurate inner thought pictures. I tried to imagine myself floating up from my birthplace to a position above the Sunndal cliffs. Then came the moment at which I had to be careful not to fall either asleep or out of the meditation. Instead I had to enter into a realm totally void of thoughts or pictures while retaining consciousness of self. Formerly for years this was where I had experienced in various ways the imperfections of my own soul forces. Rudolf Steiner often described the patience with which one must wait for spiritual experiences. This patience in meditation creates in the Consciousness soul* the first beginnings of what he termed the Imagination-soul.

In September 1996, while following my biography backwards to my earliest memory, I had my spiritual breakthrough, which I have already described in the Prologue to this book—a vivid world of moving pictures which I regarded as an Imagination. At that moment I understood the meaning of the concepts 'spirit-remembering', 'spirit-considering' and 'spirit-beholding' which Rudolf Steiner used in the *Foundation Stone Meditation*† during the Christmas Conference of 1923–24.

Anyone practising this biographical karma exercise might have

---

* This is a technical term which refers to a particular aspect of the human being's developing self. See further in *Theosophy*, New York: Anthroposophic Press 1994.

† On refounding the Anthroposophical Society at Christmas/New Year 1923/24, Steiner formulated a meditation as a new 'foundation stone' for the Society. For the full version and commentary see *The Foundation Stone/The Life, Nature and Cultivation of Anthroposophy*, London: Rudolf Steiner Press 1996.

his or her first Imagination in a similar way, with the meditant waking up in 'spirit-remembering' at a specific location and moment, or in a sequence of events from one or more earlier lives that correspond with the present memories selected. No doubt the manner in which the inner jolt happens at the transition from memory consciousness to Imagination consciousness will be different for different individuals. Perhaps there need not necessarily be a jolt at all.*

The four-day karma exercise

In my ongoing work, and alternating with the biographical karma exercise described above, I did the four-day karma exercise† focussing on many individuals in my karmic environment without most of them knowing I was doing this. In the lecture in question Steiner described doing a meditation focussed on an encounter or an event and then waiting in some way until the fourth day for an Imagination. He described in detail how the memory picture—through spiritual processes which always take place in the unconscious—becomes transformed and, as it were, draws towards itself another picture from the spiritual environment. Over the years I have done this exercise in a form which I have tailored to my own needs.

It happened frequently that I forgot about the exercise as the four days progressed, or else that I fell asleep on the first evening before finishing it. Having discovered this weakness many days

---

* I think that the self can orientate in karmic Imaginations—or even Inspirations or Intuitions—brought about by one's own efforts with far greater assurance than in those arising with the help of a regression therapist. Strong feelings and the re-experiencing of feelings such as joy, pain and sadness are always a part of true karmic Imaginations pertaining to oneself. I do believe, however, that genuine Imaginations can also come about through regression therapy (see page 91).
† See note on page 1.

or weeks later, I decided in the summer of 1996 to strengthen the exercise in its form and rhythm. I added a second and third evening meditation in which I included experiences I had had on waking up in the morning. After following this procedure I received—in the same week as the one described above—a karmic Imagination which showed a link between today and the Middle Ages.

From an encounter with a woman which had generated the deepest sympathy in me I shaped within me a clear, coloured memory picture as my first evening meditation. I cultivated this memory of the actual encounter over three days, paying concentrated meditative attention to it in the evenings. I also succeeded in including in the evening meditation the feelings and sense impressions which occurred in my soul and physical body when I awoke next morning.

On the fourth morning I woke up, got dressed and sat down on a chair with my eyes closed. Knowing that I was still within the four-day exercise I adopted a quiet, meditative mood without thinking of anything and without calling up the earlier memory. I found myself entering a kind of soul emptiness. I felt entirely empty, and the following thought came to me from the outside: 'I myself do not have the strength to call up anything karmic.' I wanted to think that I would have to resign myself to not achieving any karmic knowledge, but I could not do this. My thought life was hit as though with a boomerang by the power of my own will which I had exercised through my consciousness of self during the three days of the exercise. I felt paralysed in my soul.

Then suddenly, before my inner eyes, there appeared a medieval knight in the style and colours characteristic of the time in a region of northern Italy not far from Modena. I knew that at that time, about the mid-1170s, this person was my favourite companion. And I myself was Christian von Buch! My present self was there in the self of that time. I was able to find my way around a region that I have never visited in my present life. I knew the route we would have to follow towards Modena with our troupe of knights in order to avoid being ambushed by our enemies.

These two successes meant that I had reached a stage which gave me the strength and inspiration to begin an individual meditative practice which led on further from what I at that time knew of Steiner's suggestions. I entered what was for me new terrain. Only later on did I discover that my experiences conformed absolutely with Steiner's statements. After a while I recognized the knight as a certain Willibald who, according to further meditative research, had belonged to the circle of Christian von Buch, Archbishop of Mainz, for many years. Other Imaginations even revealed that his death in an ambush could not be prevented because Christian, who had been wounded, and another knight called Giorgio, had left him in the lurch in order to save their own lives. Sad to say, I have so far not found any historical record of either Willibald or Giorgio.

I felt that even these very first Imaginations confirmed my earlier meditative studies. Nevertheless I kept an open mind about the results and checked everything that was revealed in the Imaginations.

The jazz singer

An Imagination can be described as a light-soul-process,* an intimate subjective-objective process of the consciousness soul.

As one develops the various soul and karma exercises further a faculty is created which enables spontaneous Imaginations to arise through the presence of spirit in everyday life. The following

---

* See Chapter 6 'The faculty of Imagination as a light-soul-process'.

example clearly depicts the karmic connection between two lives of someone I had not met before. The abundance of objective information, which is in my opinion a sign of a genuine Imagination, is obvious once again in this example.

During a jazz concert I was listening to a female Danish singer performing her own lyrics in a melodious voice while accompanying her singing with gentle hand-movements. She was a typically nordic individual despite her rhythmical liveliness and black hair. With my eyes closed I asked in my thoughts: How did she come by her wonderful voice? The reply I received took the form of an inner impression.

A strong black man is standing up to his hips in the water of an ocean, about 20 metres from the shore. His upper body is naked and his arms and hands hang motionless. He is standing quite still, with his lips pressed together, awaiting what is to come in full presence of mind. Outside my field of vision but nevertheless clearly in my consciousness a large number of the man's enemies stand nearby on the shore. Their weapons, bows and arrows, are aimed at the fugitive.

Clearly I hear the leader of the pursuers call out: 'If you don't tell us where your comrades are hiding we will kill you!' The stillness of the solitary man increases as he shows in his whole attitude of body and countenance that he will never betray his friends. Seconds pass and then, at the sound of a command, arrows whir from various directions and I see them pierce the man's body. Blood flows down and stains the water around him. For a moment he stands there, looking down at the arrows sticking out of his body, before sinking slowly into the water. The mood generated by the calm blue sea with the red blood and the black face of the dead man fades away in a beautiful evening twilight. The Imagination also tells me in that moment that the man's friends were never discovered.

The question that this individual's present voice as a jazz singer had generated received a dramatic and almost mythical reply. And for the duration of the Imagination I continued to hear that voice which afterwards I found even more beautiful.

Rudolf Steiner spoke about the way in which our good or bad thoughts about our fellow human beings denote an objective process in the universe. The good will in our meditative thoughts about our fellow human beings, said Steiner, fades away in the universal ether. When, either through practice or as the result of our destiny, a consciousness or an organ develops in us which can observe these objective processes taking place in the world ether, then many-layered Imaginations of this kind can appear either spontaneously or in meditation.

Imaginations are more concise and at the same time more transparent than ordinary memory pictures. The latter have to do with our own experiences and thoughts which rise up once again in our thinking after a period of time: we remember them. Memories are always personal and subjective.

In Imaginations like the one I have just described, however, themes are shown which one cannot oneself have experienced in that place and at that time, even if one was actually alive then. A 'light-soul-process' arises during the Imagination which makes a connection between what is subjective in one's own soul (in the above example my present experience of an unknown person combined with a questioning attitude of thought) and what is objective in the world ether. As the Imagination lights up in the soul temporary access to the Akashic Record is obtained.

Memories are more like film sequences playing in the soul. They are close enough to touch and yet invisible as they come and go in the midst of a conversation or some other everyday activity. Imaginations, on the other hand, resemble living, moving, transparent pictures lazured on a wall; they can generate an ever greater depth of space or longer sequence of time. I have discovered that in meditation and spiritual research I can experience an ongoing development of myself which enables me to follow up what I want to discover by means of a questioning attitude. I have been able to observe the same themes and persons several times or see situations from varying standpoints, either from within the personality at the time, or from the outside.

Experience of a regression method

In the 1980s it was fashionable to consult clairvoyants or regression therapists to find out something of one's earlier lives. Some of my friends did this, and I found it interesting while not wanting it myself in this form. I felt that if the exercises recommended by Rudolf Steiner did not lead to any results this would mean that I was not yet mature enough for such knowledge. After I had had my own experiences of Imagination, however, a regression therapist suddenly appeared on the scene just as I arrived back at Umeå in between two jobs.

I was acquainted with this man, who was a friend from the 1970s and a Steiner Waldorf teacher. He had trained in a regression method which he used in combination with his anthroposophical way of thinking. This had enabled him to help many people discover pictures from their past lives, and he had also extended his knowledge about his own karma to cover several lifetimes. We told one another about our experiences and our own karmic memories. This was quite an intimate conversation during which I decided to ask him if he would act as a guide in a regression experiment. I thought that if I were to receive pictures with his help, it might be interesting to compare the two methods. I saw this as an opportunity given me by destiny to conduct a personal scientific experiment.

Several picture sequences did indeed appear for me. Amongst a number of situations in my life as Christian von Buch was one in which I saw him/myself riding over the Alps to Italy. The journey ended in a town I recognized as Pisa. Then came images from another life showing situations with elephants, and from a third life there was a very sad scene in which I was standing by a stretch of water carrying a young woman dressed in white in my arms. I was fleeing from something, and these pictures made me weep bitterly.

For our second session the next day we made preparations which involved my thinking about questions concerning the future. Further Imaginations from possible former lives appeared, and there was also a kind of symbolic Imagination which I was not able to interpret at the time, although several months later I did discover what it meant. During this session I also came to realize that it was permissible for me to search meditatively for friends who had died. As a result of my meeting with this former friend I was also encouraged to develop a new main meditation to accompany Steiner's karma exercises.

'Building a hut' in the elemental world

After 25 years of looking at art, working with art in a general way and specifically working with colour design, lazure painting and making murals in rooms of very varying shapes and sizes architecturally, I had achieved a level of preparation on which I now endeavoured to draw in my meditative work. Just as an integration of the various arts can come about, so now in my meditations I made various fragments, parts or links between mantras, verses, texts, forms, images and memories come together in full consciousness in order to seek in them a new harmony, a new consonance.

I shall here describe some of my steps in this meditative work which I found necessary in order to obtain any kind of sense for the truth in the great variety of material I now had, and in order to create a feeling of being-at-home in the supersensible realm.

It was at this time that I became aware of the theme of 'building a hut'. I had been experimenting—if this is a term one can use in this connection—with the flexibility and mobility of the self-aware astral body in the elemental world and had experienced, not without fear, certain incipient breakthroughs of higher ways of knowing. This made me realize that in meditation I could now visit a specific geographical location which I knew well in the natural world. By clear thinking I used memories of that place and imagined meditatively the path leading to it with all its details of pebbles, cow pats, a meadow, the wood, the hill, and a higher hill further up. I positioned myself in this meadow on the hill and looked around at the landscape, the fiord below, the islands across the fiord, and the western horizon. This was where I wanted to build a house for meditation. I had brought a few boards with me and now stepped out the dimensions of the house on the ground. I positioned myself at the spot where I wanted the door to be and tried to imagine what the simple round building with a domed roof would look like from the outside. I went inside and tried to imagine the inner space with an alcove, coloured windows, and a skylight.

Having carried out my initiative in this way and having through this received various Imaginations, I turned once more to a passage in Rudolf Steiner's book *How to Know Higher Worlds*. I realized that what I had done probably resembled what he there describes as 'building a home or a hut'. I had gone in thought to an actual hill in Norway and carried out the specific imaginative building project. Since this activity has a special place in esoteric anthroposophy I shall describe my building project as accurately as necessary from my own experience.

My decision to build a hut in the elemental world first arose from a question I asked of a dead friend in connection with ongoing karmic Imaginations. During one meditation I had a

strong feeling of her presence and immediately asked her how I
could go on meeting her and how, if possible, she could best help
me find common karmic links between us. I also tried to find out
what I could do for her. She gave me to understand that I should
create a spiritual space in such a way that it would contain in
thought the coloured windows from the first Goetheanum. In an
enclosed space of this kind, filled with flooding colours, she
would easily be able to find me and pass on my karmic questions
in the right way to spirits of higher worlds.

I first began to work on this matter of a spiritual hut in the
autumn of 1996. Then another dead friend, Rut Nilson, entered
my thoughts. I was now able to see her theme about the future in
an entirely new interpretation.

In subsequent weeks I returned again and again to this meditative building project, and I found that the building and interior
work appeared to progress on its own in the intervening periods.

I added further motifs to the meditative room of colour, for
instance to do with the *Foundation Stone Meditation*—especially
the Trinity—in which I immersed myself, and to do with the First
Class of the School of Spiritual Science. There in that room in the
months that followed I had many encounters, teachings and
Imaginations which led on from initial fragmentary Imaginations
via Inspirations right up to Intuitions of a higher kind.

In order to give the reader a more concrete idea of this work of
body, soul and spirit, which I carried out with much joy and
seriousness, I shall cite a few examples of my meetings with those
who have died. First, though, I must enlarge on the theme of a
spiritual home or hut.

Spiritual trials

The inner creative path is usually deeply solitary, and in order to
show how very serious it is and how much will-power it requires I

shall describe certain circumstances that made the further construction of a supersensible home very difficult for me but which
also greatly strengthened my courage to go on working.

One day when I approached the place where my hut was
situated I found the whole wonderfully and artistically constructed building, where so many encounters had taken place
and where I had done so much research, completely destroyed!
There it lay on the hillside, flat as a pancake, like a collapsed tent.

After the initial shock I realized that this was an inner trial that
must be tackled immediately. I went down on all fours—yes, even
in spirit this can be done—and fingered the peculiar substance
that lay on the ground. I searched for and found the entrance and
then, in meditation, I rebuilt the whole structure from the inside.
I pushed the rubbery walls and roof upwards and outwards and
they did not collapse again. As a result of this trial a new up-
bearing force had been created. My spiritual brothers and sisters
came and rejoiced at my exertions!

Another time, about a week later, I approached the site from
the east and saw a dark forest covering the whole hill including
my building. As I moved towards the phenomenon I realized
immediately that the dark trees were living spiritual figures who
wanted to exert their power over my place of schooling. I saw that
my current strength was insufficient for me to force my way
through, so I ended the meditation in the usual way and then
tried in thought to find other paths leading to the building.

Even before these events, when my building still lacked a door,
I had met with several surprises inside it. On one occasion a black
bird startled me in the middle of my meditation. For a while, until
I had invented a modern door which opened automatically when
I spoke certain meditative words, my own angel acted as door-
keeper. I had simply asked my angel to do this for me.

As the situation grew more critical I discovered that various
things which can be experienced supersensibly can be compared

with events or facts in the physical world or, more accurately: spiritual realities gave me a new understanding of what I already knew in physical reality. I discovered that meditative work can be regarded as an artistic skill and that a genuine spiritual ability can be developed out of this kind of artistic skill which has grown in an imaginative way. Conversations with a friend, a student of Rudolf Steiner, who works in graphics and sculpture helped me formulate this understanding more clearly and recognize this connection between spiritual and physical processes.

I began to understand that I needed to invent something spiritual which would be like a mirror image of the cyber world's '*virtual* reality'. I needed an instrument which I could use in the spiritual world because it had '*real* reality' in that world. So, using my physical hands as the symbol and starting point, I created a miniature etheric–astral means of communication through which I could remake contact with my hut as a base as well as with its spiritual furnishings and co-workers. Or, to be more exact, I created this possibility as an inner artistic idea and then asked the spiritual world whether it would function as I intended. I did indeed receive the help I needed, and after a while this spiritual invention led to new possibilities for me: Wherever I might be on my travels, in a train, an aeroplane or just walking along a road, it became possible for me to enter into a con-centrated, meditative direction via my hands. When I put my hands to my face, even in the daytime, they were transformed through the childlike 'urge to play' into a door or window into the spiritual world. This was a very satisfactory further development of my studies of Schiller which I had begun in the 1980s.

The lesser guardian

For my son's birthday party a few years ago I tried to design some outdoor games suitable for small children. To this end I made up a simple story which arose out of a particular connection with the natural surroundings of Järna. The story that developed was about a gnome-king called Shilbur and his daughter Da'ananda who had been captured by a wicked gnome.

The boys and girls who came to the party joined in the game of helping Shilbur—played by my daughter in suitable fancy dress—to rescue Da'ananda by triumphing in certain tests in the forest and also to persuade the wicked gnome to give up his evil ways.

Some time later I built a shed for the angora goats we kept at that time, and when I wanted to carve its name on the beam across the door the name 'Shilbur' once again came to my lips. Closing my eyes, inhaling the fragrance of the freshly sawn wood, and hearing the goats grazing nearby, I asked in a mood of quiet sympathy: 'Are you perhaps an actual being, Shilbur?' Thereupon a figure like a double* appeared, dressed in garments of red and blue. This double resembled a medieval king's jester. On his head he wore a crown that sparkled in a peculiar way, not because it was made of gold but because it kept shooting off many little coloured stars in every direction. I recognized this spiritual being as one who existed in his own right but who was appearing to me as an image of my own most intimate characteristics. I recognized the giving off of the stars as an image of my best traits which, though, if not properly managed by me, could become unfruitful or even destructive for others.

It was not a long encounter, but while it lasted I realized that this being had for a short while acted as a kind of captain of various elemental peoples in my immediate natural vicinity. I had lived in this district for about 17 years and worked a great deal in the neighbouring woodland. The being said to me: 'I am prepared once again to support you as your companion if you are

---

* Popularly known as the *doppelgänger*, the shadow aspect of the human being.

willing to collaborate consciously with me and if you want to share the light of your archetypal self with other human beings. In the far distant days of Atlantis I became separated off from your ether body in consequence of necessary but tragic circumstances which you must research yourself. Now, though, the time is ripe for us once again to relate consciously with one another.'

Since that initial encounter with this being whom I called Shilbur—and I will continue to do so in this context—we have accompanied one another. I recognized him as my lesser guardian of the threshold to the spiritual world. I hope to show by examples, in which I shall not always mention him specifically, how an encounter such as this is necessary for the spiritual pupil who wants to find his or her way in the supersensible world.

Shilbur has aided me marvellously and to an immensely great extent in my further endeavours and also my work with other good helpers. He also set me many trials. In turn I have tried by meditative means to set him free from tasks to which he has been bound for long ages. In all this he has led me to many different elemental beings and their work in nature, but also to the situations of distress they are finding themselves in on account of human civilization. Sometimes I have been able to help the being in question, thus extending the sphere in which we are mutually aware of each other.

Two elemental beings at work in November

One November day I was working in the garden. It was raining and I would really have preferred to be indoors in the warm reading a good novel or looking at art books. But there was still a lot of work to be done before the winter. The machines needed to be stowed under cover and the goats were waiting for their daily feed. In the midst of the work and despite the awful weather I suddenly felt glad I had begun.

I stopped plodding back and forth along the muddy path and asked inwardly: What do the elemental beings do on a rainy day like this? I knelt down and looked at the sloping woodland floor. A lot of dead leaves covered the ground, the rain flowed down the hill in little rivulets and I felt the smell of rotting vegetation in my nose. Closing my eyes with my hands before my face I directed a questioning attitude of soul towards the inner darkness.

Gentle movement and an aura of light began to take shape before my inner vision. Then suddenly a kind female figure stood before me. I saw her delicate frame quite distinctly. First I noticed her tears. Her eyes were all tears, and her whole attitude stemmed from this. Thousands of tears ran down from those tearful eyes, seeping into the ground through the soles of her large feet which were turned outwards. She was entirely immersed in her weeping, yet in her inmost being she was glad. A faint light streamed upwards out of her brown figure as though she wanted to say to me: 'I know my work is only temporary, but today is the day it has to be done.'

It came to me in that moment that in accord with ancient wisdom nature is still filled with beings in the process of developing, so I realized she was not alone. I glanced to the left where I knew there were some tufts of grass and bilberry bushes in the physical realm.

There I saw another picture. Deep in thought sat a grey gentleman paying no attention whatever to the rain or the other being's labours of transformation. His legs were crossed and he held his hands across his chest as if trying to conceal something. His whole figure right up to his hat which resembled a tiara played a part in this protective gesture. I wanted to ask what he was doing but before I even managed to formulate the question he looked at me with his head on one side and sent a stream of wise sayings into my consciousness which were very difficult to understand or put into words.

At the same time he opened his hands a little and allowed me to look into his heart. What I saw there was the most wonderful blue colour I had ever seen in the whole of my life as an artist. There is nothing as beautiful as that in the physical world, I said to myself. He was letting me know that he would have to go on sitting there cherishing this colour in his heart—*as* his heart, actually—until next spring. It was his duty to maintain awareness of it on behalf of this particular plant until it would be able to take it upon itself once more. Or, put in another way: He must now carry his awareness over into next spring as though that spring were already here, as though he were already present in that future spring mood while merely remembering our present autumn. This complicated interrelationship of timing was as far as I could follow him with my understanding, and in that same second he vanished.

Elemental beings in the forests of Thuringia

In the spring of 1997 I went for a walking holiday in the Thuringian Forest. I was trudging up a little valley in which, as I discovered later, a small stream had its source. The path and the forest floor to either side were covered in drifts of fallen beech leaves from the previous autumn. The trees stretched up like pillars against the blue sky, and the shadows and slanting sunlight stained their trunks in many shades of grey and mauve. The buds on every twig were just about ready to burst open. A breeze gusted over the golden-brown carpet of fallen leaves lifting some of them now here, now there, and dropping them again in another spot.

Then I stood still, wondering at this marvellous play of nature. Covering my eyes with my hands against the bright light of day— I must have looked a bit like Käthe Kollwitz's sculpture *Lament* except that my inner mood was positive and joyous—I waited for an after-image in an attitude of enquiry. After a short while the following Imagination arose:

A small evidently male figure came rushing up to me and in doing so immediately made his important task obvious. I saw two rakes with which he prodded some of the leaves to a spot where they must continue to cover the earth. As he held his long arms up to me I realized that he had transformed his own hands and fingers into his tools. He told me that he and thousands of his friends must continue this task over the next few days to protect the earth's warmth beings from having to rise up just yet. Then he pointed to the beings of the wind flying around and working with them. All day long they told tales and jokes as they tumbled about, so that the rake-men would stick at their boring spring task and not run away. From this spiritual point of view the wind consisted of hovering, soaring beings dancing amongst the rake-men making comical gestures. A sketch in pastel chalks merely hinting at the external colours in nature gave those elemental beings much pleasure and new strength to carry on with their work.

Seeing elemental beings in Imagination in this way appears to arise from a coming together of a number of those 'crossing points', as described by Rudolf Steiner in his lecture of 30 November 1919 about the 'new yoga will'.* The crossing points are of course invisible, for they are qualitative and spiritual. When the human will streams out of the inmost soul towards the universal thoughts in our elemental environment, the weaker this will is, the weaker—or indeed invisible—will be the Imagination.

It is understandable, therefore, that the new yoga will—which can give us enthusiasm for many and varied artistic, meditative and even physical exercises—does not of itself bring about a

---

* See *The Archangel Michael. His Mission and Ours.* New York: Anthroposophic Press 1994, discussed further in Chapter 6.

permanent new faculty of clairvoyance. It is rather a matter of constant practice in bringing these capabilities towards the spiritual world. If we do this, then, as pupils and researchers of the spirit, we shall receive the assistance we need, which will be entirely on a level with our own individual exercises and trials.

Encounters with people who have died

As I worked on karma research I reached a point when it seemed that it might be right to give other people information I had discovered. First, though, in my meditation building, I asked some of my closest friends amongst those who had died whether it would be a good thing to pass on concrete karmic knowledge. These dead friends, who at different locations in life had known several of those for whom I might have information, confirmed in the following way that it would be the right thing to do.

The impression I had been given left no room for doubt that in their present position those individuals were in agreement with my publishing their names and giving indications about their former incarnations. Entirely on my own responsibility I therefore venture to do so herewith. In later chapters I shall return to these three individuals again.

Åslaug Nysæther, already mentioned in Chapter 1, was the friend who had encouraged me to 'build a hut'. In her recent life she was a Norwegian special needs teacher and a teacher of handcrafts. While meditating I had an intuitive experience in which 'Åslaug' embraced me,* letting floods of warmth flow right through me and especially into the lower part of my arms; I felt this right down into my physical body. The whole process was interwoven by a consenting sense of trust as an answer to my question.

---

* In the following I shall show the names of those who have died in inverted commas when spiritual situations are being described.

In life Jørgen Smit had been one of my most important teachers. In my questioning frame of mind he approached me not as the tall man to whom I had always had to raise my eyes but as someone whom I had to find by looking downwards. 'Jørgen' was kneeling on a kind of carpet that had suddenly appeared several steps below me. His interest was directed entirely towards my feet and shins while he poured warmth and life into my whole being through his hands. When he turned his face towards me his glance spoke as follows: 'You will do well to mediate these things to the world, but speak only of what is most essential when you have tested in thought through your own self-knowledge whatever it is you want to say.'

Then I felt the presence of a third dead friend. In life he had once asked me to organize an educational exhibition for the 50th anniversary celebration of the Steiner Waldorf school in Bergen. Although he was Danish, Stig Pedersen had worked as a Waldorf teacher in Norway before joining the Danish section of the well-known Dutch firm of social consultants (NPI) known in Scandinavia as SEA. I tried to see 'Stig' in a shape that resembled mine in size, but once again I had to look downwards. Deep inside the earth, like a point, I saw a will-impulse which rushed up towards me in a flash and then stretched through the roof of my building right up to the sky as a pillar of light many kilometres high. I recognized 'Stig' as a being of sound speaking out of this apparition in a gentle voice: 'I am a pillar of social impulse. I stand by anyone who needs my help in social initiatives.'

These and other dead friends have appeared to me since then with great intimacy in all manner of forms; they have accompanied me and upheld me and it has always been rewarding to call on them and request their assistance. These experiences, together with my progressing meditative work, meant that a new phase in the cultivation of prayer began in my life.

In light-soul-processes which accompany the difficult circumstances of loneliness and bereavement in this age of modern initiation, the spirit-souls of human beings not in incarnation come to those who are incarnated and help them prepare in the right way through meditation for events in earlier lives before they later actually see them.

Later I shall describe other such encounters with friends I have known in life but who have since died. I shall show, for example, how they told me by means of Imaginations about their own karmic connections. This kind of spiritual collaboration means that karma research has become for me a spiritual-social challenge.

Researching my sequence of incarnations

After my meeting with the woman which led to the Imagination about the medieval knight Willibald, I wanted to try and follow up further relations between us. I found myself in Egyptian times and was able to take further the tragic story of the woman I had seen myself carrying in my arms during the regression session. Having reached isolated incidents from various incarnations and gone back to Atlantean and, as I thought probable, Lemurian circumstances, I decided to make a coherent 'research trip' from Lemuria right up to the present time.

I prepared myself by turning to certain individuals who had died, especially my mother 'Turid', with whom I had already had encounters; and I turned to the spiritual beings Christ and Michael because I had sensed their helpful presence in my place of spiritual schooling. My question was: May I be permitted to see those events which in each earth life were the principal ones leading over to the next life, and may I also be permitted to see how I tackled the respective tasks in those incarnations?

What arose was a sequential series of Imaginations which were also steeped in Inspiration and Intuition. The starting point was a life in Lemuria and this led on to a life after the middle of Atlantean times. Then I recognized two more lives in late Atlantean times, but it did not seem important for me to follow those up just then. The sequence proceeded to India and China followed by a larger leap to Egypt and then Greece, Rome and the Middle Ages. I expected the next thing to be the life in America which I had seen in the experience when I was young, so I was astonished and initially shocked to find a life as a woman in the midst of historically known events at the time of the Counter-Reformation. I allowed all this to come close to me, and only after that did I see events in the nineteenth century which related to the experience in my youth. The investigation, which had taken nearly three hours, then finally led to my present life.

Over subsequent weeks—while my circumstances allowed me to meditate and do research three times a day—I first investigated the medieval and Egyptian lives, which I felt to be my task at that moment. I have always tried to take as my starting point the situation in my present life and the people in the destiny group close to me. If figures appeared in the Imaginations whom I could not immediately identify I tried to repeat those Imaginations in order patiently to question the spiritual world through the strength of my own self. Gradually the work led to the discovery of karmic relationships with over one hundred people between the Middle Ages and the present time, all of whom I have known personally, or still know because they are alive today. Then I turned to the other incarnations and—before referring to historical sources and literature—tried to obtain a coherent biography from the Akashic Record.

During the autumn of 1996 I thus succeeded in obtaining life themes from 12 incarnations which I recognized to have been my own former lives. In addition I was able to enter the life after death that followed several of those lives. I was able to follow up detailed transformation themes in the spiritual world between my incarnation as Christian von Buch and the life as a woman in the sixteenth century. In Chapter 3 I shall draw on the abundance of Imaginations to narrate those incarnations in sequence.

The Akashic Record—a spiritual archive

It was in that period that I endeavoured to gain entry to the 'spiritual archive' which Rudolf Steiner had also referred to by its ancient Indian name, the 'Akashic Record'. I felt that my Imaginations came from the realm of astral light which emanates from spiritual beings of the higher hierarchies. When I approached the beings who constitute the Akashic Record by preparing very carefully and adopting the required attitude in my meditation— helped by those who had died—the Imaginations that came were so clear and multi-layered that information covering vast stretches of time were communicated in an instant.

On a number of occasions I endeavoured to look right into and through this stream of images without focussing on their content. My experience in the use of transparent layers of colour in lazure painting helped me to discover a kind of multi-dimensional effect. The Akashic Record was woven out of layers with each layer having been as though created by one individual. It was a wonderful tapestry of the most beautifully transparent colours such as we would never find in the physical world. Only a rainbow can hint at what it is like. I was as though in a still space in the midst of the akashic fabric while at the same time maintaining a distance from the various links between the layers.

The mood I experienced with Åslaug Nysæther at Rostadheimen as she set up her loom, passing each thread through the correct eye in the harness, is something I can compare with the work of those beings of the spiritual hierarchies as they impress our earthly destinies into the astral light. Each karmic thread passes through spiritual openings in the Akashic Record, right back to every event in former times; all are still present there.

A sequence of lessons on the cultural epochs

In November 1996 I was asked to lead a painting project at the Steiner Waldorf School at Moss in Norway. The classroom doors needed mending and re-lazuring and the work was to be done under my guidance with the help of parents and some teachers. Shortly before this was due to begin a teacher rang up and asked whether I could also teach the twelfth class and stay an extra week. They should be having an architecture main lesson, but the teacher was ill. Could I help? With previous twelfth classes at the school I had already twice run mural painting projects with some success; perhaps I could do something similar this time? I decided to teach the class during the main lesson slot and run the practical work on the doors in the afternoons.

More mural work would have been too much of a good thing, so I decided to give a main lesson on the cultural epochs combined with painting. I wanted to try and describe examples of my own karmic development in connection with art history and culture without letting the pupils guess that it was myself I was speaking about. To do this I would need the help of the spiritual world and I requested those who had died to support me.

Having arrived in Oslo I then had to take the bus to the centre of town, passing around Bygdøy, where Sigrid Mørch-Reiersen had lived. I glanced in the direction of her house and inwardly turned to my memories of her. The result of this was a kind of experience I had not had before:

I felt the human soul and spirit of 'Sigrid' approach me by hovering all around me. I sensed that we would be able to converse in thoughts and that she had approached me because she had noticed that I would need her strength for the coming lessons I would be giving.

Sitting there in the bus I asked her whether she would help me. She confirmed that she would and said she would envelope me throughout the whole main lesson period. I sensed that this was possible and sent her my complete trust and deep gratitude.

Because of the short notice I had been given, and also my other tasks at Umeå, I had only made fragmentary preparations. So now I began both projects at once, that of painting the doors and that of teaching the twelfth class. Three times a day I went into my meditative building where I always found 'Sigrid' ready to help me find the necessary information in the Akashic Record. Once she brought a large pot of balm with which she treated me, whereupon my soul grew very calm and full of confidence. In the afternoon, in the evening before going to sleep and early in the morning before getting up I did the preparation for the next lesson, on every occasion together with 'Sigrid' in my Michael school.

In the classroom she was always with me, enveloping me in a way that enabled me to bring forward suitable themes which the youngsters would be able to take in. It was even possible to talk about aspects of sexuality, for example from ancient Chinese culture, without disconcerting or embarrassing the young people too much, so far as I could tell.

The ship that can travel across land and sea

It was during this period that the idea of a fictitious ship that can travel through the millennia occurred to me. That such an idea can be taken up by the elemental world and transformed into a spiritual reality might appear rather crazy. Yet this did indeed happen, in the midst of my working life, and I shall now try to describe it.

I had made contact with my former friend from Garnes. I was due to help her do some painting during the coming month and we were discussing dates. We talked several more times and she told me about her life-crisis. One of the themes in her story was connected with an old oak tree which a building project at the institute she directed made it necessary to fell. Opinions differed as to the strength of the tree to go on living. Some were on the side of those who thought it still had many decades of life left in it and the house could just as well be build elsewhere. The others accepted a report that declared the tree to be dead.

My friend, who had the casting vote, felt she had to uphold the report, so she had the oak felled, but it turned out that the report had been mistaken. The arguments continued and as the director of the institute she took the whole responsibility on herself.

In my meditation I went to the place where the oak had stood and there I saw waves of wonderful light streaming up out of the earth's organism. But the light was a kind of prison for the elemental beings there. I called on Shilbur and asked whether I could set the beings free by taking the still existing life forces of the felled oak tree and making a ship out of them to use in my lessons at the Steiner Waldorf school. He said: 'Go to bed and wait until the morning.'

In my meditation next morning I went back to the same place and found there a wonderful ship which I was allowed to take away with me. This ship was able to bring forth new ships out of itself and it could also be as small or as large as a human thought.

In ten main lessons I recounted to the pupils sequential biographical and general details from Atlantis, India, China, Egypt, Greece, Rome, the Middle Ages, the Counter-Reformation and the wars against the American Indians. Each morning we entered the ship together, so to speak, and journeyed from one place to the next. At the end of the course I told them the Norwegian folk-tale about the good helpers, as a kind of bridge for each pupil back to the time spent in the first class at school.

On the final day I gave a spiritual gift to each of those present. Invisibly it passed from my hands to theirs. Into each gift I impressed inaudibly the name of the higher self of the pupil receiving it. In Chapter 4 I shall have more to say about this theme of the human being's archetypal name and Christian name. I shall there also return to my spiritual experiences with 'Sigrid'.

During those two weeks at Moss in the second half of November 1996 I also practised initiation exercises on my own initiative. These are only comprehensible against a background of the whole sequence of my incarnations.

My initiation story

In Chapter 3 I shall be giving detailed accounts of the Atlantean oracles.* In order to help readers understand these in connection with my karma let me first tell the Norwegian folk-tale which I was able to discover in my life-tableau.

The tale is entitled 'The Cinder Lad and the Good Helpers'. As do many Norwegian stories, this one begins with three brothers, of whom the two eldest are always hard-working and receive much help from their father. The youngest, Espen Askeladden or 'Cinder Lad', spends all his time in front of the fireplace looking for yesterday's embers amongst the cinders. The king sends out a proclamation to be announced in the churchyards up and down the country. He wants a ship that can travel as well on land as it can on water, and whoever makes this ship for him will be given the princess and half the kingdom.

One after the other the two older brothers go into the forest to build the ship, well equipped with a bundle of tasty food and a

---

* Also known as 'mystery centres' or places of initiation into spiritual mysteries.

sharp axe. In the forest they meet a woodman who asks them questions. When he asks what they have brought to eat both brothers say they have cowpats. Later, when they want to eat their food, they find that it has changed into cowpats. When the woodman asks what they are going to build they say it will be a kneading trough. However much they try to build a ship, all they manage to produce is a kneading trough.

When Espen sets off into the forest his father only gives him dry bread to take with him. So off he sets with a crust of dry bread and an old axe. He, too, meets the woodman. On being asked what food he has brought with him he answers truthfully and shares his bread with the woodman. Thereupon the woodman tells him to lie down and go to sleep, saying that in the meantime he will build the ship by the next day. Next morning the wood-man explains how Espen must steer the miraculous ship and advises him to give a lift to anyone he meets. Joyfully Espen bids him farewell and sets off on his journey to the king's palace.

He drives over land and over sea, and one after another he sees six men down below whom he invites to join him in his ship. They become his good helpers when he meets with the king, for instead of giving him the princess the king keeps on setting him new trials. The man who eats stones on account of his huge appetite helps him eat up the store of meat. The man who is so thirsty that he sucks the fir-cones dry helps him drink up the store of wine in the cellar. The man who has to weigh himself down with weights on his legs because he would otherwise fly to the end of the earth in less than ten minutes helps him fetch the water for the princess's morning tea from the well at the world's end. The man who can hear the grass growing hears that the fast-running helper has been put into a deep sleep by a giant. The man who is a first-class sharp-shooter hits the distant giant with his arrow. The man who holds his hand in front of his mouth has fifteen winters and ten summers inside him when Espen has to burn the wood to heat the water in the bath-house. The last winter is used for the king, who then finally gives his daughter to the ship's helmsman.

It will be found that this 'initiation story', if I may use the term, describes in pictures exactly the steps to be taken by someone who was once connected with the Atlantean Mercury Oracle and now wants to do research into karma.

It was in the members' supplement of the journal *Das Goetheanum* (Nos. 8, 9 & 10 in 1998) that I first described the six Atlantean oracles grouped around the Sun Oracle. Later in this book they will be described again. In comparing the six good helpers with those six Atlantean oracles grouped around the Sun Oracle it is not difficult to recognize the Mars Oracle in the man hungry for meat, the Venus Oracle in the man thirsty for wine, the Mercury Oracle in the quick runner, the Jupiter Oracle in the man who hears the grass growing, the Saturn Oracle in the sharp-shooter, and the Vulcan Oracle in the man with the fifteen winters and the ten summers. My experience with the life-tableau taught me that many folk-tales contain ancient Atlantean wisdom.

This is the level at which one can do genuine research into one's own incarnations as well as those of other individuals, reaching right back to Atlantis and Lemuria.

Having discovered my destiny story I realized that the period from 1986 to 1996 corresponds with the scene of Espen at home by the fire. His encounter with the woodman corresponds with my meditative breakthrough in the autumn of 1996 when I received the first Imaginations and encounters with those who have died, with elemental beings and with my lesser guardian.

Reasons for publishing

After careful consideration, and with knowledge of possible consequences and reactions, I have decided to write about my experiences of former incarnations in order to help others whose destiny in life makes them want to enter into the modern mysteries. In my opinion every general schooling, including the anthroposophical path, reaches its limits when one enters deeper threshold experiences. The best help at that point is to hear from others what happened to them when they were having similar experiences. In that sense this book is intended to be a 'midwife' for those who seek their higher self in order to share in shaping the future. Through viewing former incarnations we can rediscover the archetypal wisdom living in each one of us, which can then be individualized in a modern language. Now that we have reached the edge of the abyss of materialistic civilization, such wisdom can help us seek and traverse new paths.

The schooling words of the Chartres teacher and Platonist Bernard can be heard in one's own soul language when individualization has reached the point it has to reach if earlier incarnations are to become so clearly recognizable as to be describable as they are here. This is my way of saying that I regard this publication of my former incarnations as a gift from a present-day representative of the Platonic stream to representatives of the Aristotelian stream,* challenging them to begin exchanging their thoughts and experiences with me and my Platonist friends. Such an exchange has hitherto been very little cultivated, if at all.

---

* For background on these spiritual streams see *Karmic Relationships, Vol. VI*, London: Rudolf Steiner Press 1989.

3

Episodes from past lives

O Guardian of the Gate,
make wide the way for me,
that I may dwell at the place of my intent.
Egyptian Book of the Dead (from Verse 52)

The 'shrouded' human being in Paradise

Once again I want to stress that I am not publishing this karmic research in order to make myself out to be something exceptional. Every human individual is exceptional within the context of human evolution. My purpose is simply to use myself as a concrete example by means of which to illustrate from an individual point of view the great steps in evolution about which Rudolf Steiner spoke. It would be pointless to deny that in doing this I have come upon several historically known figures, and it would be wrong to remove these from the sequence. On the contrary, it will become apparent that descriptions of known historical events will have to be partially revised on the basis of these karmic perspectives. Indeed, when other karma researchers also begin to present the results of their work we shall see that a good many more historical accounts will need revising.

The following Imaginations, which I regard as being connected with what occurred before my entry into a first incarnation in Lemurian times, are much more difficult to characterize than anything that happened later in relation to circumstances on the earth.

I shall initially give the designation 'stellar exercises' to the state I experienced. I found myself coming together with a being who was human. Enwrapped in etheric-astral swathes—I shall call him the 'shrouded' human being—this entity floats in a permanent state of pleasure. Reposing in the spiritual world he feels constantly embraced by good impulses and higher beings and also by other 'shrouded' human beings close by who surge around and through him. Then I found that this 'shrouded' human being—for whom I received the name 'Arjuna'—was being called by someone who was no longer spiritually in the vicinity. Arjuna does not comprehend that the caller has been led away into a first incarnation. Understanding of this only dawns later when his angel tells him this is so. The name Arjuna is known in connection with the *Mahabharata*, the great Indian epic poem, but here there is not necessarily any direct connection with the poem. I believe there is always a whole group of human individuals who were created out of the same titular configuration and then continue to bear the same archetypal name.

A motif then appears that covers a longer span of time. It is an inner conversation in soul between Arjuna, who is not incarnated, and his sister-soul, here called Miriam. Miriam is living as a man in the culture of Lemuria. In a kind of prayer she describes what life on earth is like. Miriam speaks to Arjuna, asking him for help which he can send down out of the spiritual world.

I have taken great pains, working with my angel, to receive this Lemurian prayer and a translation which my angel brought to me through eurythmy because I could not reach it through direct consciousness in Inspiration:

Tamaga tagala Miriam mada,
Arjuna Gala, Baman; tha Gada!
Sam mada Gada Bamila.
Shima baga; gathada!

Timaga Dathamaga Shida! Thagawan!
Bethaman Shada Shagamila thada.
Jimaga Dathamila! Fafaga Datila!
Shustafila Thadagawan, Shama Maga!
Ara jatila, Gamamiram Iram.
Shabatila Giram! Amathidam!
Fidafatigam Iraman; tha Miriam!
Aratha Man, Arjuna!
Thada Thigam, Ma Miriam.

In translation:

Miriam sends a prayer streaming up to you,
    her friend Arjuna, who possesses divine fire:
Let gentleheartedness descend!
We receive it in the divine council's circle.
Earth's pathways lie open before us; guide us forward!
Victory for the mercy of world-manifoldness;
    strengthen our hands with forces of form!
We receive human beings skilled in tilling earth and heaven,
    in depths, in widths.
May world-forms show us mercy, and protect us with
    stillness!
With our hands let us gather our daily food, to our
    satisfaction in purity!
Earthly hills spread out for us, to the delight of human souls,
    in favourable winds.
Give shelter for human groups! Give healing power!
Many will find human dignity; give it also to Miriam!
Come Arjuna, to earth as a human being!
Miriam, your mother, receives your spirit's flame.

Even though Miriam appears as a man in the Imagination he
nevertheless presents himself in the prayer as the mother of

Arjuna. This may be in keeping with specific Lemurian conditions which I did not follow up.

After Miriam's first incarnation the two souls meet in their primeval spiritual home which gains a new quality for Arjuna through the arrival of Miriam who has been incarnated once. Now Miriam becomes a woman and Arjuna's mother. Thus Arjuna begins his earthly journey as a man, now named Retana.

Boatbuilder in Lemuria

Retana's life can be described briefly as follows:

He grows up in a landscape that is as though flooded in warmth, but it is difficult to discern whether this is a land containing thousands of souls or a sea with thousands of islands. Everywhere land merges into water and water into land. There are places resembling lagoons where wonderful small woodlands situated between the land and the water provide human beings with what they need in order to live, and they actually live there as well.

Water is Retana's favourite element, which is why the priestesses appoint him to be a boatbuilder. On one occasion when I saw him he looked like a Neanderthaler. Having just finished making a boat he was shrinking his size. His physical body seems very pliant; it can react to influences from his soul and life forces and thus take on different shapes. He is sitting on the ground, pressing his stone axe to his chest. Now he looks quite different, more like a small child, and immense gratitude streams from him in three directions: outward towards the circumference of the earth, downward towards the earth, and upward towards the heavens.

I see these Lemurian conditions and realize that physical facts then were quite different from those of today. And I also see that the relationship between the elements is quite different from that which came into being after the Lemurian catastrophe. As though arranged by mathematical laws, the stone head of the axe is placed in the correct position in relation to the soft and light wooden handle. This reveals a culture that is not physically primitive at all, but rather highly spiritual like a kind of seed.

Later I see Retana taking his family, a woman and two children, on a trial run in a boat. Suddenly he is caught by a hot whirlpool and the boat capsizes. The woman drowns but being an incredibly good swimmer he saves himself and the two children. He is told to take the children and give them back to the divine mother. Knowing that they cannot grow up without their earthly mother he has no hesitation in doing what the 'Gada'—the council of gods—decrees.

Then I see Retana, accompanied by representatives of his people, carrying the children on their shoulders to a volcanic lake on an island. He throws both children into the lake and witnesses their earthly mother, in spiritual form, receiving them with open arms. Happily he then takes a new wife and improves his boats to meet the approval of the Gada.

Spiritual pupil of the Mercury Sphere

Between that first incarnation as Retana in Lemurian times and the next one I found, as Shamu'radhin in Atlantean times, the 'shrouded' human being Arjuna was in the spiritual school of the Mercury Sphere, having undergone the necessary transformation after death.

My ongoing research indicates that every human soul who was to be led into progressive development after the Lemurian catastrophe first had to be born out of one of the planetary oracles. These oracles were in existence before a population spread out across the Atlantean continent. In their early stages all the other oracles had been created by the Sun Oracle in a 'mystery of birth';

the respective planetary spheres were to be mirrored by them on the earth.

When I tried to follow up what it was like to be in the Mercury Sphere I gained the following knowledge which I shall endeavour to describe in pictures as follows:

Arjuna is lying upon the hands of a being of the higher hierarchies. He must learn to blow 'shrouds' out of himself when that being sends his breath towards him. These 'shrouds', which look like shreds of thin paper, are distributed by other beings into small ships in the spiritual world.

In a subsequent phase Arjuna—I shall continue to give him this name when he is in spiritual realms after death—has to travel along starry thoroughfares and gather up the ships that belong to him. This is how he gains information about the places to which he goes, because his ships have there been given certain distinguishing marks. He must bring each one of these ships to his home and impress his Mercury seal upon them before returning them to their specific locations which he now knows.

Not until all the ships with their seals upon them have returned to him once more from those locations can he turn towards the earth, trusting that he will be born into the Mercury Oracle.

Atlantis and the divine Tau'wa

In the following sections I shall give detailed accounts of the Atlantean oracles and the conditions for living there. I do this for a number of reasons.

My initiation story has already been mentioned. In something like an etheric prototype the biographical themes from my first Atlantean incarnation provide a karmic background for my present life. This etheric prototype runs its course in a kind of reverse time process. I shall return in later chapters to this complicated but remarkable connection with present-day possibilities of initiation.

The conditions in Atlantis also yield new understanding for many of the mysterious factors that appear in my post-Atlantean incarnations. They can be regarded as initiatives and expressions of the various cultures in which my gallery of individuals—if I many call it thus—has been incarnated. Frequent references back to Atlantean wisdom, themes and capabilities occur in later incarnations.

I also dare to hope that my descriptions of Atlantis might attract researchers, archaeologists and sponsors for new professional archaeological investigations at certain locations beneath the ocean and on land, for example the Azores and the Bermudas. What I have seen in my Imaginations leads me to claim that certain signs and objects of that culture can be found in the caldera on the island of Corvo, one of the Azores.

Many of the situations described in the following will appear not only foreign but even perhaps suspect or barbaric to our present-day way of thinking. Nevertheless I shall describe what I saw and hope that a better understanding will arise from the fuller picture. The Atlantean way of life in the oracles had features quite unlike those of a modern city today. Human beings, animals and plants, even matter itself, formed a totality with the creative gods and the elemental world. Everything the Atlanteans did with one another and with nature and the animals must thus be seen as belonging to a greater whole that was for them holy and of divine significance.

The Atlanteans had a picture consciousness that made them feel as though the divinity working in the pictures was within themselves. This divinity manifested everywhere in nature: in the rustling of leaves in the forest, in the sighing of the wind, in their inner soul pictures when they had the urge to look up towards a lofty future for humanity. These experiences of a great divine wholeness which always pointed towards the future was called TAO by the Atlanteans or, as I think more accurately: TAU'WA. To think with our modern consciousness of this divine wholeness still at work in our time means seeingly to remember the Atlantean past, and from this spirit-remembering to draw strength for the future. This is TAO today.

Tauwa'dorraman—the Mercury Oracle

My research led me to an incarnation after the mid-part of Atlantean times. Delving into this incarnation turned out to be decisive for any further karma research I did, and I spent much time and energy on going into it. Close collaboration with my spiritual helpers gave me an overview of that life of the Mercury initiate Shamu'radhin and much insight into the oracle centres of Atlantis.

The names of people and places often came to me in the consciousness of Inspiration at the moment of researching them. Or my angel, if asked, imparted them to me by means of eurythmy gestures. The frequent division of names into two parts arose from the custom of giving an individual a title to be added to his birth name after he had been initiated into the sphere of his life's task. Radhin means 'He who travels everywhere', and the title Shamu 'He who is permitted to form something out of the forces of life'.

In conversation with my angel I concluded that reckoning backwards from today the incarnation lasted from 14393 to 14313 BC, i.e. during the final third of the fourth Atlantean cultural epoch. You have to take care not to imagine such exact dating physically, for you reach the correct figure by counting the seasons backwards. Time is a living and pliant process, so having reached back to Atlantean times we must imagine time somehow stretching out more and more the further back we go, until finally we reach the point when the moon departed, before which it is no longer meaningful to consider time in the way we count it today.

The impression I received was that in Shamu'radhin's day there was still a degree of uniformity in the whole of Atlantean culture and that all culture emanated from the Sun Oracle. At first I was able to follow the lives of the Mercury initiate Shamu'radhin and those who lived with him in the Mercury Oasis. Later I also saw others in the other oracles as well as the ordinary people outside the oracles whom he and his companions met on the journeys connected with their work.

Having learnt how to relive my travels across the Atlantean continent I once tried to gain a geographical overview. I concentrated my attention around the Azores as they are known today and tried to rise up 'high' enough to give me an overall picture of where my journeys had taken me. What I saw was a huge continent covering almost the whole of what is today the northern part of the Atlantic ocean, reaching north-west as far as the Labrador Sea, north-east to include Ireland, eastwards probably to include the Atlas Mountains in today's Morocco and Algeria, southwards at least to the Romanche trench, south-west probably to include the Guiana highlands in today's South America and westwards to include the Bermudas. I was not able to discern from the overview whether other parts of today's western Europe and northern America belonged to this continent. It was not easy to determine its exact contour because the coastlines of Europe, Africa and America were quite different then.

The name of the Mercury Oracle is Tauwa'dorraman which translates as 'Companion of Gods and Men'. This oracle is situated on an ancient volcanic island in a gulf of the south-eastern coast of the Atlantean continent. Craggy mountain formations rise to the west while to the east the ocean flows right into caves in the cliffs and rounded gorges of the lower mountains. Through these travel Shamu'radhin and his companions as well as other itinerant groups. This has been going on for generations over many thousands of years.

About 2000 people live inside this protected cultural centre. The natural world there is wonderful, with lakes, marshes, woods, settlements, gardens, streams and little valleys in which children slide down the damp, mossy slopes on something like skates made of tortoise-shell.

This Mercury community lives a life that is divided into work, festivals and play. In the west there is a shrine in a cliff and the children make shoes from cork and bark which they bring to it as gifts. The adults use the bark of a tall, straight tree which they dry and then roll up, before binding the bundles with tough, thin roots and steeping them in oil. This is how they make torches for religious processions as well as for some of their work, e.g. painting inside the caves.

This sanctuary, the actual Mercury Oracle, sends out all the impulses needed by the twelve Mercury working communities which have to do with various ways of cultivating interrelationships, art, nature, and body and soul.

Organic architecture and seed cultivation

One of Shamu'radhin's friends is Traggetana, 'She who can pass to others what she has carefully curled'. She works with others, men and women, in a kind of plantation. They wear long smocks and boots or stockings that congeal on their legs when they dip them in liquid rubber. There is a special workshop for these preparations which are needed as a protection against certain kinds of water creature. When they are ready the people wade through the water and gather large root fruits with stalks. These fruits have a thick skin which can be peeled off in one piece. Inside the fruits are seeds resembling carrots which are used in the preparation of dyes.

The thick skins are also utilized. They possess very many etheric forces and are used to wrap up the black stems of a different plant that resemble chess pieces and are covered with countless growth points. Wrapping them up in those skins makes these stems elastic enough to be stretched out to lengths of several metres. Two such stems are bent over and both ends are planted in the earth side by side about three feet apart so that they enclose a kind of inner space. Shoots soon sprout from these bent stems, and once they are long enough they too are bent down in an oval curve and planted in the ground. This is how an organic hut is built. Other fast-growing leafy plants are added to obtain firm, watertight walls. Entrances are later cut into both ends between the two original arches. These small buildings serve various purposes. Some, called 'bagitagam', provide housing for tortoises, for example. Tortoise-shell finds many uses, among others as drinking vessels and, as above, those skates.

A man named Tragge'mitram, 'He who wraps himself up when he passes something on', gathers large seed-pods from which he removes the seeds. With these seeds he builds small compost heaps on the ground. As they dry out a hard skin forms over the heaps inside which an extract arises that is used as a dye. This dye serves as face-paint for festivals and ceremonies, a kind of cultic decoration, to which is added a feathered headdress similar to that used by the North American Hopi and Lakota tribes. The feathers were collected from the coastal cliffs on the outside of the Mercury Oracle by groups of youngsters when whole communities made trips to the seaside to bathe at certain times of year.

Mitregana Gaman—the spring festival

The ceremony of fertilization every spring, Mitregana Gaman, is another special festival. In agreement with the priests a man and a woman are often chosen for one another by their parents while they are still children. After puberty the women wear a kind of leather apron round their waist. The ceremony involves the man carrying the woman a long way into the forest. The first coitus takes place in a plant hut or tent. For many days and nights both are in a state of sleep induced by a narcotic substance that makes them lethargic, and the whole process is watched over by priests. The man walks about in his sleep carrying the woman. The whole oracle community participates in this festival.

At other places on the Atlantean continent some women and men have already performed the sexual act independently, but this is strictly forbidden, and children arising from such untimely unions are not allowed to live.

Gamamila—the flying vehicle

In his description of Atlantean culture in *Cosmic Memory*, Rudolf Steiner described the Atlanteans as having flying vehicles. When I discovered the possibility of meditatively following up this statement, which seems so unlikely to a materialistic way of thinking, I wanted to find out as much as I could about it. In what follows I describe my research into those Atlantean vehicles and the way they were made.

As far as I could make out it was only Mercury initiates who practised the organic art of making the flying vehicles or ships, which were called 'gamamila'. This name means something like 'Remaining so intimately united with those one has sent forth that they will find their way home again'. Thus the ship bears a name which denotes a spiritual-soul activity of those initiates in the Mercury Oracle who remain at home but maintain an inner link with those who have been sent on a journey. By remaining in the gamamila or quite close to it, those who have been sent forth retain a feeling of connection with their home oracle.

These vehicles were used for thousands of years by journeying Mercury initiates, right up to later times when the magic arts were no longer available and other forms of building had been developed. Special ships were also constructed for the Sun Oracle, for it, too, required a means of transport. Building a gamamila involved skilled collaboration between gods, elemental spirits, human beings and plant processes—over a period of forty days and nights. Approximately what happened at the physical level can be described as follows:

Many preparations have already been made on a kind of small meadow near to the Oracle centre where a gamamila is to be 'built'. All around there are special plantations with various types of plant that are to provide the building material. Shamu'radhin, who is at this time 'first helmsman' for one of the many travelling groups, sits, lies and moves inside an organic shape which is gradually developed into a gamamila. The substance from which the form is moulded comes from the various kinds of plant that are fetched one after the other from the plantations. First, large leaves from a cactus-like yet pliant plant are used. Shamu'radhin—rather like the Egyptian hieroglyph 'via' meaning vehicle—is wrapped up in these as he sits with both hands between his thighs as the rudder. Through his rhythmical movements and using all his bodily fluids—sweat, saliva, tears, even semen and blood—which he exudes, the gamamila is shaped from within. Fellow workers—who will later be his passengers—mould it from the outside with their hands and plant oils, adding more and more plant material. All around there is dancing, singing, music and spoken choruses that imbue the vehicle with all the Mercury impulses which Atlantean human beings possess.

One of the verses which I was allowed to take down goes something like this:

Tami maga, thamaga gamala,
Magi Thagawan, shamaga Damila;
Magi magala, Lathada Gamiron.
Thada Shamirada, Gamamiron.
Bethila thada, gamathi Dana,
Methi; Ramada Gamamila Thani.
Shamu Radhinila, Mithila don.
Gamu Radhina, mamamila Thidiron,
Migara danamila, Shustafila Biron.
Mina thada, gamamila Thidilarion.
Shamu'radhin imidatila Mistira.
Methada thada, Gamamila Wivavira.
Shila Uraman, Xandorra Tauwan.

In translation:

Trusting in creation's strength we receive the power
    of growing seeds,
To give them shape by our hands' strength for journeys;
And by excretions from our body as food for Gods and men.
We receive from spirits of earth spiritual mother's milk.
Forward impetus we receive, forces of uprightness in time,
And in gratitude from firmness we receive the vehicle.
The one who forms it will find the way with the goal
    before his eyes.
United with his passengers he ever returns from his
    destinations,
With new tasks, food and gifts for the community.
We receive our own, and the vehicle, after the circling
    journey.
Shamu'radhin is initiated into new connections.
Receptivity we receive, the vehicle as a whole with
    winged flight.

Praised be the art of our forefathers, the blessing of
the holy Oracle of the Sun.

The finished gamamila is big enough to transport thirteen people plus luggage. It usually moves through an atmosphere that has a consistency somewhere between rarefied water and dense air. Its speed is between 20 and 50 km/h. By letting their hands hang down from the open stern those in the vehicle retain contact with the elemental world. This brings about the forward motion and, by means of a kind of 'conveyor belt' linked to the two wing-sails, enables steerage to left or right.

The Atlantean atmosphere at that time can be described as follows: The air was denser than today, like mist, but of a kind that allowed the sunlight to stream through it in a way quite different from the mist we have today. Although the air was much more humid one did not get wet. The air was mixed with the water in such a way that I would like to compare it with a kind of mucous secretion. The air was pliant and absorbed and passed on every movement, whether caused by man, animal or speech. Hearing and smelling by animals and human beings was almost like touching.

Xandorra'tauwa—the Sun Oracle

Shamu'radhin journeys with his passengers to the Sun Oracle in the north. Ambassadors of the Mercury Oracle are responsible for all the interrelationships between the Atlantean oracles. Especially important is the dissemination of new impulses to all the Atlantean settlements and tribes by means of installations and techniques of civilization developed by the Sun Oracle.

Gamamilas travel over land and water along special elemental roads in the air which initiates have been building for thousands of years in collaboration with the spiritual world. These roads could be described as a circulatory system of the earth where the flowing of the various kinds of ether differs from that in the surrounding vicinity.

The journey northwards follows the eastern coastline through thick, misty air. Shamu'radhin uses a flute made from a large pod to chase away animals but also to announce the gamamila's arrival near the dwelling caves in the cliffs or at the Oracle centre being visited. (He himself has made the flute by carefully sticking his magical hands and fingers into the growing fruit in order to create holes from the inside. Once the fruit has been dried he produces different notes by blowing in or out.)

On reaching a settlement the people greet one another by raising their hands. The Mercury travellers either make a short stop in order to distribute gifts or, to the great delight of the inhabitants, they accept an invitation to stay the night. Usually, though, they take it in turns to sleep in the travelling gamamila. I shall say more about the food they carry with them when I describe the Venus Oracle.

After travelling for ten or twelve days the great moment arrives at last when they reach the drive that spirals up to the highest volcano of the whole continent. (Or at least this is how it appears to me from seeing the overall geography of the continent at that time.) No one can scale these heights without a flying vehicle. I have rediscovered this mountain as today's island of Corvo, the smallest of the Azores, where to my knowledge no archaeological investigation has so far been undertaken.

On the journey in question Shamu'radhin is accompanied by a young Mercury initiate, Tamu'thamas, 'He who entrusts to others what he has received from God'. It is his first journey of this kind, and now he experiences a wondrous marvel:

Most Atlanteans have never seen either the sun, the planets, the stars or the blue sky or a rainbow. However, hot gases constantly stream upwards out of the Sun Volcano with the holy name of

Xandorra'tauwa—'Sun Place of God's Blessing'. These gases clear the air above it. As the gamamila ascends to the rim of the crater, young Tamu'thamas sees the blue sky and the sun for the first time. At first the apparition is too powerful for him, but he has with him expressly for this purpose a reindeer antler with a thin fish-skin stretched across it under which he can shelter. Having reached the rim of the crater the gamamila rides down towards the Sun Oracle within the volcano. There are mountainous shapes all around, and in the centre the 'Sun Staircase'. There are lakeside parks, canals and plantations, and twelve different workshops distributed around the whole rim.

Sun arts and sun impulses

The Mercury travellers dwell here for a time, cared for and entertained by the Sun people. First they call upon the Sun initiate, Tami'tame'sham, 'The gods trust him to give form to power'. Although born in the Mars Oracle, as an adult he was called to the Sun Oracle where it became his duty to represent outwardly the power of the secret inner leaders of the Sun Oracle. His clothes are of asses leather, and antlers crown his head. As the procession mounts the Sun Staircase, white-garbed temple maidens stand on the right accompanying the ascent with upward-pointing gestures. For the descent they stand on the right again, their gestures pointing downward.

A special ceremony greets the newcomer Tamu'thamas, the young Mercury initiate, and he is entrusted with the task of bringing a new masonry technique to the Vulcan Oracle. The Sun Oracle is sending out an impulse: all over Atlantis huge ovens are to be built for the purpose of dispersing the dense atmosphere. Over subsequent millennia it is around these oven temples that Atlantean settlements and towns congregate. The round towers of Ireland and Scotland are late reminders of those Vulcan temples.

Impulses for art and culture also emanated from the Sun Oracle. For example the wooden fibres of a bamboo-like stem were pulled apart so that a flat stone could be inserted. This led to the stem developing a bulge at the point where the stone was positioned. When it was ready the stem was cut apart in the middle of the bulge and the stone extracted. The result was two trumpet-shaped wind instruments. Even in those days dried seed pods were used as rattles. For the manufacture of such instruments the processes of growth were thus utilized to obtain specific effects.

Near the coast of Africa women from the Mercury community who had been initiated into swimming and diving collected spiral shells. These were taken to the Sun Oracle and used as moulds for special crystal goblets. The craftsman Tamu'shadhin, 'He who entrusts to others what he has shaped by his breath', took crystal dust into his mouth and through a tube blew it on to the spiral moulds that were suspended above a round oven out of which hot volcanic gases rose. The dust congealed on the shells that could be 'screwed' out once the deposit had dried. The resulting delicate yet hard glass goblet was then placed on a wooden tripod and served as a drinking vessel for ceremonial feasts.

Tamu'thamas remains behind after the visit of the Mercury people to the Sun Oracle: he is to be initiated more deeply into various matters to do with the Oracle. It will take some time for him to learn the new masonry technique, after which he will teach it at the Vulcan Oracle in the south-west. This will be described later.

On this visit to the Sun Oracle Shamu'radhin meets the high priestess for female temple services, Tame'xan'dima, 'She who guides the fair maidens of the gods'. Although it is not springtime they have a love-encounter in a grotto resulting in Tame'xan'dima becoming pregnant. In my meditative investigation of this episode I was able to rediscover the new feelings engendered in

Shamu'radhin's soul resulting from this coitus taking place in consciousness. The priests who work in the School of Pre-existence are indignant about this unpermitted pregnancy. However, when the power of the secret Sun Initiate enables Tami'tame'sham to see which spirit-soul is going to incarnate, he allows Shamu'radhin to take the pregnant priestess back to the Mercury Oracle with him.

A male child is born after nine months. The full name he is later given is Tame'mani'sham, 'He who has strength to stride while standing still and creating something new'. Later he becomes Tame'tami'sham's successor as the highest externally visible Sun Initiate.

Tonnaman'texila—the Mars Oracle

Together with their chief helmsman Shamu'radhin who acts as the mediator between them, the Mercury travellers mentioned above have spent a good deal of time preparing for a journey to the Mars Oracle in a new gamamila. In some ways the vehicle resembles the much later Viking ships. The figure of a dragon was more prominent in ships in those days; indeed, in his soul a clairvoyant could experience the flying gamamila as a living dragon. The image of the astral being of a spiritual dragon had been so transformed by mercurial magic that in the gamamila it could become a ship capable of carrying human beings over land and sea by flying along special elemental channels.

From the Mercury Oasis, Tauwan'dorraman, the travellers journey northwards, traversing the ravines in the east and the waters of the gulf, and then moving along the eastern coastline of the great continent to a place where a wide fiord cuts inland into a mountainous region. At a special place they cross the fiord and then follow the northern coastal cliffs westwards.

To the north rises a huge flat-topped mountain, Tauwa Gimala.

The gamamila travels along a valley in a north-westerly direction. The mountains on the left rise up to the heavens and when a cold wind blows down on the Mercury travellers it awakens in their common memory their knowledge of the pointed summits up there, which they call Gitaxa'gila. There are several settlements in the Tonnam'gala river valley which by degrees runs up to the fertile high plateau.

Here there are extensive forests and undulating savannahs on which herds of various animals graze. Mist is everywhere, but the people know what is around them through their picture-consciousness: animal noises and plant fragrances conjure up soul pictures mirroring the external situation.

The Mars Oracle, 'Servant of Human and Animal Rights', lies on an island in the midst of a lake on the high plateau. During the early history of the earth this place had been created by the impact of a meteorite. On crags already existing in the centre of the island human hands have erected a building with four staircases facing the four quarters of the compass. On its summit a holy flame burns incessantly, nourished by the priests with various animal remains and plant sacrifices. Around this holy place of steps stand the temples of the twelve schools of initiation.

The Mars community awaits the Mercury travellers in a state of high anticipation, for they will help them build new bagita-gams, plant huts, and pass on new impulses from the holy Sun Oracle Xandorra'tauwa. During the welcoming ceremony a number of new trumpets are presented as a gift from the Sun Oracle, while the Mercury Oracle has sent several flutes made from pods, and many rattles. Children and young people receive baskets of snails and the feathers of sea-birds with which they immediately begin to play and decorate themselves delightedly. Over the next few days a festive procession winds through the countryside using the trumpets and other new instruments;

people from the surrounding land are allowed to participate in this.

The central impulse of the Mars Oracle is to connect the animal kingdom with human beings. This oracle cultivates and develops everything that has to do with hunting and the utilization of animals. Thus there are workshops that process bones and horns to make needles, arrows, knives and other tools as well as musical instruments for which skulls are also used. A whole group of workshops is occupied in the making of leather. Skins and furs that are needed for temple work are removed from animals that have been stunned with poisoned arrows.

Tame'mani'sham, who was later to become the chief initiate for the external work of the Sun Oracle, had to be initiated into all the other oracles. One of his trials was to catch an ass with his own hands, stun it and skin it alive, and then wake it up again, after which he had to sing while it died. His initiate's soul must profoundly absorb the pain of the flayed animal. From the ass's skin he then had to make his first mantle.

There is a workshop in a small wood on the Mars island where menstruating women manufacture special leather aprons which absorb the menstrual blood. Then they hang the aprons on branches to dry. In the larger forests they also collect beeswax with which to soften the dried straps. The Mercury travellers bring these aprons which young women wear as a protection round their waist as gifts to the people of the continent and those in the other oracle centres.

The children of the Mars Oracle love all animals and often sit in the trees on thick branches waiting to catch lizards.

Youngsters bathe and fish in the streams coming down from the Gitaxa'gila mountains. They are accompanied by young men skilled in bird lore who are awaiting initiation. Before puberty girls and boys go naked, wearing only a red leather band round their waist as a sign of their ancestry.

Hamma'fafagama—the Vulcan Oracle

On another, very special occasion the Mercury travellers set out on a southward journey round the Atlantean continent to a part in the south-west where active volcanos are forming a chain of growing islands around the quieter mainland. Warm, subterranean rivers have formed a huge lake on the continent itself. On the western edge of this lake rise vertical cliffs several hundred metres high, filled with clefts.

The gamamila approaches this place from the direction of the lake: it is the Vulcan Oracle Hamma'fafagama, 'Protector of Souls through Masterly Building'. All around over water and land warm steam rises from the hot springs of the district. The Mercury travellers have announced their approach by notes from a flute, but the holy place appears deserted. Profound stillness sets the mood now experienced by Shamu'radhin and his twelve companions, the Radhinila.

Slowly hundreds of Vulcan people appear from underground holes and caves; speaking in chorus they greet the Mercury travellers. The many male and female voices echo from the surrounding mountainsides and carry far across the lake:

> Ugama—ugama, Giramma Magala,
> Methi mada, shamaga Maga Tau'wa.
> Ma methida, Shamu'ra Fafagama.
> Hi'ramma Lama, Shimaga mada,
> Thrusteri'gama, Mari, Methilati.
> Wivavira Uraman, Hamma masda,
> Teth tuda—tuda, Gala—Gala.
> Henki fafa, isti Sila, Tau'wa
> Xandorra, Gada—Gada.
> Umaha—umaha.
> Uma Hamma.

The whole population gathers around the gamamila. Inquisitive girls and boys arrive in wooden canoes; the youngest have only heard the adults tell of the flying ships, but have never yet seen one. Soon they begin to make folded boats in imitation of the gamamila out of large, waxy leaves.

In the Vulcan Oracle the mysteries of the earth and of fire are equally cultivated and protected. To this day we hear of people in Tibet using magic to switch off the force of gravity, an art that was originally practised in the Vulcan Oracle of Atlantis. When building is in progress certain initiates stand on a rocky shelf projecting from a high mountainside and cause huge blocks of stone to rise up in the air without any external aids. The High Priest guides the procedure from on high, using music and singing; others stand on both sides on tall wooden ladders.

The Vulcan people know the depths of the earth with its clefts and caves. They know where to find precious gems, and they have also laid the foundations of what will become the knowledge about working with metals in post-Atlantean times.

Fafagatimir—the fire temple

On this visit the Mercury travellers instruct the Vulcan people in the new masonry technique. Their highest initiate, Trinni'dadama, 'He who can draw through the eye of a needle something that is spread out', enters into a close association with Tamu'thamas who gives him the new wisdom to the accompaniment of singing and dancing performed by groups from both oracles. Out of this interchange between the two arises a fire ceremony that continues to be used for thousands of years whenever a fire temple is erected.

They come together at a spot on a high plateau where the first fire temple of this kind is to be established. Based on the ceremony described it receives the name 'Fafagatimir'.

Selected stones from the volcanic surroundings are gathered and shaped with stone axes, and slow-drying lava is collected from special volcanic geysers to be used as mortar. The men sit round the geyser waiting for a discharge of lava: special preparations enable these initiates to tolerate the otherwise life-threatening heat of the lava drops. They spread an animal skin over the volcanic hole to catch the stream of lava which they then quickly carry to the building site where it is immediately used by those doing the masonry work.

Stone by stone a round building rises to a height of about five metres, narrowing towards the top to form the chimney. The entrance to the fafagatimir is closed with a door made of stone. Every crack is sealed with lava and moss, and the building is then covered with a skin made of fast-growing plants that can tolerate high temperatures. The fire is set on a stone ring in the middle of the floor inside. The fire initiates, both men and women, sit round the fire on stone benches singing to the fire spirits in the earth and in the starry universe, and also worshipping them.

Dried wood for burning is collected in the woods and along the shores. Later special firewood depots are established. Even during Shamu'radhin's lifetime several such fire temples were erected on the Atlantean continent. They were further developed by initiates of the Mars Oracle especially on the high plateau to the west of the Tauwa Gimala mountain.

Later forms of this Vulcan temple reached heights of 12 or even 14 metres. They were cleverly constructed furnaces with double walls, air vents and reversed combustion from above downwards. A huge column of fire and hot air rose into the atmosphere from these fafagatimirs, yielding the desired effect of clearing the air of mist in the vicinity of the temple.

Ambassadors from all the Atlantean oracles came south for a festive ceremony to view and experience this new marvel. Such a large-scale expedition meant a lot of work for the people of the

Mercury Oracle since many new gamamilas had to be manufactured to transport the chosen initiates to their destination.

Tauwa'mami'tagawan—cave painting

The art of rock and cave painting harks back to early Atlantean times and arose, I think, from collaboration between the oracles of Mercury, Mars and Vulcan. The impulse originated in the Sun Oracle and—through the threefold confluence of various initiatives and skills in the oracles mentioned—became the special task of the Mars Oracle.

Initiation into zoology was the responsibility of Mars initiates; the manufacture of paints and the skill of applying them was practised by Mercury initiates; and Vulcan initiates brought charcoal and selected suitable sites for such artistic projects, which were very much a part of initiation culture.

The work was carried out by people from all three oracles who had first undergone special schooling. In later Atlantean times rock painting was also taken up by people from the oracles of Jupiter and Saturn and linked in other ways to their special tasks. In Shamu'radhin's day there was, to my knowledge, at least one school specially devoted to cave painting; it was located in the Mars Oracle. The chief master of hunting, Abra'muthin, directed this school for a while before going over to the new building projects connected with the Vulcan Oracle. The Mercury initiate Shamu'radhin associated himself profoundly with the cave painting impulse.

The impulse to paint animals on rocks in such a wonderful way—as, for example, in the cave discovered at Chauvet in France in 1994—arose from the experience of Sun initiates that human and animal souls spring from the same origins. The animals had entered the earthly world first, and the Atlanteans knew that for human beings to do the same in the right way they must lovingly take the ways and lives of animals into the inner life of their own souls. To obtain permission from the godhead Tauwa to use animal products in their culture they must first find new ways of replacing the old form of burnt offerings. So the cave paintings were felt to be acts of worship as well as an education for human beings who must prepare themselves for future incarnations and tasks connected with the domestication of animals.

Mami'tagaman—the Venus Oracle

The Venus Oracle Mami'tagaman, 'Embrace of Human Souls', was the centre nearest to the Mercury Oracle. Gentle hills and uplands arise where the gulf meets the inland part of the southern Atlantean continent with huge primeval forests.

At a certain spot a river flows from the ocean into the jungle, a remarkable fact visible to clairvoyant vision: the river flows backwards and disappears into the depths of the earth. Then at various locations water re-emerges from the ground in fountains, ponds, streams and rivers.

Various mineral, plant-etheric and spiritual qualities are used by the mostly female leaders and carers of the Venus Oracle for bathing the body and also for the improvement of vegetables and fruits. The whole of human life from cradle to grave, in so far as the continuation of the human race on earth is concerned, appears to be influenced by these water mysteries.

For example various vegetable items are wrapped in long leaves and placed in a spring round a mineral stalagmite. This treatment makes them edible and easy to transport in a gamamila. So they are either given to the Mercury travellers as food on their journey or sent with them as gifts to other oracles.

Children are born while mothers are submerged in other springs. Midwives are special initiates called mamiugama. Children from other oracles destined for specific initiation later on are also brought to these nurses. Midwives also go to other oracles and settlements to do their work.

Sun Oracle and Venus Oracle share responsibility for the spring festival Mitregana Gaman in the whole of Atlantis. Venus initiates work everywhere in these mysteries and are also present in winter when the children are born. Sun initiates of the incarnation mysteries, called Tami'ugama'gada, have the task of accompanying incarnating human souls from their spiritual stellar homes to their correct destination on earth. Representatives of this Sun Council lead the youth festivals already mentioned at which the relationships between father and son or mother and daughter are confirmed.

The Venus Oracle also cultivates certain mysteries of dying and special ways of handling the corpse. It seems to me that the post-Atlantean art of medicine in its early beginnings must have arisen out of an association between the wisdom of the Venus Oracle and that of the Mercury Oracle.

Datila'casturaman—the Jupiter Oracle

The Jupiter Oracle sends its influence out from a place in the north-west of the continent. Its main tasks are the mysteries of rhythm and of education. In a tract of land between an inland sea and the western coast there is a landscape of great forests above which rises an enormous high plateau. This can only be reached by strenuous travel on foot and via ladder-bridges slung between huge trees. Around this acropolis live many thousands of people in various settlements, with a main group on the coast of the inland sea.

The Jupiter Oracle itself appears to be constantly coming into being anew not so much in specific spatial situations as in time and activity. Those responsible for the Jupiter Mysteries cultivate lively connections with the whole population for example by arranging festivals at certain times or setting up schooling situations for young people or other age-groups. With the young people, for example, the initiates go to the acropolis where for a time they engage in various gymnastic and acrobatic exercises. The mysteries of rhythm in human life and nature are constantly taken up anew in the various communities around the acropolis, which is called Datila'casturaman, 'Resting Place of Human Judgement'.

Remnants of this high plateau remaining after the Atlantean catastrophe are to be found in the Bermudas. Perhaps this is where the formative spirits of the divine hierarchies have preserved geographical landscapes for future tasks in educating the human race.

Tsuckbal'dawagan—the Saturn Oracle

Whereas the Jupiter Oracle has more to do with aspects of time, the Saturn Oracle cultivates rather the mysteries of space and place. Tsuckbal'dawagan, 'Finder of Form in Earthly Depths', lies in the northern part of the Atlantean continent. A great waterfall with many tributaries plunges from the high mountains into a valley running northwards. On the northern coast itself the valley meets sand dunes, quicksand, caves and cliffs with spaces between which generate special wind currents and aerial conditions.

Having seen this tremendously long valley of the Saturn Oracle I was later able to rediscover it on a map of the Atlantic's ocean floor. It is the North-west Atlantic Mid-Ocean Canyon which stretches in a north-westerly direction for thousands of kilometres, beginning at the Flemish Cap on the eastern coast of Newfoundland and ending in several side valleys like long fingers on a hand, in the ocean floor of the Labrador Sea.

There I saw a man cutting thin slices of softwood out of which he fashioned kites. One form of schooling involves children being carried high into the air by these kites using strong currents of wind. In other situations people practise on the waterfall, in river rapids, on quicksand, in underground caves or climbing up the cliffs.

These Imaginations suggest initiations that prepared people for life situations in various natural conditions in later incarnations. These trials in nature challenge the human body and soul at various levels that correspond to different professions and forms of society. In this sense the Saturn Oracle can also be termed the Mystery of Civilization.

The central focus of the Saturn Oracle takes place in a huge cave. Initiates sit and move around a large purification pond in the middle. Many stalactites and precious stones sparkle in the light of the flaming torches. Either on rafts or in the water different arts and dances are practised. All the various exercises followed outside in nature in this great northern land are combined in a wonderful spectacle which brings a cult of community into being. Descendants of these Saturn people—many so-called primitive tribes such as Red Indians and Lapps—have retained the community-building power of this cult to the present day. An evolutionary mystery to which I shall return later lies hidden behind these traditions.

Destiny of a Mercury initiate

Shamu'radhin was born in 14393 BC in the vicinity of the Mercury Oracle. His father's name was Tadga'menerthin, 'He who is imbued by what he has absorbed', and he was an initiate of the Mercury Oracle. His mother hailed from the Mars Oracle. In his youth he learned many of the skills practised by the Mercury Oracle, but his favourite was helping the adults who manufactured coloured paints. His father arranged for him to be accepted into the service of the temple and initiated as a gamamila helmsman.

As described, he had many contacts with other oracles. Initially, in the Sun Oracle under the guidance of Tami'tame'sham, he was taught how to cultivate links first with the Venus Oracle and then with the Mars Oracle. Later, through Tamu'thamas, the chief teacher of the new masonry technique, he had frequent contact with the Vulcan Oracle. He did not have much to do with the Saturn Oracle and even less with the Jupiter Oracle.

Only later in life did he meet ordinary people from outside the temple precinct with any frequency. However, in his early years as a helmsman, on a return trip, he once met a woman with two children on the eastern coast beside a cliff and brought them back to the Mercury Oracle where they were taken in. The woman had lost her husband, a hunter, and been cast out by her tribe. Later she was one of the circle closest to Shamu'radhin.

A special event, not only for Shamu'radhin but for all the communities led by the Sun Oracle at the time, was the out-of-season birth of Tame'mani'sham, later the high priest of the Sun Oracle. He grew up in the Mercury Oracle but was taken to the Sun Oracle at puberty. Later he travelled with his father Shamu'radhin to all the oracles. His initiation in the Mars Oracle involving an ass has been described above.

Great changes are on the way for Shamu'radhin and some of his friends and colleagues as he approaches middle life. Together with several representatives of the Sun Oracle—e.g. the master of masks Miriam'akatila and the master of sacrifices Trusteri'gamon—he spends some time at the Mars Oracle in order to make specific preparations for the imminent change-over of high priest at the Sun Oracle.

In this Shamu'radhin becomes more closely involved with various Mars initiates, such as the master of the hunt and leader of the school of cave painting Abtra'muthin. Other Mars initiates have names like Mantor'agila, Katha'mardin, Milti'magisan and Magni'magisan.

Shamu'radhin is a particular favourite of the Mars people on account of the flutes he makes out of pods, which he continues to develop and improve. It now becomes necessary to catch certain animals, ibexes that live high up in the Gitaxa'gila mountains. To this end, groups of Sun, Mercury and Mars initiates live together up in the mountains for many days and nights. In doing so they develop into a new community, one that does not bear any of the usual characteristics of Atlantean communities.

On the whole this has a favourable effect karmically for the individuals involved as far as their future incarnations are concerned, but in the life in question it has catastrophic consequences for their magical abilities.

The power of his hands, Magi Thagawan, gradually drains from Shamu'radhin's ether body because he becomes too involved with the concerns of the Mars initiates. The astral urge to play results in their going in for various antics with the animals of the high Gitaxa'gila. With no inner or outer purpose they chase many of the animals into the ravines where their cries of pain are drowned by the shouts and laughter of the people. Then, when later on Shamu'radhin wants to set off for the Sun Oracle with his load of ibex skins, he finds he can no longer set the gamamila in motion. His spiritual intermediary to the elemental beings has withdrawn from him. Wailing and lamenting resounds for days across the length and breadth of the whole region.

When the whole misfortune reaches the ears of old Tami'ta-me'sham, the Sun Oracle's highest initiate, he cannot but pronounce a punishment on Shamu'radhin and his fellow travellers, including those from the Sun Oracle: For the remainder of their present life they may never be given the opportunity of seeing their home oracle again!

This is the real reason why Shamu'radhin becomes more

involved with the Mars Oracle and is taken into the school for cave painting there. Later, with the rest of the travellers, the Radhinila, and also others from various oracles and from amongst the ordinary people, he founds a new settlement to the north-west of Tauwa Gimala. Henceforth his name is Gamu'radhin, 'United with his fellow travellers'.

He and the others are not alone in experiencing a turning-point in their lives, for changes also come about for those in the Mercury Oracle who are connected with him. Gamu'radhin's father, old Tadga'menerthin, resigns his office and travels with a group of younger Mercury people to the Mars Oracle where he joins forces with his son. The old gamamila initiate's deed of joining forces with his son in this way brings about a karmic link between the two of them which again and again has positive consequences right into post-Atlantean times. He becomes one of the co-founders of the new settlement where, after some time, he dies.

This new settlement comes into being around one of the earliest of the higher form of Fafagatimir. When he is very old, Gamu'radhin leaves this town called Timir'dorraman, in order to promulgate cave painting more widely towards the north. In 14313, aged 80, he dies in the Saturn Oracle. The highest Sun initiate, Tame'mani'sham, orders that his burial shall take place in Tauwa'dorraman.

Thus it came about that the memory of this former Mercury initiate, who had begun his career in the south with his hands and ended it in the north with his feet, continued to be kept alive in the Mercury Oracle. Many similar destinies began in that place before the Atlantean floods destroyed it.

Interim remark

During the period when I was researching the Atlantean oracles and the life and times of Shamu'radhin, later Gamu'radhin, and following him and those karmically connected with him into further incarnations, I was not yet able to enter more deeply into what happens after death. Not until one is capable of following up the spiritual continuity by doing so, however, can one truly depict a number of incarnations as belonging together as a sequence. Later I shall make this good by describing some post-mortem themes in connection with a number of incarnations. There are also other motifs which I shall mention that show the links between incarnations.

I shall show how the Atlantean incarnation described in some detail above can serve as a kind of karmic key to subsequent lives. It will enable us to retain in our awareness the idea that the higher self—called Arjuna—of the individual in question either opens or closes something with this key through the destiny events of the relevant incarnation.

From Atlantis to Alaska

On the continent of Atlantis, which still exists but is now smaller, there is a place in the north belonging to the Saturn Oracle. In the twelfth millennium before Christ a girl is born there named Tanamira. To use modern terminology, she is a very sanguine child.

I saw Tanamira playing with mostly older children in various places amongst the mountains. She develops a wonderful mobility in her limbs, a characteristic for which her people are generally known and admired far and wide. In a number of neighbouring kingdoms this capacity is even utilized socially.

At the beginning of her second seven-year period she falls off a cliff and both her legs are damaged. For many months she lies there with her legs wrapped in herbal compresses but once the treatment ends she can still not stand. Her legs are paralysed and no physician is able to help her.

At this time the leading initiates of the Sun Oracle which reigns over her people send out a command similar to one which other communities received some time ago. They are to divide up into groups with an exact number of participants and set off on a journey westwards in order to find new land on another continent. They are given a description of that distant land and also documents made out of animal skins showing distinguishing features along the way.

Tanamira's father is instructed to hand her over to another group with whom she will be able to emigrate when she is well enough to walk. But he loves her too much and disobeys the order. He takes her with him, carrying her on a stretcher with the help of an older brother.

The girl's paralysis has still not improved when the group reach the north-western coast of the continent after many months of hardship struggling through unknown territory. They are taken in by a local tribe who have been forewarned that they should receive them hospitably. They are shipbuilders, and over the coming autumn and winter they instruct Tanamira's people in shipbuilding, sailing and life with the sea. Still the girl's health does not improve. Her father now comes under pressure because his disobedience to the leaders of his people has been discovered. Profound sorrow overcomes Tanamira as she sees her family and relatives set out in wooden boats and disappear over the western horizon towards the setting sun.

This sorrow gradually transforms her inwardly and after a number of years, through her own efforts and the love that grows in her towards her new environment, she regains her health. She can no longer remember her own people; they only appear to her on certain occasions in pictures that are like dreams. She goes to the seashore at sunset and there Imaginations rise up of people she feels she knows. She watches her blood relatives going about in foreign lands and encountering strange animals. Then she begins to sing of these Imaginations to those who are now her companions. They support her gift and build her a hut on stilts in the water near the shore. At sunset no one is allowed to disturb her.

Over the next two or three years she is taken there and brought back in a little canoe. At festival times people come from far away to hear her sing, but only the initiates know that her stories are about the external experiences of her own people.

One day a group arrives who are to travel onwards across the sea. Her memories suddenly clear and she realizes where she belongs. She tries unsuccessfully to mingle with the seafarers. She is not one of them and the leaders sternly turn her back even though many would love to take her beautiful songs with them, 'in the flesh' as it were.

A young man called Simagil, the leader of a small group of youngsters of both sexes, falls in love with Tanamira. He has a secret chamber built into the bottom of his boat in which Tanamira hides. She is only discovered once it is too late to turn back. On reaching the new continent, Tanamira and Simagil are joined in wedlock and she is accepted by his people.

Her life unfolds among them as they journey on and on. High points arise when they meet another group travelling along a different route. Then they live together for a while, exchanging all their songs and stories, experiences and skills. Tanamira's group only reaches its destination in Alaska when she is very old. Her husband is no longer alive, but she meets with her original brothers and sisters who have arrived at the same location. Her parents are long since dead; she is aware of this through her own manner of seeing. In this rather beautiful way a final Atlantean incarnation ends, almost as in a fairy tale.

From Ireland to Crete

Towards the end of the tenth or the beginning of the ninth millennium before Christ—I have been unable to pinpoint the exact time—an initiate called Mani'mac'mahan journeys eastwards via Ireland with about 800 others from various Atlantean peoples. Ireland is still connected via an isthmus to the northern part of the Atlantean region which now consists of several large islands.

In these Imaginations I am following the weather interpreter Areldingun who lived in Ireland. It was his task to observe meteorological changes such as atmospheric conditions, clouds, thunderstorms, rainbows and so on. He and his group of magicians had to keep watch on all the ever-changing weather patterns which crossed the country, usually from west to east. The divine-elemental gifts brought by these natural phenomena of the air were to be linked with specific locations on the ground, and for this purpose special plants, bushes and trees were grown in such places.

Mani'mac'mahan takes Areldingun and several others of his people with him as he journeys onwards. The leader of this migrating group intends to take them to the far-distant east. First they travel across the sea in a south-easterly direction before crossing territories we now call France. They journey for many years, and as they travel they take with them more people from the inhabited regions they pass through, for some of their travelling companions die along the way. Thus their number remains more or less constant. Mirimana is the name of a woman who is allowed to join them. She belongs to a kind of oracle community which is now taken over by Mani'mac'mahan.

The travelling group stays for some time in the region of southern France where cave painting had been practised in earlier Atlantean times. Mani'mac'mahan and his companions lead a selected group of men, among them Areldingun, down into the caves. As he contemplates the animal paintings and listens to special songs Areldingun begins to yearn in his soul for an encounter in this life with creatures such as these.

But the journey continues as far as the island of Crete. Here various adventures bring Areldingun and Mirimana close to one another. One day, while taking part in a festival with the inhabitants of Crete, they have walked away from the settlement and now encounter the wild animals they have been told about. Mirimana is frightened of the great bulls and climbs up a tree, but Areldingun is enchanted by their strength and beauty. Taking hold of a fallen branch he tries to approach them, but they gallop away, leaving the astonished weather interpreter standing in a cloud of dust.

While the travellers are preparing for their onward journey eastwards by boat Areldingun has climbed up into the mountains with Cretan huntsmen. He cannot forget about his encounter with those new animals. He and some of his friends gain the permission of both groups to remain behind. Taking leave of Mirimana is only a brief interruption of sadness in his new life on the island of the bulls. She stays with the group who go with Mani'mac'mahan to the innermost reaches of the Mongolian uplands where as time goes by a smaller circle gathers around the great Manu, about whom Rudolf Steiner spoke. Over the next few thousand years the larger group who have arrived from the west, together with their descendants, form a protective circle around the sun initiates who are preparing and creating the new post-Atlantean cultural impulses within the inner circle.

Areldingun and his friends are absorbed into the early Akkadian people of Crete. He begins to pursue the herds of wild cattle with the intention of catching and trying to tame the leading bulls. The familiarity with atmospheric phenomena he had developed back in Ireland always helps him pick up the animals' tracks. An early attempt to catch a great bull alive misfires when he is cornered and fatally wounded by one of them in a narrow mountainous cleft from which there is no escape. In the years that follow his companions also fail to catch and tame those wild beasts. They die in such numbers that the king of the country forbids any further exploits.

The memory of those first tragic attempts to domesticate animals on Crete remained with the people for a very long time. A stone was erected wherever someone had been killed. Several thousand years later animal tamers who were initiates were brought in from distant Persia. They introduced new methods of animal husbandry.

An Indian elephant tamer

Having described the previous two lifetimes more briefly than I did the first Atlantean incarnation, I shall now once again depict certain events and circumstances in greater detail. We have arrived at the first post-Atlantean culture, round about the last third of ancient Indian civilization in approximately 5700 BC. These Imaginations about the woman Ramishanda took me to the north-western part of central India.

Her parents belong to the caste of protectors of the people whose forefathers had come from the north. Now large areas with many villages and settlements on both sides of a river flowing westwards are under cultivation. The people are still hunters and gatherers while at the same time already cultivating the land. In Ramishanda's village I saw domestic animals such as cows, pigs, hens and dogs.

The young girl wanders further and further afield around the village and her parents know that she loves to spend the whole day in a treetop. There she listens to mysterious animal noises, for Ramishanda has discovered the kings and queens of the wild animals: elephants. She would love to play with the baby elephants and tries to get near to them, but her parents forbid her to follow this urge. She tries to find her own ways of approaching them without success, for she has no good ideas.

One day she awakens from a dream knowing who can help her: her uncle Bugtamar. He lives upriver and works at pottery and basketry. He tells her to bring a sacrifice for the goddess Shiva, to put her in a good mood. He also gives her a pottery bowl as an offering and advises her to tell neither her parents nor anyone else. She promises and after embracing her uncle sets off straight away to the Shiva temple by a circuitous route. The temple lies beside a small lake on flat ground protected by rocks. She makes her offering and prays to the goddess in a whisper with her eyes closed. Then she strikes up a conversation with some priests, asking them without further ado how she can play with the elephants. Having glanced at one another in surprise they speak together for a moment and then ask her to wait before disappearing into the inner chambers of the temple. Soon the high priest Tadgathiwan emerges. She knows him already, for at festivals he has always regarded her kindly. Now he speaks to her in a gentle voice:

'Dear daughter of the good man Gumatamar, gentle protector of the Tomthawan. Dear daughter of proud Muritama, protector of our daily activities. The goddess looks down upon you, Ramishanda. Shiva will show you the way to her beloved children in the jungle. But first you must grow as strong as the elephants, so you must learn to live the life of the elephants.'

Throughout her youth Ramishanda then undergoes special preparation under the guidance of the Shiva temple, first in secret but later with the full approval of her family and the whole community. She lies on a crystalline bed made of quartz and zircon, she bathes and swims in muddy water. Clinging to lianas she swings from tree to tree, she rides on bulls. Standing upright on the back of a bull and holding on to his long horns she forces him to go long distances, to a river where she throws herself into the water and swims to the other bank.

Her elder sister, Gangatami, plays the flute. A group of female musicians helps her accustom the elephants to human civilization by walking round them day and night in a great circle without frightening them.

After many years the great day comes at last. Ramishanda, now almost grown up, has been taught how to be an elephant tamer. Will she pass the great test? Or will the leading female elephant break her with her trunk like a clump of dried mud or crush her under one of her great feet?

The whole population has gathered while Gangatami and the other musicians play delicately and harmoniously on flutes, sistrums and drums. In the background stand Tadgathiwan and the Shiva priests together with priests from other cults. Incense made from dried elephant-grass and sweet fruits floats upwards while a group incessantly recites the ancient songs.

Naked and alone Ramishanda, nearly nineteen years old, stands on the village side of the lake. The sun is at its zenith in the blue sky. A single cloud pauses directly above the young tamer who does not see it, for her eyes are directed to the forest. The leading female elephant emerges, followed by the others, the young ones holding on to the tails of the older ones with their trunks. As they enter the water Ramishanda does so too. The elephants take no notice of her and continue to drink, bathe and play as usual. The young ones show no fear for neither do the older ones. Ramishanda does what the elephants do, and after a while she swims across the lake, climbs out of the water and then stands and waits, covered in mud, on the bank where the elephants are. The mud dries in the hot sun and gives her a new skin. Finally the leading female sees her and gives a signal, whereupon all the others quickly withdraw. Now the human being Ramishanda and the queen of all earth's animals confront one another.

Quietly and with courage the tamer stands and waits. The elephant approaches and seizes her round the waist with her trunk. She lifts her up and makes a movement that looks as though she is going to dash her to the ground. The crowd gasps and the music stops for a second. The single cloud evaporates and disappears into the blue. But Ramishanda is not dashed down!

She speaks in a high voice: 'You are Shiva's daughter. I am Shiva's daughter. So we are sisters. I would like to play with you and I would also like to play with your children.'

Ramishanda looks into the elephant's left eye. There she sees the eye of the earth with the blue sky reflected in it. There are no clouds. A rainbow arches over the deep well of the elephant's eye. All this Ramishanda sees, and she thanks Shiva for her life. The elephant, now tamed, stands the tamer on her back while Ramishanda continues to speak to her: 'I am Shiva's daughter. My name is Ramishanda. You are Shiva's daughter. I name you Latabaga.' What happened on a higher plane at that moment I shall describe later when I follow up the connection between human beings and animals from other angles.

The elephant kneels and allows the human tamer to slide down her trunk. She recalls the other elephants and for the rest of the day Ramishanda plays with them, including the young ones. At sunset, when the elephants return to the forest the woman swims back to the other shore of the lake where she is greeted and celebrated as a heroine. After this success one of the princes of the Tomthawan, Margathudin, does not let her out of his sight. She becomes his wife, and they are the ancestors of many later female elephant tamers and riders. I discovered during my research that for thousands of years it was the women who continued to domesticate elephants, until the times of pre-history, when men took over the task.

I also saw the wedding feast of Ramishanda and Margathudin. After the celebrations he carries her up a ladder into a little hut. It is square and built between four tall tree trunks. The living branches with green leaves have been cunningly tied to create a roofed chamber that is like a balcony in that the walls do not reach up to the roof. Here they consummate their marriage.

Throughout her whole adult life Ramishanda and her people work with the help of the elephants to tame the jungle and make canals that carry water to artificial ponds situated near orchards. When she is not working with the elephants she enjoys taking her rake to till the enclosures thus created. To protect her from the sun she wears a wide hat made from reeds rather like the ones still used today in eastern Asia.

In the decades that follow this culture spreads south-east-wards. Many days' march from Ramishanda's home, on a plateau with a climate that suits certain crops and fruits, a house is built for her and her family.

Beyond some low hills live other northern communities belonging to another southern civilization whose people have darker skins. For several years in succession these southern people suffer famine and distress on account of a drought, but thanks to their irrigation systems the people in the north can grow enough to eat. People from the south are forced to go north, but when their request for help is turned down they begin to plunder. Many times they attack the northern plantations at night and since these are not guarded they can gather good stores. But Ramishanda's people do not suffer this challenge without retaliating.

Riding on an elephant Ramishanda leads an elephant army through the southern regions and villages where they are opposed by brave foot soldiers. Many humans on both sides, and some elephants, lose their lives. The survivors flee from the centre of that culture and hide in the mountains for many months. Such warlike measures create a gulf between the two peoples which remains unbridged during Ramishanda's lifetime.

The high priest of the southern people has saved his life by remaining quietly in his hut during the battle. His name is Brahmakatzar. He waits in the devastated village for several days, but when no one returns he sets off into the jungle with a burning censor. Day and night he travels southwards, but when his strength fails him he sits down in the middle of the forest where he remains for several more days keeping the censor burning with dried flower petals and seeds which he takes from a little pouch. Thus dies Brahmakatzar.

A few days later some members of his tribe see the smoke from higher up the mountain. They venture down and find their master still sitting there. He is dead, but his censor still burns. A little bird sits on his hand, takes seeds from the pouch and lays them in the vessel. For several thousand years, perhaps even still today, the censor continues to burn in that place. People build a huge stupa there and around this temple new impulses arise for a further development of that special culture of southern India.

A Chinese silk worker

We now move forward to the time of the third post-Atlantean civilization. I shall try to explain later why in my case I have found no incarnation in the second, the Persian period.

Shida Dong lives about 2400 BC in a hill village by the western shore of a huge and very long Chinese lake. From large maps of modern China I have been able to identify this as the Dong-ting (or Tung-ting) lake. The village itself, consisting of several hundred round houses, is called Dong'du after the clan to which Shida Dong belongs. The more prosperous families can be recognized by the extra rooms of their houses that have been attached to the central unit in a semi-circle. The roofs look like reed hats. The inhabitants are mainly occupied with the craft of working with silk.

Rolling hills stretch away to the west. A cart-track leads northwards along the shore of the lake to the distant temple and market town several travelling days distant. King Wang resides still further to the north-west. His servants regularly ride through Dong'du either northwards or southwards to where the king's family oracle is sited not very far away.

No one from Dong'du has access to the holy areas of this oracle near the sacred waterfall Shamintaga'nga. The children of Dong'du, however, like bathing in the lake and want to explore further afield. Thus one day they find themselves at the edge of the holy wood on the shore of the sound that runs along the perimeter of the oracle's temple. They look at the image of the holy place mirrored in the still water and do not understand why the king has built two temples, one on land and another in the water. As they stand there talking about this a dragon rises out of the water and shows them its fiery jaws. Shida and her friends run away in alarm.

Many years later Shida ventures to that place once again, this time alone and approaching from the lake. She paddles her canoe on the still water, and now she realizes the link between the temple and its reflection. She stands before the sacred waterfall further back in the valley beyond the oracle. It is divided into two streams and tumbles down in stages. Nothing untoward occurs, and she happily paddles back home where, however, something unexpected has indeed been prepared for her.

A stranger, a young man called Djingotan, has arrived from another people up north. He is her future husband, chosen by the family council. Once the two have been paraded through the village as a wedded couple Djingotan picks her up in his strong arms and carries her to the specially prepared visitors' hut. Immediately he begins to prepare for the first act of love. He is lighthearted and loving. Shida accepts everything, in anticipation of all the wonders she has been told about. Entwined with one another they lie on the bed of straw and Shida experiences a wonderful encounter between the heavenly god Shinto'shin and the earth spirit Diago'shan. Djingotan takes his knife and makes a deep cut on her left thigh. Blood flows and he fills both her and the open wound with his seed. This holy act makes this woman his property for the whole of his life. No other man can later intervene, for Shida has been marked for life with the sign of her husband.

Despite this dramatic beginning the young wife is not alarmed. Djingotan proves a good husband to her. He carries her to a little stream where he continues to care for her over the coming days, and she becomes pregnant immediately. Following her first confinement with all its accompanying feelings and details was quite a special research experience. When the time for the birth draws near all the close relatives in Dong'du gather at the house of her grandfather, Bami Dong. This tremendously fat man is to be the midwife at the birth. They all sit or stand around Shida in the middle of the round house. The child arrives and Bami Dong holds it up in front of Shida. She sees a screaming mouth and realizes that something is missing. Then she feels the earth open up beneath her and she sinks through darkness into unconsciousness.

On waking up later on she finds herself on her own balcony looking out over the lake. Djingotan immediately comes to her side and lovingly strokes her right shoulder and the back of her neck. He tells her about the dead child but she already knows. His tame bird with the beautiful coloured feathers flies up from the fence and perches beside her, touching her hand lightly with its beak. Looking at the flowering plum tree she falls asleep.

The couple live harmoniously together and have several children all of whom survive. Shida works in the silk craft and Djingotan offers his skills as a fisherman to other inhabitants of the village. He swims in the lake with his harpoons and delights the villagers with his fisherman's luck. Since he is a boatbuilder as well, a special commission comes his way one day.

King Wang has had a most beautiful wooden altar made for his family oracle, and he commissions Djingotan to build a boat that can carry it across the great lake. He is delighted to accept the task, and many people gather from the surrounding region to see this marvellous vessel that has been built for this one special occasion. An even greater crowd gathers on the day of the festival. Only the altar-boat and the other royal ships are on the water, for none other may travel. The king has arrived and sails with his court on the alter-boat which Djingotan himself is to steer. His helpers are a few seafarers from his own tribe who have also come specially for this occasion.

But when Djingotan reaches the spot where the children once saw the dragon a great wind gets up and his boat sinks. The altar cannot be saved and goes to the bottom. Djingotan dives after it but cannot do anything. He immediately realizes what this means so he swims further underwater and then hides in the depths of the forest. The king as well as the others think he has drowned, but he is found by the royal guards and thrown into the palace prison. Only when King Wang himself dies after many years is Djingotan executed together with other prisoners and buried in the king's grave.

With her beloved husband in prison Shida falls into a state of mourning that lasts for many years and also brings misfortune in her work. She has been working in the dyeing department of the silk works for some time. One day in her misery and anger she empties several pots of dye into a stream in which other women are doing their washing lower down. The family council takes a dim view of this. On another occasion she is reprimanded again, but for a different reason. She has taken her eldest sons with her to market. Instead of going home with her they climbed up on to the roof of the Shinto temple in the late evening in order to peep in through the air vents. They were discovered by the guards and punished accordingly. After this episode Shida decides to go to the king and beg for her husband's freedom.

All alone she walks the many hundred kilometre stretch to the royal city in the north. It takes her many weeks, spending the nights up trees, in caves or with kind people. She now benefits from what Djingotan has taught her about nature. Finally she reaches the royal city and is permitted to enter the palace. The great round central hall is encircled by a wide gallery on which beautifully clothed elderly men with long beards and hair in the Mongolian style sit in silence on small thrones. At the spot where the gallery is open to the central hall sits King Wang himself, on a higher throne. Shida is allowed to walk past all these men and stand before the king. They greet each other, for many years ago a greeting once passed between them in Dong'du.

She states the reason for her visit: 'Highly esteemed king of my people in Dong'du. I, Shida Dong, wish to beg for the return of my dear husband Djingotan. He is still young enough to build more ships.' The king interrupts her: 'You have come with justifiable human wishes, but your husband was judged many years ago by the god of the wind when our altar was taken by the god of the water. Your request and your journey have thus been in vain. Of course you may visit Djingotan today, but tomorrow you must set out on your return journey.' The audience is at an end, and Shida is led to her husband.

I saw the final meeting between Shida and Djingotan, but I shall leave readers to find it for themselves in the Akashic Record if they so wish. The meeting did not help Shida to overcome her chronic state of soul, and when she arrived at her home all she wanted to do was lie down and die.

A priest at the temple of the heavenly god Shinto'shin called Ranga Jia has heard about all this. When the inhabitants of Dong'du persuade Shida Dong to go to the temple with them the temple servant approaches her in the forecourt just as she is handing over her gifts. He says: 'Instead of your lost husband Djingotan, Shinto'shin will give you a friend, Shivabei. She will follow you back to Dong'du, bringing with her the eunuch Barigong. You shall learn a new craft making lamps and vessels for fruit offerings for our temple. Shivabei will also heal your soul.'

And so it happens. Slowly Shivabei brings Shida out of the profound melancholy into which she has fallen since her husband's misfortune. She teaches her the new craft and also the art of caring for the body and the art of the divine touch: acupuncture. From the forest Barigong fetches pieces of wood suitable for making the temple vessels and even ventures into the forbidden royal woods. By the fire in the evening he plays and sings for the two elderly women and also for the whole village community.

Having reached a ripe old age Shida stands once more in the garden plucking mulberry leaves. She feels her end approaching and is taken to her round house. As she lies on her deathbed the whole family gathers while Shivabei brings beautiful cloths and unguents and Barigong plays gently on the sitar. The temple priest Ranga Jia and another priest Tanga'ngam have come from the temple city this very morning to collect lamps and vessels for fruit offerings. They sing the hymns for the dying.

Death comes to Shida Dong at the moment when the blossoms on the plum tree by the balcony open. The tame bird who has always accompanied her spreads its wings and is never seen in Dong'du again. The guards at the Wang oracle in the valley of the

Shamintaga'nga waterfall, however, now daily see a new visitor perching on the gable end of the temple roof.

I have been able to learn some things about Shida Dong's life after death. Her spirit-soul leaves her corpse and floats above the lake. She views Dong'du and thinks certain thoughts: 'I have learnt something about reconciliation. I have come up against the power of men. I once wanted to try and unite temple impulses with the life of ordinary people. This has been my life this time. I thank you, the god above, the god below and the god all around that I have had some success in this.' The spirit-soul watches as Shivabei and Barigong prepare the body. It is wrapped in silken shrouds and at the burying place is hung head down in a mulberry tree like the cocoon of a silk worm. There it hangs for several days and nights, watched by the living. Gentle music keeps birds and animals away. Finally the corpse is placed in the grave in the earth, which means it is given over into the keeping of the earth spirit Diag now that all the bodily fluids have drained away.

An Egyptian scribe in the reign of Rameses II

The following is another life which I found in addition to those already described. It is about a person who lived under Rameses II during the XIXth dynasty. In the autumn of 1996, after having discovered this connection through meditation, I read about the work of the archaeologist Kent R. Weeks in the Valley of the Kings where, it seems, he discovered the so-called 'graves of the princes'. It had long been known that this pharaoh had had about 50 sons and 40 daughters. Now that these graves have been found, more will be learnt about all those princes and princesses from the paintings and other treasures they contain. Before the new findings are published I feel I can give detailed descriptions of the life of one of the princes, whom I call Ray. Perhaps my spiritual research will one day be corroborated by the archaeologists' findings.

Ray is born around 1277 BC. In giving this date I am going by the standard for Egyptian dynasties applied by Christiane Destroches Noblescourt. I have tried to compare what I saw with the historical facts she describes in her book *Ramses—Sonne Ägyptens* (Rameses, Sun of Egypt), as well as endeavouring to fit in with her dating system. Ray's father is the pharaoh Rameses II, who has been in office for two years. His mother is one of the many concubines and I have interpreted her name as being Entramada. I experienced her in the Imaginations as being a good mother who lives with her son in the capital city in the delta near the palace.

At the age of about five the boy is to be brought before the pharaoh, his father, and he has been told exactly how he must behave. Somehow he expects that he will be permitted to sit on his father's knee. Having made various pronouncements to him, Rameses then says: 'Your father is Osiris.' Thereupon the boy turns round and runs into his mother's arms.

Ray is sent to the school for scribes and learns everything there is to know about the papyrus plant. I see him sitting on the ground with other boys. He is painting on plant leaves with his fingers and drawing pictures with his finger-nails; he also writes hieroglyphs on slabs of soft stone. I saw how later on his thumbnail becomes his most important writing tool for giving certain hieroglyphs the correct character in the papyrus scrolls that are many metres long. My guess is that, should Ray's mummified body ever be examined, his fingers will still make this obvious. From published drawings of the princes' graves I am able to pinpoint the location of his grave accurately, towards the left of the entry shaft.

As an adult Ray goes to Karnak and Luxor in connection with different tasks. In the House of Life, over a period of several years, he rises via various phases of workmanship and crafts-manship to become 'setter of the seal'. In this Egyptian institution new papyri are manufactured and stored, and also copied. I saw about 40 scribes standing along the same side of a long writing table, Ray being almost at the left-hand end of the row. Daylight streams down from the opening in the middle of the ceiling above their heads. Pillars all around the rectangular room carry the roof that also extends above neighbouring chambers. It is darker and cooler behind the pillars where the scribes chat together during breaks in their work. At the end of this large workroom, a long way from where Ray is standing, I imagine the papyrus archive. While the scribes write, priests or lectors oversee everything and read aloud. The scribes' patrol also recites everything before and after each phase of the work.

Over the next few years, between about 1250 and 1243 BC, Ray rises in rank and receives commissions in connection with a number of building projects, for which, as we know, Rameses II became famous. From ancient documents he supplies texts for use in murals and reliefs. He works down south under the old vizier Chaj who would like to have him as his successor as the Vizier of Wawat and Kusch in Nubia which is held under permanent occupation by Egypt.

However, Chaj's successor, Setau, is not chosen as usual from the corps of officers but because of his services as the former 'Scribe of Horned Beasts' and his career in the administration of the state. There are several such deserving men on Chaj's staff, one among them being his favourite, Ray. Chaj sets him up in a position for which he is not properly qualified. In order to silence Menerthin, the man whose true position it is (connected with certain building works in the south), Ray sells him a very ancient, valuable papyrus document. This is of course totally forbidden and would be punished by death if it ever came to light, but since Ray himself is the overseer of the archive, from which he has taken the document, nothing can ever be found out until after his death anyway.

I saw both men standing on a cliff after having concluded this transaction. The scribe is smaller but wiry while the master-builder is much bigger and stronger. Menerthin seizes Ray, who is now his superior, around his naked chest and dangles him with outstretched arms above the valley in which the building works are making much dust and noise. Menerthin says: 'Now swear never to speak of this transaction.' Ray promises. Within a few days Chaj dies. The large sum of money Ray has received from Menerthin enables him to set up good contacts in dynastic circles in the ensuing struggle to succeed the vizier.

His rival Setau hears about the sale of the document from a master sculptor called Muustragathichaem who has been given hints by Menerthin himself. Setau persuades Menerthin, who would prefer to see him rather than Ray as the new vizier, to enter into further arrangements, for after all, the master-builder himself could be in trouble if everything were to be discovered. So circumstances turn against Ray in that rumours begin to circulate hinting that Menerthin declined Ray's offer to sell him the document. Ray quickly travels to the capital city in the delta in order to clear himself of the reproach before the pharaoh. After all, he is a son of Rameses; surely the pharaoh would prefer to see him above some stranger as the vizier of Wawat and Kusch.

Rameses II receives him at once, and listens calmly and kindly to Ray's accounts of his many works in Nubia. Then comes the moment when it is customary for the subject to kiss the feet of the pharaoh. Instead, Rameses II places his right foot firmly on the head of his son Ray who experiences pain and punishment, but not self-pity. He remains prone for some moments after the pharaoh has left the audience hall with his officers and servants. Some of Ray's brothers who have witnessed the scene show their amusement, and the pharaoh also laughs mockingly. The unfortunate scribe knows exactly what is to be his fate. Rameses has not imposed the death penalty; in fact, he has saved his life by his action which means, however, that Ray must go far away for some time, until the whole affair is forgotten and tempers have cooled. But where should he go?

The answer is not long in coming, for behind a curtain Maathorneferure has been listening to the proceedings. This former Hittite princess has been living in Pi-Ramessu—the palace city on the Nile delta—for some years as one of pharaoh's wives. While Ray is still lying on the ground she steps forward and says to him: 'Ray Kharama, my son, I come as your protector. Go to the land of my father in the north where a task awaits you. I shall furnish you with a letter of recommendation, a staff and four bearers.'

Ray could never have imagined such a solution. He embraces the beautiful Maathorneferure and sets off northwards before the sun sets.

In Hattusas he is invited to join the school of scribes where he shares in the work of carrying on the copious correspondence between the Hittite kingdom and Egypt. Wichtagar, a musician and instrument-maker, introduces him to the customs and practices of Hattusas which are quite different from those of Egypt.

There he remains for several years until the discord in the south has calmed down and Setau is established in his new position as vizier. Ray makes contact with him and they settle their differences, and Ray now becomes one of Setau's advisers. Around the year 1237 BC—aged about 40—he is made a kind of governor in Upper Nubia where he becomes more closely involved with the black Nubians.

A Nubian prince, Gubomba, is to marry a young woman, Chaembasa. Before the wedding the bride's mother, Kamitirida, takes Ray aside and asks whether her daughter pleases him. Ray, who has known these people for nearly a year, replies in the affirmative. 'Then you shall take her away and save her from Gubomba, who is wicked.' These words spoken by this black woman, still beautiful despite her age, enchant the Egyptian.

Helped by the mother, Ray carries off the bride Chaembasa, who is already dressed in her finery, and flees northwards down the river. He is planning to make for Dendera where he once made many friends at the Hathor temple while carrying out a number of commissions there. When they are halfway there they rest for a few days in a royal residence on the island of Elephantine. They are now very much in love with one another and go for a ride on a raft on the Nile. When they have made love she lies on the raft while he swims in the river, pushing the raft before him. She dangles her right foot and ankle in the waters of the Nile and they lose track of space and time as the raft drifts downriver nearly to Kom Ombo.

Suddenly she is dragged from the raft by a crocodile that has seized hold of her leg. Ray dives and searches for his beloved. First he tries to drag her from the animal's jaws but when this fails he takes his knife and, sitting astride its back, stabs it many times between the eyes until it dies. He manages to extricate the wounded leg and swims with Chaembasa to the river bank, where he pulls her out of the blood-stained water.

Carrying her in his arms he runs upriver, begging the water-side inhabitants for help. He sends some youths to go swiftly and fetch physicians while he himself, weeping, continues to run upriver with her. Her white dress dries in the warm air, but her wounded leg hangs limp. They talk to one another. She: 'Never leave me, my protector.' He: 'I shall follow you always, even if you die.' Whereupon the beautiful Chaembasa dies in his arms before any physician arrives. She has lost too much blood, and all Ray's efforts to revive her are in vain. Others can do no better, for none of them possess magical powers of sufficient strength.

Some members of Chaembasa's family, but especially Gubomba and his people, are now filled with hatred. There is a revolt which is severely quashed by the Egyptians. Historical annals tell of a Nubian revolt around the year 1236 BC which was put down by Setau. Hermann A. Schlögl (*Ramses II*, Reinbek 1993) writes: 'In the 44th year of the reign there was a small incident in Nubia. Apparently a group of revolutionaries attacked some gold workers in Wadi Alaqi. Setau reacted with a military punishment raid which he made out to be a great act of war...' I think the reason for that Nubian attack was the incident I have described above.

Ray takes Chaembasa's body to Dendera where he arranges for her funeral. He uses his remaining funds and some good contacts he still has in dynastic circles to pay for having her embalmed and for an appropriately ornamented grave.

After these tragic experiences he remains at the Hathor temple in Dendera as a pupil. Over the next four or five years his tasks, among other things, involve taking part in the annual festival when the Goddess Hathor, in the form of a statue, is taken in a ceremonial ship to visit various temples on the Nile. He discovers the significance of divine rhythms in music expressed by means of a special sistrum or rattle.

He receives the Hathor initiation. It was a remarkable moment in my research when Ray, awakening after the third day of his initiation sleep, received a drink poured into his open mouth from the trunk of an elephant. He is lying in an open sarcophagus. The elephant strides slowly along the high temple hall and takes the extract from a golden vessel that is carried forward by the high priest. When the elephant has stepped over the sleeping pupil and gone out, Ray is awakened by calls. In the next phase he is supposed to recount what he has experienced in the spiritual world. He does so, but for the initiates who are present a shattering moment arrives when he ends what he has to say with the cry: 'I could not find my beloved Chaembasa. If only I could die this instant.'

After his initiation Ray's sorrow deepens. The leaders of the Hathor temple, under Maanthorthebin and Amarthitina, have to regard his initiation as a failure. In a kind of euthanasia the priestess Dendraa helps him to die around the year 1232 BC. Ray lies with his back bent on a table-like bed underneath which a sharp metal obelisk is attached which is movable. His hands lie on his chest, the right below the left. Dendraa places her hands on his and slowly presses downwards. At the same time she operates the mechanism of the obelisk with her foot, making it move upwards. It pierces Ray's body, and because he has turned to the right its point emerges through his left nipple and passes between the thumb and first finger of his right hand. His last words are: 'I see her; my bride has come for me...'

The background to Ray's death would not have been made known and therefore would not be mentioned in the inscription on his grave. After his death as an initiate of Dendera his princely rank, of which he has been stripped for many years, is reinstated by Rameses II. As with other members of the royal family, the pharaoh has a grave prepared for him in the Valley of the Kings. As I have said, I hope that research into the 'graves of the princes' which were discovered on 2 February 1995 will show whether the results of my meditative research into the life of the scribe Ray contain the truth.

Charioteer at Delphi, messenger for Pericles, and master organizer of the Eleusinian Mysteries

Around 490 BC a son, Agamon, is born to a family of vintners to the north of Delphi. His life encompasses the age of Pericles (465–429 BC) in ancient Greece. The incarnation I shall now recount is the one to which the Imaginations about the

Eleusinian Mysteries refer which I received after doing the bio-graphical karma exercises already described. I have found nothing in historical sources about anyone called Agamon at that time or in fact that show the name Agamon to have been in use in ancient Greece.

I saw the boy lying, day in day out, on a cliff overhanging the temple of Delphi and watching the goings-on in the place of the oracle below. More often, though, his eyes are directed towards the stadium, for he wants to learn to be a charioteer. Throughout his boyhood and youth he plays all kinds of games with his relations and friends in the village with the aim of developing his physical strength and testing his skills. The terrain around Delphi is as though purpose-made by the gods to accommodate games of this kind. A kind uncle lets the boys have a few wooden wine-barrels which they roll downhill while they balance on them either alone or two on one barrel. But first they have to roll the heavy barrels uphill, which certainly develops strong arm and leg muscles. They practise standing on tree trunks carried down-stream by mountain torrents. They treck for many miles among the slopes of Parnassus hunting birds which they shoot with crossbows.

As a youth Agamon is accepted by the Delphi gymnasium where he trains to be a charioteer. In addition to their gymnastic and olympic exercises, the young athletes also have to serve in the temple precincts and work in the gardens. Already at Delphi, but also later at Olympia and Sparta, Agamon is admired as a charioteer and marathon runner. One of the charioteers at Olympia is called Trapestarion. Another sportsman is Haftoteles, who becomes his friend for life.

He lives in Sparta for a number of years, taking part in the gymnastic education of young athletes. Under one of the representatives of Spartan interests, the administrator Marion, he first learns about being an express messenger. With Haftoteles he attends the great theatre performances at Epidaurus where he gets to know Elitania, a serving woman in the sanctuary of Aphaea. Both athletes are permitted to join the theatre chorus at Epidaurus and later in Athens. Agamon is seriously injured in an accident during a chariot race and Elitania arranges for him to return to Epidaurus where he is cared for by the women of the Asclepius temple who cure him. One of the priestesses there, Mirtilia, has him instructed in the secrets of healing remedies.

During the year he spends at Epidaurus he comes to realize that he has passed the age when he can be an athlete. He decides to go to Athens and try his luck there, where the leadership of Pericles is beginning to blossom. He joins the chorus of a theatre, and it is in these years that he gets to know, among others, the tragedian Sophocles. He also finds new friends amongst the sculptors working on the many building projects on and near the Acropolis. One of these is Amterion. It is through this circle that he gains an introduction to the government leader Pericles. When Pericles hears of his knowledge of Delphi he asks whether Agamon would like to go there as his messenger to glean advice from the oracle. Agamon agrees immediately, and there follow many years of work as a messenger for Pericles.

His first journey takes him to Delphi where the priests of Apollo's temple remember him and therefore receive him very favourably. Those consulting the oracle receive its answers through the priests and never directly from the Pythia who receives them by direct inspiration from the gods. When I was trying to research the work of the Pythia in my meditations—who was named Dithelia at that time—I saw and experienced the following: that the place of the oracle was separated off by textile walls and a ceiling resembling a tent. The air is filled with smoke rising up from the earth beneath a tripod in the middle of the room; incense makes the atmosphere even denser. In a deep trance, the Pythia sits on the tripod whose legs are shaped like serpents. Around her stand the priests who can translate her utterances into human language. I realize that the individual who was once the highest initiate of the Vulcan Oracle of Atlantis is now incarnated in this Pythia.

During an earlier stay in Delphi Agamon had made the acquaintance of a woman who was there on a visit. She came from Athens and was called Deidera. A close relationship developed and a son was born to them, Emterion. With his little family, over the coming years, Agamon travels extensively as a messenger for Pericles in the Mediterranean region around Greece, for instance to the Greek colony of Sybaris and to Pergamon in Asia Minor.

One day while he is in Athens he receives a message from Delphi telling him that his father is ill. He sets off for Delphi immediately, the quickest means of transport being his own two feet. Having run across valleys and hills along the familiar pathways he pauses for breath at a spot to the south of Delphi. He looks down on his homeland and the valley and, closing his eyes, remembers his boyhood. Once when he was looking at the stadium a stone had fallen down the mountainside. The idea that this might have caused some terrible accident had troubled him so much that his grandmother sent him to the temple to confess to having been the cause of the stone falling. However, nothing had in fact happened, and a smiling temple servant had sent the boy home.

A great roar rouses Agamon from his reverie. Glancing up he finds himself looking into the eyes of a wild bull. Quick as lightning he jumps up and hurries down the hill with the bull after him. It can run faster than the one-time charioteer and is about to stick its pointed horns into his back. Agamon ducks from side to side and suddenly remembers: 'That deep river pool must be just down there.' Feeling as though Apollo is lending him wings he leaps from the cliff's edge and lands in the water where he can swim across to the other side uninjured while the bull falls and is killed. Helped by several uncles and other relatives Agamon is thus able to come to his sick father laden with gifts of fresh meat. But neither this nor the medicines from Epidaurus can save him and after a good conversation about the deeds of Pericles he dies in his son's arms.

Years pass without any other dramatic events, and Agamon's son grows up to be a youth. Free of family duties and being too old to continue acting as a messenger, Agamon looks around for new tasks. For many years he has been participating in the public festivals of Dionysus which involve a procession of many thousands of people winding its way from Athens to Eleusis. Unattached participants can join in various trials and watch dramatized versions of the divine mysteries along the way. Agamon now seeks admission to the second stage of the Eleusinian Mysteries and is accepted. I have already described the moment when Agamon was lying in a kind of cart resembling a ship which was set in motion by four bearers. I recognized the man at the front on the right as the Athenian Amterion. The cart travels on wheels through subterranean galleries where the neophyte experiences various encounters with spiritual beings dramatized by actors.

Agamon has his first encounter with the Mystery School of Eleusis around the year 447 BC and he continues to belong to this school until his death around 418 BC. First he works for the public festivals before later becoming the master organizer of the closed mystery celebrations. There he makes close friends with a lady of the wardrobe, Mitami, who is much older than he is. She tells him many things about the history of Eleusis.

A dramatic incident occurs in which Agamon is not involved. There is a disagreement between some of the actors and the leaders as a result of which one of the actresses, Lysistrate, kills

Lagomenes who is the head of a family. She in turn has to pay with her life.

During the first tenth of this period Agamon still makes many journeys to Athens. After certain dramatic events at Eleusis, about which it is not permitted to speak, he renews his contact with Sophocles. I watched them standing at the foot of the Acropolis as he tells Sophocles many secrets about the Eleusinian mystery tradition. One of these secrets is connected with the mystery of the world soul and the world cross. I have not been able to follow up whether and in what form these matters reappear in the plays of Sophocles. It is likely that the play *Oedipus Rex*, written some years after the death of Pericles in 429 BC, was influenced by them. Something tells me that in those conversations with Agamon Sophocles was given Eleusinian interpretations of that ancient myth.

At a ripe old age the former athlete from Delphi sits on the temple hill of Eleusis cutting and polishing crystals which his son Emterion sells in Athens as offerings for Delphi. Of all the incarnations I have found, this one as Agamon strikes me as being one of the happiest.

The mother of a Roman Emperor becomes a clandestine Christian

We now come to the life of a woman that unfolded in the midst of well-known historical events. She was the daughter of Marcus Antonius and Octavia and was called Antonia *minor*, or 'the younger'. She is mentioned in numerous sources, but I had never heard of a Roman woman named Antonia *minor* when my Imaginations first showed me many events in her life.

After exhaustive work with those Imaginations I turned to historical sources where I found the very events I already knew about from the Akashic Record. With spiritual sight, however, I had also seen other motifs which throw an entirely new light on many known facts or even, if they are true, would make it necessary to rewrite history. Before describing what I saw I shall put forward a few historical facts in order to complete the picture.

Antonia *minor* was born in 36 BC. Her older sister was called Antonia *maior*. Her mother Octavia was a sister of Octavian, known historically as Caesar Augustus. For a while her father Marcus Antonius (Mark Antony) ruled the eastern part of the empire while Octavian ruled the west. When Mark Antony took up with and later married the Egyptian queen Cleopatra and had children by her, his marriage with Octavia was dissolved. After the dramatic deaths of Antony and Cleopatra in Alexandria, Octavia brought up their children together with her own in Rome.

As was customary at that time, Antonia was married to Drusus at a young age. Among those of their children who survived were Livilla, Germanicus and Claudius Drusus. Together with her husband, who was an army commander for example in Gaul and Germania, she experienced life in the provinces. Drusus died in 9 BC after falling from his horse. Out of love for this highly appreciated commander Antonia did not marry again, although she was still young. For many years she lived with her children on the Palatine Hill, the royal residential area to the south-west of the Roman Forum, in fact until the death in AD 29 of Julia Augusta, the female head of the family.

Antonia enjoyed the peaceful era of Caesar Augustus and became one of the guardians of his cult in Rome. With interest she followed the military successes and exertions of her favourite son Germanicus in Germania, but also his tragic death in mysterious circumstances in Egypt. She took his son, her grandson Gaius (later to become the Emperor Caligula), into her house when his mother, Agrippina *maior*, was placed under house

arrest by Tiberius. Her bad relationship with her eldest son
Claudius (who succeeded Caligula as Emperor) has been made
world-famous through the novels of Robert Graves.

The Roman historian Suetonius records that on her own
initiative Antonia murdered her daughter Livilla by withholding
food from her as a punishment in connection with intrigues
around Tiberius in which Livilla had become involved. Antonia
minor, so say historians, died in AD 38 or 39 by her own hand as a
consequence of increasing disagreements between herself and
Caligula.

My own account of Antonia will include other facts which lead
to the assumption that she did not die until AD 55. There are
several stories that point to the possible continuation of her life in
secret and I shall begin by describing the following encounter
which I saw in Imagination.

Antonia, aged perhaps 35, is on one of her customary shopping trips in town, dressed simply as usual to avoid being
recognized. On her way home she hears the sound of weeping
coming from a side-street. Going down the dark alley she finds a
strong young woman sitting alone, and listens to her story. Her
name is Agoria and she has been driven from the house of the
banker Gaius Praetorius for supposedly being his illegitimate
daughter. Having had financial dealings with Gaius Praetorius,
Antonia is familiar with that name. She takes Agoria home with
her and then finds her somewhere to live and employment in a
bakery of which she knows the owner. Agoria becomes respected
as a capable baker and after some years even takes over the
bakery from the owner.

Antonia remains in contact with the banker but does not
mention the matter of Agoria. There is an occasion when she is in
need of money for repairs necessitated by a small fire started by
her lively grandson Gaius. When the banker refuses her a loan
she uses sexual means to persuade him. She goes about this so

discretely that nothing has ever been discovered about it by historians.

Walking in the Forum one evening she finds a small book someone has dropped. She takes it home and discovers that it belongs to Gaius Praetorius. Normally Antonia is entirely trustworthy in such matters (several of her contemporaries have confirmed this) but in this instance she reads the diary from beginning to end, thus gaining first-hand evidence of the banker's many love affairs with Roman women. In his own words she reads about several illegitimate children whom he is obliged to support secretly. Antonia finds this rather at odds with the way he has treated Agoria. She goes straight to the banker's house and gives him a piece of her mind. In the years that follow, the diary provides her with a useful hold over Gaius Praetorius if he refuses her financial help when she needs it.

There are several Jews in Antonia's household. Even while Herod the Great was still alive (he is presumed to have died in 4 BC) she had got to know many people from Palestine who frequently visited Rome or spent several years living there. She is constantly in touch in person or by letter with Berenice and her son Herod Agrippa, king of Judaea from AD 37 to 44, who is a close friend of Caligula and Claudius but an opponent of Tiberius.

One of Antonia's chambermaids is the Jewish woman Priscilla who is married to the tentmaker Aquila. Priscilla has got to know Agoria in her bakery, and Agoria accompanies Priscilla to her Jewish gatherings and feels at home there. Through these two women Antonia comes into contact with Jewish teachings and Christian beliefs taught by a Jewish scholar, Hermas, from Alexandria. Here the elderly Roman woman also hears about the Jewish idea of reincarnation which it is hoped will not be contradicted by the new faith. Antonia has very little to do with the other Christian group that meets in the house of the Roman senator Rufus Pudens to which the Apostle Peter came later. But she knew Pudens from earlier in her life.

Round about the year AD 38 (Caligula has been ruling for some time) a Greek orator already known to the Romans is on a visit to Rome. He is a philosopher and has a seat on the Areopagus Council; he is a kind of counsellor who can advise people and politicians alike in difficult situations. His name is Dionysius. He gives an oration standing on a terrace above the crowd (possibly the Forum of Augustus). Among the crowd are Antonia and her friends. As he tells a parable about the salt of the earth, Dionysius takes some salt from a cup on the marble altar beside him and scatters it over his audience with his left hand. A grain lands on Antonia's forehead. Lost in thought, she is somehow startled into action and runs home as though with the legs of a youngster. (It is said of her that the older she got, the more nimble she became on her feet.)

At this point I shall quote from a lecture Rudolf Steiner gave in Hamburg on 19 May 1908 published in *The Gospel of St John*:

> I have often pointed out that Paul, the great apostle of Christianity, used his powerful, fiery gift of eloquence to teach Christianity to the people, but that at the same time he founded an esoteric school, the director of which was Dionysius the Areopagite, mentioned in the Acts of the Apostles (17,34). In this Christian Esoteric School at Athens, which was directly founded by Paul himself, the purest spiritual science was taught.

The other women wait until the oration is finished before going home to find her. She is lying in bed looking ill and both legs are paralysed up to the hip. On the second evening, at her request, Agoria and Priscilla carry her to the Jewish cemetery which is situated underground in a catacomb. Here she partakes of her first Christian communion. In this simple place, a candle-lit underground meeting room, old Antonia undergoes a kind of transformation. Next morning she walks back home on her own two feet without any assistance.

Now she decides to take steps which will remove her from external Roman life. She brings the diary to Gaius Praetorius and sells it back to him for a large sum of money. She prepares every detail of a pretended suicide, even buying a corpse so that nothing shall be discovered subsequently. Some time later she begins a new life with a new identity and a new name, Ioana, in Greece, near Corinth.

When both Jews and Christians are expelled from Rome in AD 46 by her son Claudius she joins forces with her women friends who have come to Corinth with Aquila. Here, and possibly also on journeys to Athens and Ephesus, she meets a number of Christians who were present at the events in Palestine.

In her new identity Antonia sends a messenger, Menos, to try and retrieve her correspondence of many years with the former Roman governor in Syria, Pomponius Flaccus of Moesia, who died in AD 33. Menos is unsuccessful in this mission, but he makes contact with one of the many women named Salome and also other Christians. On returning to Corinth he brings with him reports and greetings from the Christians in the Holy Land and even directly from a Salome whom Antonia had met many years before in Rome. Antonia *minor* alias Ioana dies a Christian, aged over 90, round about the time when the son of her grand-daughter Agripina, the new Emperor Nero, is forcing the priests at Delphi to initiate him into the Apollonian mysteries. The year is AD 55.

Later on I shall return to this period two thousand years ago around the Mystery of Golgotha (Rudolf Steiner's term for the life, death and resurrection of Jesus Christ). It will be important for me to show what consequences can result in later incarnations from the manner in which an individual does or does not accept Christianity. First, though, I must complete my account of the sequence of incarnations. The next step takes us to the time before and after the Second Crusade in the twelfth century.

German Chancellor, Archbishop of Mainz, imperial legate in Italy

As I have already mentioned, working with the indications Rudolf Steiner gave in his lectures on karma concerning the teachers and pupils of Chartres led me to make quite a comprehensive study of the twelfth century during which I first became aware of Christian von Buch. Subsequently many of the results of these studies were confirmed by my meditative research.

As with the previous life story, I shall distinguish between what I discovered meditatively in Imagination and the information I gleaned from historical sources. Having made a more thorough study of this incarnation and the period in which it took place I shall describe both events and persons at greater length.

On his mother's side Christian von Buch is known to have descended from a Thuringian family from Bucha near Querfort, about 40 kilometres north of Weimar. There are records of Christian as a provost of Merseburg in the late 1150s. After the assassination in 1160 of Arnold von Seelenhofen, Archbishop of Mainz, a diet of princes including Landgrave Ludwig II of Thuringia 'the Hard', and Conrad of Hohenstaufen, Count Palatine of the Rhine, put Christian forward as the new Archbishop, against the choice of the church in Mainz. Frederick I Barbarossa refused. (I have already mentioned these matters in Chapter 1.)

In 1162 Christian succeeded Rainald von Dassel as Chancellor, a position he held until 1166. When Conrad I von Wittelsbach finally took the side of Alexander III in 1165, Christian von

Buch became Archbishop of Mainz, which he remained until his death.

As Christian I of Mainz he continued to function as Frederick Barbarossa's legate and ambassador in Italy. In 1167 he travelled to Germany with Duke Berthold IV of Zähringen in order to mediate between the rebellious Saxons and Duke Henry the Lion. In 1168, with Henry the Lion and the Archbishop of Cologne, Philipp von Heinsberg, he visited the Kings of England and France on diplomatic missions. In 1170 he was sent on a similar mission to the court of Emperor Manuel I Comnenus in Byzantium. His greatest achievement as a diplomat is regarded as his participation in the negotiations leading to the Peace of Venice in 1177 in which Pope Alexander III was finally recognized by the Germans. During the latter years of his life he continued to work in central Italy representing German interests and winning broader support among the princes. He personally supported the new Pope, Lucius III. Ernst W. Wies wrote about this in his book *Kaiser Friedrich Barbarossa, Mythos und Wirklichkeit*, Munich 1990 (Emperor Frederick Barbarossa, Myth and Reality).

> Pope Alexander died on 30 August 1181. The cardinals chose Archbishop Hubald of Ostia, a companion of Alexander and participant in the negotiations for the Peace of Venice, as his successor. He ascended the papal throne as Lucius III. His position in Rome was weak and he was only able to hold his own politically thanks to the Emperor's sword-arm and legate in Italy, Archbishop Christian of Mainz, who hurried to his protection and fought off the Romans ... Terror at hearing his name alone was enough to drive them off. This powerful individual, heroic soldier, diplomat, archbishop, scholar with a knowledge of many languages who had translated the story of Prester John during a mission to Greece, lover of women and life, died of a fever on 25 August 1183. He had begun by being a bitter opponent of the popes, but now he was their protector. Pope Lucius ordered all German collegiate

churches to hold a 30-day funeral mass for Christian of Mainz. His person provides an example of the remarkable turnaround that occurred during Frederick Barbarossa's final decade.

From among my meditative experiences of Christian von Buch, I will recount those Imaginations which supplement what is known historically. This will provide an overall picture of his life. I will then also describe some individuals from among his circle, both helpers and adversaries.

For his seventh birthday Christian's maternal grandfather gives him a silver knife with a leather sheath and belt. This knife accompanies him throughout his life in all kinds of destiny situations.

Aged about nine he is standing by his father's deathbed. His father has always served the church and since his elder son has been taken on as one of Landgrave Ludwig II's knights the younger son, Christian, will have to become a priest as soon as he is old enough. The boy promises to do this and the father then dies in peace. Probably in 1147, when Christian is 12, King Conrad III is travelling around Germany mobilizing followers and knights for the Second Crusade. In Merseburg he calls for men to take up the cross, and the men of Thuringia come out of their houses to join the crusade, while those who are either too old or too young at least want to catch a glimpse of the King. Landgrave Ludwig gives Christian permission to ride northwards by the side of his brother. For the first time he is on a horse of his own, and seeing the wonderfully caparisoned knights riding in the King's vicinity he longs to be one of those who may ride beside him.

After their meal in the open air on the plain to the south-west of Merseburg, Ludwig 'the Hard' catches hold of Christian around the waist and swings him up into the air declaring: 'I'll take you like your brother to be one of my closest knights.' With his feet back on the ground the youngster replies: 'I fear that won't be possible for I promised my father on his deathbed three years ago to become a true man of the church.' 'Very well, my son,' replies the Landgrave, 'in that case I shall make you a prince of the church and we shall make common cause.'

I saw the growing boy playing in the river valley with his cousin Johanna, who is two years his senior. Their favourite place is near the mill where the miller, called Wulf, likes it when the children are around for he can then send them off on errands. During the milling season he has to mind his mill all day long and has too little time to attend to his other duties. The children have to get out of the way when the peasants come to deliver their grain. Usually they climb to the dark upper floor where they sit above the heads of the men and eavesdrop on all the gossip and rumours about what is going on in county and empire. This 'school of the miller' is where young Christian first learns about the rise of the young Duke Henry, later to be known as 'the Lion'; about the quarrels between Henry's uncle, Duke Welf VI and King Conrad; about the schism in the church, with Pope and anti-Pope; about why the Landgrave who was so kind and tolerant to everyone in his youth has meanwhile become 'the Hard'; and about many other stories and legends as well.

The first radical change in his life comes in his fifteenth year. The Landgrave has arranged a place for him in the abbey of Corvey. I see him before he departs, going round the village taking leave of relations and friends. At first he cannot find Johanna. He goes to the mill to say goodbye to Wulf and has hardly entered the dark building before he hears Johanna whimpering behind the sacks of flour. He immediately knows what is going on. With his knife in his hand he creeps forward, slitting open one of the sacks. (The strange thing is that during the Imagination I hear the faint sound of flour running out and forming a little pile on the floor.) With bare feet wet with sweat and his knife held high the youth steps over the flour. He stands for a moment behind the miller who is lying on top of the unfortunate maiden, his back naked and his trousers down. At the moment of ejaculation Christian cuts a cross on the miller's back. Wulf jumps up and his cry can be heard far and wide across the county. Christian takes Johanna in his arms and runs down to the river with her, where he washes her tenderly. I see some flour mixed with the miller's blood on the surface of the water; it has rinsed off Christian's feet, and begins to travel downstream as it mingles with the froth on the water.

After this dramatic happening young Christian von Buch finds his way to the abbey of Corvey of which Wibald of Stavelot has been the abbot since 1146. He is already over 50 and is an influential statesman, a counsellor to King Conrad and a close friend of Pope Eugenius III and later Pope Adrian IV.

Not long ago I visited Corvey for the first time and found myself in the area that had once been the monastery garden. I succeeded in reaching an Imagination: A monk is showing young Christian various herbs, and he has to make a piece of ground ready for sowing by raking it carefully. His favourite spot, however, is the library where the monk Eloph lets him read secret books on the three Greek forms of love, agape, eros and sexus. Over the next few years, under the supervision of Wibald, Christian learns several languages: Latin, French, Italian, and even Greek.

There is much discussion at Corvey about the reform preacher Arnold of Brescia, anathematized by Pope Eugenius III in Rome and hanged and his body burnt in 1155 during the reign of his successor, Adrian IV. Abbot Wibald, who is a close friend of both popes, hints during conversations with Christian and other monks that he has some sympathy for certain of the ideas Arnold is expressing. As a vehement critic of papal power, Arnold of

Brescia had started a republican movement in Rome which was quashed by both Pope and Emperor.

In 1158 Christian von Buch, now 23 years old, accompanies Abbot Wibald on a diplomatic mission to Byzantium. The abbot has been sent by Emperor Frederick Barbarossa to negotiate with Emperor Manuel. Christian, the young interpreter, enjoys conversing with the German-born Empress Irene, formerly Bertha von Sulzbach, and it is from her that he hears of the above-mentioned manuscript about the legendary Prester John. On this first visit to the eastern Empire Christian makes good contacts with Emperor Manuel and some of his counsellors, contacts which turn out to be useful later on when he is working from Italy.

On the return journey Wibald, who has fallen ill, asks the young diplomat whether he would like to be his successor as abbot, saying that if he agrees he will instruct him in all the tasks as soon as they reach their own country. Christian asks for a few days in which to reflect on this, but meanwhile Wibald dies, and posterity has never heard anything about this conversation. As it is, Christian does not want to be abbot, which Wibald in his turn does not realize before he dies.

Christian is now appointed cathedral provost in Merseburg. I see him instructing young clerics in the cathedral school. Among these I discover a number who later stand by Wickmann von Zeitz, Archbishop of Magdeburg, when some Slav border territories are to be annexed by the church. As soon as he has fulfilled his duties to the church, Christian finds his way to Margrave Otto von Meissen, who later became known as 'the Rich', riding with him to inspect his estates. Later he receives much support from Otto, also in the form of knights to follow him to Italy.

The first of the Margrave's knights he encounters is Friedrich von Haussen, knight and minnesinger, who later accompanies him for many years in Italy. I shall mention him again. Friedrich provides Christian with a good contact to Wickmann who has been the minnesinger's tutor.

Having assassinated their archbishop in 1160, the citizens of Mainz had begun to realize that the Emperor would make them do penance for this murder. Ernst W. Wies (see above) had this to say:

> They searched among the great families for a successor who, they hoped, would afford them protection. They elected Rudolf von Zähringen. He was not only a brother of Duke Berthold von Zähringen but also a brother-in-law of Henry the Lion, as well as being related to the Emperor ... However, a diet of princes headed by Rainald von Dassel, archbishop and chancellor, annulled the election and ex-communicated the citizens of Mainz.

Rudolf and Berthold von Zähringen's sister Clementia was Henry the Lion's wife until 1162. Their daughter Gertrude became the wife of Friedrich von Rothenburg, the young Duke of Swabia, a son of the former King Conrad III. Duke Friedrich, with a number of others, died in Rome in 1167 in the outbreak of malaria to be mentioned later. In the autumn of that year Christian von Buch rode with Berthold von Zähringen to Saxony as a peacemaker. They probably brought Gertrude news of her husband's death on their way through Swabia.

As mentioned in Chapter 1, while I was studying medieval history in the early 1990s a friend made certain suggestions in which she told me about some specific karmic connections between the members of a family who were involved in a family drama in the Middle Ages. My studies led me to the circle of the individuals mentioned above, and my Imaginations subsequently confirmed that the lady in question had indeed formerly been Gertrude. Since Gertrude later married the pretender to the Danish throne, who became King Canute VI, it can be assumed that Christian von Buch played a part in the negotiations for this marriage, because his earlier missions had already brought him into contact with the Danes.

During the seven years from 1160 to 1167 Christian von Buch was closely involved with Rainald von Dassel. It is said that the political views of the former were indistinguishable from those of the latter. Historians have found no hint in the records of any rivalry between Rainald and Christian. In fact the prevailing impression is one of fundamental agreement in political matters. The Italian chronicler Acerbus Morena from Lodi described Rainald von Dassel as follows (quoted by Wies, see above):

> Rainald, the chosen Archbishop of Cologne, formerly called Chancellor and then Arch-Chancellor for Italy, was of medium height and powerfully built; his countenance was pleasing and his complexion fresh; his limbs were evenly-formed and well-proportioned; his hair was thick and fair; he was well-spoken and highly educated, eloquent, circumspect, and very acute and discerning; he was extremely desirous of elevating the honour of the Emperor, so much so that the Emperor lent his ear to none but him; he was also generous, cheerful, sociable, magnanimous, and patient in hardship; the glory of the Emperor was tremendously enhanced by his acumen and effort.

I came to realize that it was during his time as a cleric in Corvey that Christian got to know Rainald through Abbot Wibald.

Rainald made many enemies in the Alexandrine camp in the years following the beginning of the schism in the church in 1159, during which he became one of the most zealous opponents of the Gregorian idea of the supremacy of Pope over Emperor. His bitterest enemy John of Salisbury, the English philosopher and later Bishop of Chartres, wrote that his criticism was directed not against the faith but only against the different constitution of the church.

The schism worsened in 1166 during Barbarossa's fourth

Italian expedition when the German princes crossed the Alps with huge armies. But Rainald was ill and could not join the Emperor's army in Lombardy until several months later. The main aim of the expedition was to conquer Pope Alexander III, install Paschal, the anti-Pope who favoured the Emperor, in Rome and then conquer southern Italy and Sicily. All modern biographies written by reputable historians describe Rainald von Dassel as Pope Alexander's strongest opponent. He died in the malaria outbreak of August 1167 and thus did not live to see the resolution of the schism.

The registers of the medieval Archbishops of Cologne were collected and published in the nineteenth century. There is a passage in these which could be interpreted as hinting that before he fell ill in Cologne, Rainald may have reached the conclusion that the schism could be resolved without force and by means of a compromise. This idea arose from his connection with a certain Master Girard Pucelle who had been his adviser in Cologne in 1166. The following is what my research through meditation revealed:

Rainald is lying weak and exhausted in bed, having recently vomited. He has his right hand on his stomach while his left arm lies across his body so that the left hand dangles down on his right side. A beautifully embroidered cross adorns his nightshirt. A man in dark garments with a sleeveless jerkin stands on the left side of the bed. He is wearing a mortar-board with the characteristic tassel such as we are still familiar with today. He is immediately recognizable to me as being Girard Pucelle.

He is telling the sick archbishop about his most recent letters to the English King Henry II and his friend John of Salisbury who is in exile in France. In them he has described the situation in the empire and given the latest news about Emperor Frederick's expedition against Pope Alexander. Rainald lifts his left arm and points at the speaker with his little finger. Recently he has understood Pucelle to be willing to impress the German view on the party of Alexander; but now he realizes that the Master perhaps has other plans. Girard places his right hand on Rainald's right and says something like:

'This expedition against the rightful Pope, if he is driven from his throne by force, will be not only an expedition against his own person and a part of the Holy Church, but against Christ himself. If you are prepared to disarm this expedition I shall immediately be able to persuade Alexander to a compromise.' Rainald has let his arm fall, but now he raises his hand again, speaking in a low voice and no longer pointing with his little finger:

'In my condition I now recognize how right you are. I shall use every means within my power to achieve an ending of the schism.' This conversation contradicts everything that is historically known about Rainald von Dassel. In the subsequent events mentioned in the sources there is no hint that any negotiation based on it might have taken place between him and Pope Alexander.

In meditation I have followed in detail his path after the illness, his relationship with Christian von Buch during the last year of his life and the dramatic events in Rome before his death. And I have compared the historical descriptions with what I saw in my Imaginations. I shall report on some surprising themes that emerge, and also give karmic details. But first let me follow and quote Ernst W. Wies on his historical investigations. I think it is important for us to understand the events of 1167 if we want to develop an eye for karmic connections, which is why I am going into so much detail in this instance.

Wies tells of the Emperor setting off for Rome in January 1167 although 'the two princes of the church, Rainald von Dassel and Christian of Mainz had failed to establish peace...' The Emperor was determined to enter Rome, 'end the schism and extend imperial power over Rome and the church'. His progress was not impeded by the founding of the Lombard League which more and more towns flocked to join, driving out all his commanders 'on an agreed date'. He 'ignored the conflagration and ... following the tried and tested practice of German emperors, split his army on the way to Rome. He himself took the main portion southwards along the Adriatic coast while the two archbishops, Rainald and Christian, were to make for Rome via Tuscany along the Tyrrhenian Sea.' But the towns of the Lombard League still stood firm. Rome itself had put together an army to oppose the Emperor's progress. Rainald had got into difficulties at Tusculum, but then his 'clerical companion-at-arms Christian of Mainz arrived with his contingent ... The Archbishop of Mainz saw that he was outnumbered and tried to negotiate.' But the Romans mocked the Germans, and thus

> began the battle on the second day of Whitsun, 29 May 1167, in the ninth hour and lasted until the evening. Christian of Mainz faced the hugely superior force of the Romans ... Nevertheless he had left a small select band in an ambush. Rainald, watching from the walls of Tusculum, saw the outnumbered Germans whom the Roman army threatened to engulf. So ... he commanded his men to sally forth. With his 300 knights of Cologne and the garrison of Tusculum he broke out through the gates and joined combat with the enemy. He himself bore the banner of St Peter and led the battle hymn *Christus qui natus* (Christ is born). The Germans attacked from the rear while Christian of Mainz burst from his ambush and split the enemy army in two.

The Emperor arrived in Rome in July 1167 accompanied by Paschal, the Pope whom he supported. Pope Alexander still held out for a while, before finally departing secretly and fleeing to Bénévent. On 1 August Pope Paschal III crowned Emperor Frederick and his Empress Beatrix, and the Emperor granted great rewards to Rainald von Dassel, Archbishop of Cologne, for services rendered.

> Then, at the pinnacle of their triumph, Emperor Frederick and his followers, believing they had bent the Occident to their will, were visited by catastrophe. It was brought about not by a hostile army, not by a new coalition of enemies, but by nature. On 2 August 1167, in the shimmering heat of summer, tremendous deluges of rain which triggered a malarial fever epidemic plunged the German army to destruction. Nearly 25,000 people were carried off as cloudbursts alternated with humid showers in the heat. The young Duke of Swabia, King Conrad's son and cousin to the Emperor, the young Duke of Welf, Heinrich of Tübingen, Count Palatinate, the Dukes of Sulzbach, Nassau, Hallermund and Lippe all died shaken by fever. The Bishops of Verden, Liège, Regensburg, Augsburg, Speyer, Zeitz and Prague also died.

'Rainald von Dassel now also ended his active career. He died on the eve of the Feast of the Assumption of Mary, 14 August 1167, having received the sacraments of the church with great piety and laid down his last will and testament.' (Wies quoting Geoffrey of Monmouth.)

I shall now put forward something of what I have seen in Imagination pertaining to the year 1167.

After his illness in the autumn of 1166, Rainald von Dassel crossed the Alps with his knights and sought out Christian in the imperial encampment outside Lodi. I see the two princes of the church in Christian's tent at a moment when he is cutting some bread with his knife. Rainald has just finished telling him about the offer made by Girard Pucelle. Christian hands him a piece of bread and says:

'Surely you realize, my friend, that the schismatic Roland (he means Pope Alexander III) will not depart from his wrong-minded standpoint. He will have to be removed from his throne before we can begin fresh negotiations.' Rainald listens patiently, slowly chewing his bread. Then he replies:

'Very well, my brother, I shall let your judgement stand until we reach Rome. Until then I shall say no more about Girard's opinion. Depending on people's positions when we arrive we shall see whether we should call on his assistance or not.' Then the two take leave of one another for the moment.

In Imagination I follow the two commanders, see their exertions with pack-horses and wagons. Christian goes towards Rome and I see him riding down from the Sabine hills. I see Rainald in the watchtower at Tusculum waiting day after day for the German reinforcements. He even wonders whether he should send out secret messengers on his own initiative to test Girard's words.

Christian's arrival turns his attention away from such thoughts, for he sees the serious threat to his brother in arms posed by the superior Roman forces. He sees dark clouds gathering in the west, then lightning flashes. His impulsive will, which he knows all too well, takes hold of him. There are trumpets and flags, and Rainald rides forward on his horse to meet Christian. Together they sing the hymn 'Christ is born' and vanquish the Roman knights, who flee. I see the prisoners and the dead, and watch as the two archbishops and their soldiers march into Rome. With them is the young Duke Welf VII whom they know well from earlier activities together. He has suddenly appeared during the final skirmishes.

Then I see the thunderstorm and the downpour. Before the storm sets in Alexander and his closest cardinals flee down the Tiber in a boat. I see him sitting on a seat beneath a canopy in the centre of the low-sided river boat that is too full of people and baggage, so that the deck is several centimetres under water. I have a close-up view of the Pope and realize that he is afraid of drowning, for he cannot swim.

His red slippers with their turned up toes suddenly attract the attention of my spiritual sight. They are under water and the golden side-seam is still visible beneath the ripples. He had no time to put on any other shoes. All he could do was throw on a monk's habit over his papal vestments. Now that he is out of danger he is once more wearing his tiara. I was able to follow up the consequences of those wet feet: Alexander caught a cold from which he never fully recovered; it weakened him for the rest of his life.

Then comes the fever epidemic after the downpour followed by more August heat. In my Imaginations I see the flies swarming everywhere, for instance on the meat laid out on wooden boards as it is prepared for eating. I watch Rainald drinking some water from a stinking gutter leaking from a well that is probably infected. When he realizes that he, too, is ill he remembers the words of Girard Pucelle. He realizes that both he and Christian have had an erroneous perception of the matter, and he takes this knowledge with him to the grave. The fact of this realization by Rainald remains unknown historically to this day.

I was able to follow Rainald's soul after death. The karmic essence which he received from his life panorama can be defined by the three words: eloquence, patience, fervour.

Thus far my attempt to describe Christian von Buch's relationship with some of his contemporaries. Building on my present relationships with certain individuals I have in my karma research also endeavoured to follow up in Imagination Christian's connections with many of those same individuals, for example Barbarossa's first wife Adele von Vohburg, his second wife Beatrix of Burgundy, Hildegard of Bingen, Henry the Lion, the brothers Conrad and Otto von Wittelsbach, Obizo Malaspina, the anti-Pope Calixtus III and many others. Instead of going into all these interesting relationships here, I shall now recount some more details out of Christian von Buch's life after the fateful summer of 1167, including his relationship with some of his closest friends and also Emperor Frederick Barbarossa.

At the end of 1175 Christian had conquered the city of Bologna, a member of the Lombard League, in battle. On 14 March 1176, at Carsoli, north-east of Rome, he conquers the troops of King William II of Sicily led by Roger of Andria and Tancred of Lecce. Eyewitnesses of the time describe Christian von Buch as follows: On his horse he leads his wild Brabançons against the enemy. Over his armour he wears a hyacinth-coloured tunic and on his head a gilded helmet. He is said to have downed nine men with a single blow of his triple-knotted club. And on one occasion he knocked out the teeth of 28 distinguished persons with a stone.

Bishops were forbidden to spill human blood, so they went into battle swordless. Contemporary attitudes, however, permitted them to smash the skulls of their enemies bloodlessly with a club. I have several times watched Christian practising the art of swinging his club.

In a number of Imaginations I see Christian, probably in the spring of 1176, riding with his knights, who are divided into several groups, down the northern side of the Apennines. They are in a territory belonging to conquered Bologna. Some Bolognese are hiding in the mountains and entice Christian's group into an ambush. His close friend, the brave knight Willibald, is surrounded and thrown from his horse. In the midst of the skirmish Christian consults with the nearest person, a knight named Giorgio, as to what they should do. Since Christian himself is wounded in the shoulder he decides on withdrawal. He sees Willibald being killed. Giorgio is given the horse of the dead knight and they retire to a monastery near Modena.

In a convent near Lodi they are then cared for by nuns for several weeks. I see Christian taking a bath in a wooden tub as a nun Maria pours warm water over him; the water is fetched by another nun. Maria tells him tales about Pope Alexander III whom she admires for his courage during his escape. He tells her about thoughts and experiences from his own life. There are several Cistercian monks in the convent who tell him of the arrival of fresh German troops brought by the Archbishop of Cologne, Philipp von Heinsberg, to Como, north of Milan. But Christian continues his rest. He is absorbed in memories of Rainald von Dassel. Rainald's words about Girard Pucelle dawn in his memory.

On this last day of May Christian hears about the defeat of Emperor Frederick at Legnano. It is not the nuns who tell him, nor his own spies, nor the Cistercian monks, but the Emperor himself. Frederick Barbarossa appears quite suddenly in Christian's guest-room in the convent. Christian leaps to his feet and embraces his lord. 'Emperor Frederick, what can I do for you?' he asks. 'I simply need your advice, Christian,' replies the Emperor, and continues, 'How can we negotiate with Alexander without losing face?' This Imagination explains the Emperor's disappearance from the battle of Legnano and his reappearance three days later in Pavia, which still mystifies historians.

How Christian von Buch continued to support his lord and Emperor from that day forth, and also how a change of attitude began to appear, in line with what Girard Pucelle had said, is shown by subsequent events which led to the Peace of Venice in 1177.

I found many other details and relationships in the life of Christian von Buch in the Akashic Record. For example: a conversation between him and Henry the Lion in 1168; the meeting between Emperor and Pope in Venice; tragic events in the household of Acerbus Morena; dramatic circumstances in an Italian monastery which led to a monk in court being punished by having his tongue cut out by the abbot; what Pope Lucius III did on witnessing the death of Christian von Buch in 1183. I shall describe a few more events that are important for an understanding of the karmic connections.

During the period following the Peace of Venice, Christian von Buch continued in Italy as an imperial governor, but now also with the agreement of Pope Alexander. The latter put all his strength into convening the greatest twelfth-century assemblage of churchmen, the third Lateran Council in the spring of 1179. Since it showed few external results, this Council is not seen as particularly significant by church historians, but from the anthroposophical point of view, owing to the presence of certain specific participants, it must be regarded as an encounter that was karmically very important for the future. Only two anecdotes have come down to us about the great teacher and *doctor universalis* at Chartres, Alanus de Insulis, and one of these pertains to this Lateran Council.

The anecdote recounts that the great humanist, who lived quietly in the Cistercian monastery of Cîteaux, was allowed to accompany his abbot to the Council in Rome, but only in the guise of his groom. Alanus, however, yearned to participate in the meeting at least only for a day and even if he had to attend incognito, in order to listen once again to his old scholar companions. The abbot took him into the gathering hidden under his cloak, but Alanus had to promise to behave quietly and say nothing. A moment arrived when no one had any answer to a question that had been asked. Alanus, however, spoke up and answered the question. Everyone immediately remarked that only the devil or Alanus could say such a thing, and the hidden philosopher had to show himself, whereupon the whole gathering did him honour.

In putting dates to Christian von Buch's life in Italy at this time I found a gap in that spring which corresponds exactly with the period occupied by the Council. It is therefore possible, indeed logical, to assume that he attended it. After the end of the schism Alexander had agreed that he should retain the see of the German primate—the diocese of Mainz having precedence over other bishoprics in Germany during the Middle Ages. The custom of the time also makes it unthinkable that he would not have been present even if he had no voting rights. Presumably attendance lists are extant, but I have to date not succeeded in seeing them.

I conducted my meditative research with this in mind, and the result was as follows:

Christian von Buch is making his way through a crowd in front of a building which I take to be the Lateran Basilica in which the Council is taking place. He enters through a door at the left of the front of the building. The hall is already over-full, and he is shown to a seat against the wall on a slightly raised platform.

He has a good view of the participants seated on raked rows of benches and of the Pope on a throne amongst his cardinals. Through the eyes of Christian I watch the scene of Alanus' sudden appearance, and see old John of Salisbury, now Bishop of Chartres, rise and give a speech.

In a quiet moment, still during the Imagination, I once again ask myself whether Alexander III can possibly be the individual in the twentieth century who my research has on a number of occasions already found and confirmed him to be. He turns to the left and looks at me. The earnest countenance of that time is transformed from within and a smiling face emerges which I recognize as that of a certain student of Rudolf Steiner to whom the karmic threads I have thus far discovered have already been leading.

I watch Christian. After the meeting he seeks out John of Salisbury and is reconciled with him. That eminent humanist of the twelfth century once wrote to a friend of his in the Alexandrine camp, describing Christian satirically as an anti-Christ.

Different though they are from one another, from today's perspective one would have to call both of them Platonists. They embrace, and I cannot help seeing that embrace as something good for their karmic starting point of today and the spiritual tasks awaiting them.

During the late summer of 1179 Christian was taken prisoner by the brothers Conrad and Rainer of Montferrat. After a dispute between Conrad and the German legate they were now his enemies and they had even reached a written agreement with the Byzantine Emperor Manuel. Manuel even wanted the much-feared military leader murdered. However, he was not killed by Conrad, who was in contact with the Templars and would later become King of Jerusalem. Christian was held prisoner for a whole year with Rainer of Montferrat as his gaoler. In September 1180 he was released after payment of a large ransom.

I see Christian sitting in a tower chamber of the castle of Aquapendente. He converses frequently with a woman named Eugenia, whom I see as a sister or relation of the brothers. He is well cared for and has plenty of time to think, read and write, occupations for which he has hitherto set little time aside in his stormy life. I think it is possible that this is where Christian von Buch translated the legend of Prester John. However, much research still remains to be done.

Much in connection with Christian must remain undescribed, but one more picture shall be recounted, one belonging in the period following his death.

The year is probably 1190. Arjuna, the spirit soul of Christian von Buch, hovers near his friend Friedrich von Haussen the minnesinger, who is still in incarnation. Since the death of his lord he has joined the knights of the young King Henry, Barbarossa's son. Now, however, he is following the Emperor on the Third Crusade. Arjuna sees his friend riding up the Taurus mountains. He sees the horse rearing and bucking, and shaking its head from side to side. The knight is thrown off forwards and to the right. Friedrich von Haussen's neck is broken and he dies forthwith. Arjuna sees a delicate bluish flame emerge from the minnesinger's open mouth. The singer's soul escapes through the mouth and passes across the threshold of death. The two spirit-souls meet. Arjuna takes the soul of his friend into his spirit 'shroud' and leads it to other encounters in the world that follows death.

A queen without a crown

The following incarnation to be described will be seen by many readers as an affront if I claim it as one of mine. Nevertheless I shall continue to give accurate descriptions of my researches that have led me to conclude that I was, in fact, that person.

As I have already mentioned, I first received an indication through Imagination about a former incarnation when I was 17 years old. That was about the life of Ronald B. Dixon in the nineteenth century, which I shall describe in due course. At the age of 41 I discovered Christian von Buch through my studies, and 19 months later came the first confirmation through Imagination of that medieval incarnation. In the same week I also received the first pointer to Agamon. The next Imaginations led to results referring to Ray, Ramishanda and Shamu'radhin. Having discovered these connections I wanted to try and go further back, into Lemurian times, with the help of spiritual friends and beings. I succeeded, and Retana came on the scene. From then on I established a questioning situation aimed at finding every incarnation and following the main karmic themes from one incarnation to the next. This resulted in the appearance of Tanamira, Areldingun, Shida Dong and Antonia. After Christian von Buch I then encountered the life of a woman which I cannot assume to be of any other than Mary Queen of Scots.

To be absolutely honest: While this was simply a fact during the meditation, I was subsequently astonished and indeed shocked. Up to that moment I had known almost nothing about that lady except the little I happened to have gleaned from *Maria Stuart*, the play by Schiller many of whose works I had read in earlier days. The journey I followed during that Imagination, which lasted several hours, finally brought me once again to Ronald B. Dixon and thence to my present life.

I decided that before I started to read about Mary in history books or biographies I would first try to find out as much as I could in Imagination from the Akashic Record. In many sequences I pieced together a kind of biographical survey: her early childhood in Scotland, her youth in France, a journey to Spain, the dramatic years in Scotland, her time in prison up to the execution, and finally certain experiences after death. Only then did I turn to the books, and found that most of what I had seen was known fact. Some things had to be described or interpreted differently; and there were some experiences which I could not find in the literature, for example the journey which I was sure had been to Spain. After a while I had to leave the whole complex matter of Mary Queen of Scots on one side. In everyday life it was all too much for me, appeared implausible and also arrogant and brazen to claim so many historically known persons as my own former incarnations.

Gradually, as various themes discovered in my own research began to link up, and as confirmation came through others who had performed karma exercises with me, the sequence of my incarnations became more familiar to me. I then created a possibility which enabled me to research the period between the death of Christian von Buch and the birth of Mary. Through this I discovered why that person, who had been active in the external world of the Middle Ages, now had to become linked with a specific impulse at the pinnacle of monarchic power at the time when the Renaissance was flourishing and before the rosicrucian tasks of the seventeenth century emerged in the future. I shall here strive to describe my researches about Mary Queen of Scots and her contemporaries without reservation. In Chapter 6 it will be necessary to show some of her karmic links to other individuals, both forwards and backwards in time.

Again I saw the spirit-soul of Christian von Buch as the spiritual individual I have from the beginning called Arjuna. The situation I followed was the one in which, surrounded and carried by higher spiritual beings, he found himself in a kind of transition stage between the former incarnation and the next. First I looked on from the outside at this part of the process, but when I experienced it as belonging to me I was able to experience everything as happening to me there and then in the present.

Hanging round his neck and resting on his chest this spirit-soul has a tool which is clearly intended for the physical world. Like a kind of symbol, Christian von Buch's knife is hung round my neck. This knife is taken away by my angel and all the powers connected with it are removed from me. My angel is then handed something else and he hangs a new symbol, a true one, round my neck: a red rose. This action leads me to understand that in my coming life as a woman different ways of behaving and different experiences of pain are awaiting me.

In another situation I stand surrounded by spiritual beings and by those individuals whom I must meet in a new way in the coming incarnation and who will cause me the relevant pain. From within my being a pillar of strength grows upwards from below, ending on top of my head in a crown-like adornment. I immediately discover what is taking place in me and cannot recognize the monarchic symbol on my head as my own impulse.

I lift up my hands and try to tip the crown off backwards. I intend this to show that I no longer want to give my support to monarchy, with which I rightfully had dealings in the Middle Ages. However, by the world of spirit around me, which is at work in the manner described and showing itself to me in Imagination, I am given to understand that a time is approaching when certain individuals can strive to transform monarchy from within. In the case of Henry VI, Barbarossa's son, Christian von Buch overstepped his karmic competence and joined in strengthening the monarchy to such a degree that it became hereditary, which is something that should not have happened. Because of this I can now take this karma upon the person I am going to become in my next incarnation.

Several times the crown on my head grows up from within me and every time I tip it off backwards. I recognize this as a lengthy process which is very painful to me as a spiritual battle. I realize that in my next life I have to be concerned in that process of transformation for karmic reasons but that I do not have to appear in the forefront of events. I am able to use my independent thinking to converse with other individuals and higher beings to help me decide which position in the relevant constellation I should choose. Thereupon I accept the choice of the symbolic situation with the crown as one which will be possible for me in the coming physical situation and place myself in the hands of the spiritual world which will make the necessary preparations.

Instruction is given me about the esoteric Christianity (what we now call the Rosicrucian Stream) which has been developing on the earth since the Middle Ages and which certain measures will cause to appear in the open during the coming seventeenth century. My karmic companions and I receive the task of giving the Catholic church new impulses, emanating from the upper echelon of European society through a special constellation of the different royal houses—impulses to enable the church to become less worldly. The whole of European society is to be prepared for Rosicrucianism.

With hindsight I have come to the conclusion that during the time of spiritual questioning which took place prior to the life of Mary, some individuals with whom I was karmically connected distanced themselves from the possibilities of undertaking those tasks together. The consequence was that others had to take their places. It is perhaps difficult to discern anything of this spiritual background in the historical processes that unfolded, but today I am tempted to attribute to this perspective much of what may be regarded as having failed.

I also experienced another Imagination which I feel belongs in that 'time' in the spiritual world. I saw myself in the post-mortem situation sitting with my friend 'Friedrich von Haussen' on my left together with thousands of other individuals receiving wonderful instruction. I recognized the situation as belonging to what Rudolf Steiner described as the 'spiritual School of Michael' in which the future time spirit Michael worked in the spiritual world on developing certain specific future tasks over several hundred years with those who had freely decided to work with him. This is how I should like to describe that process:

There is a space filled with substance-of-light which is on every side accessible to all human individuals. Those participating in what is being taught are seated side by side in rows while at the same time being within and on top of one another. Two substances from different sources are received and held, one in each hand. These can be described by the Greek words 'alpha' and 'omega'. The one comes from the past, the other from the future. I felt these spheres of substance which the angels had placed in our hands to be something like seeds radiating power. Each participant had been set the same task: to combine the two spheres together in such a way that past and present would receive a new form suited to both substances, a form that could one day become visible on the physical plane. For our earthly way of looking at things this process might be compared with combining hydrogen and oxygen in a manner suited to them both. As a result they would relinquish their gaseous state and become water. I realized that in addition to other tasks this labour of spiritual sculpture would for a long while be made available by Michael and his cohorts to human spirits during their sojourn in the spiritual world between incarnations.

This Imagination made me realize that not only those who worked on earth with Rudolf Steiner were builders of the first Goetheanum, since many others not incarnated at the time had also shared in making spiritual preparations for it. For a short while, until everything was destroyed by the fire in the night of New Year's Eve 1922, there had been visible on earth in the artistic shaping of that building what had been practised in the spiritual Michael School in the manner described.

I was given sublime Imaginations about the onward path of Arjuna in preparation for the new incarnation.

Standing beside him I experienced myself as Arjuna at the moment when he was to leave behind a higher sphere in order to begin the descent to earth. He was balancing on a small, blue sphere which drew him towards itself with indescribable force. Stretching up with arms and hands open he allowed all-embracing star wisdom to stream into himself. I cannot adequately recount the moment that followed. As Arjuna I stand in the light of stars and planets looking down at the wonderfully sparkling sphere beneath my feet. Then I discover the connection between myself and the sphere: it is the earth! I am a cosmic human being! I want to go there in order to reveal the sublime powers of the spiritual world on the earth.

The descent then follows, and it is at the same time a process of diminution. By beings of the higher hierarchies Arjuna is pressed into and through a funnel that grows ever tighter the lower down he goes. I had the idea of the angel-beings treading the incarnating human being with their feet as though treading grapes in a wine-press. It is a painful yet joyful process. At the end of the funnel a new 'vintage' of Arjuna emerges; he has his own individual angel as the guardian of his being's own new 'vintage label'.

I see a room where a man and a woman are making love in bed. Standing at the foot of the bed is the angel bearing a miniature Arjuna wrapped in warmth of soul. After the unbelievable warmth and light weaving through the previous Imaginations, there now follows one in which I almost freeze to death in the earthly cold blown by mist and wind into the chamber of a castle in Scotland. I watch a birth take place; it fills the people present with many expectations. Around the child hovers the question: 'What do these people expect of me? I cannot understand. I have forgotten something important. I feel as though it is already too late to do the right thing.'

In Imaginations I followed the growing girl named Mary through many experiences in a castle, outdoors in nature, in a convent church, on a ship, amongst beautifully dressed people and huge horses in a foreign land that became home to her. There was also a love affair, a secret journey to Spain, the return to Scotland, dancing and music in various castles, dramatic events and battle scenes, an encounter with a critical clergyman, scenes of flight, people who helped, incidents during her imprisonment, her execution and experiences after death. These Imaginations I shall recount.

Little Mary is about four years old; she is wearing a medallion on a chain around her neck. She feels at home in the large rooms in which her mother, the queen, and other kind women watch over her all the time. Her older brother James is somewhere nearby. She is thinking about her father who died shortly after her birth and whom she has only ever seen in a painting. It may be that the medallion she is wearing bears a portrait of him; I was not able to find this out. Mary goes through unlit rooms to a wing of the house which she is not allowed to visit. She knows that the chamber of the dead king is there, her father, whom she loves even though he is not here.

For a long while she stands in the darkened room trying to make out the faces in the obscure paintings hanging there. James suddenly appears beside her, saying: 'Mary, you know you're not allowed in here. As I am the future king you must pay a forfeit to me straight away for being so naughty.' Looking sternly at her he snatches the medallion from her neck. 'It's mine now. If you don't tell anyone why I've got it from you I won't say you came here without permission.' With that he quickly leaves the room where she remains behind alone. Crying she sinks to the floor where her mother finds her after a while. She does not want to tell her mother why she is so sad.

The day arrives when Mary says goodbye to her mother. She is going to her mother's homeland to visit her relatives there. She does not know the real reason for the journey, which is kept secret in Scotland. She is looking forward to all kinds of new experiences, for she always feels better outdoors in nature's sunlight than within the dark, dank walls of the castle. She spends a great deal of time out of doors on this journey. For a few days the travellers stay in a monastery on an island in a lake. The old man whom the grownups call the abbot is very nice to her. In the middle of the night, unable to sleep, she looks out of the window and sees the monks processing into the church carrying candles. She goes there too, hides in a side-chapel and listens to their beautiful singing. She falls asleep on the floor and when the abbot finds her there in the morning he asks why she has slept there. Pointing to a picture, she says, 'The Mother of God allowed me to be near her Child.' The abbot remains silent, and does not get angry. This warms her heart deeply.

As she steps aboard the rowing boat, a chained rower shouts out: 'You little symbol of the old superstitions, I wish I could row you across to France so that our country can become free.' Guards beat the man to shut him up. Later in life Mary meets that man again; he is John Knox, the enemy of her faith.

Here I shall pass over a number of situations in Mary's childhood and youth. Of the various relationships at the court of Catherine de' Medici I shall recount only one episode, involving Mary's husband Francis II of France. Historians have always maintained that because of his illness, of which he died about two-and-a-half years after the marriage, the pair had never had a sexual relationship. What I saw was the following: The newly married couple ride out to a meadow they used to play on as children. Leaving the horses to graze, they walk in the meadow amongst the tall grass and many flowers. It lies in the sunlight between a hill and a valley. The lovers walk hand in hand to a solitary great tree. In its shade, hidden in the grass, they have a loving encounter such as they will never forget in that life and the memory of which Francis will carry with him all through his illness and death right on into his next life on earth. For Mary Stuart her love for this man is something she will think about as she accompanies him in his pain before he dies and later during all the years of her imprisonment in England. Her feelings are more than she dare express.

After Francis' death, a marriage to the Spanish prince Don Carlos was discussed and negotiated. Elizabeth of Valois—a daughter of Catherine de' Medici and later the third wife of Don Carlos' father, King Philip II of Spain—had been Mary's childhood friend. I saw Mary Stuart, probably in the spring of 1561, a few months before leaving for Scotland, making a secret journey to Spain. The little group of travellers halts at a small monastery of so-called grey friars in southern France, where they can spend the night and are given fresh horses. Mary is kindly cared for by a monk.

In Spain she talks with Elizabeth for many days. They stay in a little castle which, I maintain, is located near the eastern coast. The young women bathe together and discuss the young gentlemen who come to visit them. Elizabeth already has a good deal of life experience behind her. They play in the great four-poster bed, and pretend to be 'ill' when Don Carlos and King Philip pay them a visit. However, they cannot keep the men away when they enter the room in turn. Later on I shall describe some of the karmic background shared by Mary, Elizabeth and Don Carlos.

I do not know how this journey to Spain can be fitted in with other *known* timings in Mary's life. On subsequently reading the two great biographies—Antonia Fraser's and Michel Duchein's— I realized that verification would be difficult. I am sure that in the research situation I specified the geographical location correctly and do not think I am mistaken. There was definitely a meeting of this kind between the four persons in question.

Because of circumstances on which I shall comment later, the onward life of Mary in Scotland and England still moves me very strongly. I shall therefore here skip many events which are anyway very well known historically. In Chapter 6 I shall return to her relationship with James Hepburn, Earl of Bothwell, and to the murder of her second husband, Henry Stewart, Lord Darnley. The behaviour of John Knox towards Mary is not a simple matter; I do think, however, that there is a tendency to be too negative in its interpretation.

In Imagination I saw that she had one of his books. I see them standing in front of a building and conversing about questions of faith. In a friendly manner Knox is trying to steer her away from the Catholic mass. Her contradiction is also friendly, but definite, and she then turns to mount the steps to the house. He accompanies her for a few of them, but she does not permit his intensity to influence her. Instead she changes the subject and invites him to take tea with her. He remains calm, stops mounting the steps, declines the invitation politely, bows respectfully and departs.

In order to do justice to all the doubts I myself entertained towards my recognition of my connection with Mary Queen of Scots, I wanted to see and re-experience in as much detail as possible her execution on 8 February 1587 at Fotheringhay Castle. This was a labour of spirit and soul of a very special kind.

I watch as she makes her way to the great hall on crutches because of her rheumatism. After a number of incidents—for example her maids beginning to weep—she turns round and sees the two executioners. They are wearing black hoods with eye-holes. Mary is blindfolded with a handkerchief. She kneels down and wants to lay her head on the block. She is told to turn round. She does so, and after a few more incidents she gathers herself to receive the death blow. Since she does not know where the executioner and his assistant are standing, she does not know from which side the axe will strike. Then the first blow comes from the left. She notices that she is still alive.

She remembers the black-shrouded executioners' faces with the eyeholes and knows all of a sudden where she has met these two men before. She knows that in an earlier life she was a governor in Nubia named Ray and that as Ray she once con-demned to death two Nubians accused of stealing by their Egyptian lord. Now she knows that the two were innocent when they died, and as she follows this idea in her thoughts two more blows fall and her head is finally severed.

I felt the pain and other feelings in this Imagination right down into my physical body. Nevertheless, while I was follow-ing every stage of the action I also wanted to find the two executioners and discover their present identity. I prayed to Christ to show me the Imagination backwards and repeat the moment when Mary looks into her executioners' eyes. All of this was shown to me over again in a way that enabled me to find those two former Nubians—later executioners—in my present life on earth. This knowledge threw a grace-filled light on to many episodes in my present life in which I had many beautiful experiences with those reincarnated executioners. Then the Imagination moved forward once again and I experienced the execution a second time over.

After death 'Mary', as Arjuna, remains close to her friends, endeavouring to lighten their shock, suffering and sadness. She pays attention to her favourite lapdog which had been hidden under her skirts and is now utterly bewildered. With its fur covered in her blood it is causing chaos amongst the bystanders. She draws it towards herself by weeping for it, until some understanding people set it free by ending its life.

Then she is 'fetched' by others who are already dead and by higher beings. She is laid in a spiritual boat of light that carries her 'upwards'. While 'lying' in this boat she experiences the panorama of her life. I receive her first thoughts once she has regained her inner peace after that cruel execution. To the spiritual world around her she expresses the wish: 'In another life I want to live in anonymity far from any worldly attention.'

I followed the life of 'Mary Stuart' after death still further. Looking up from the earthly angle I watched the boat of light move slowly upwards over the following centuries. It cast a kind of shadow of light down on the surface of the earth which gradually spread over Europe. I found that when Mary Stuart was their theme all the poetic writers from Pierre de Brantome to Schiller wrote out of what this shadow of light bestowed on them.

Musician, Quaker, railway engineer—member of a Red Indian nation

I have found the events of the next life in Imagination only, for to date I have not looked for any historical records. At the beginning of the 1930s there was in America a well-known anthropologist and researcher into the life of American Indians called Ronald Burrage Dixon. He was probably a younger relative of Ronald Baltimore Dixon, whose biography I shall follow here.

A boy is born in the Dixon family in Dublin, capital city of Ireland, somewhere around the year 1843. The family emigrates to America when little Ronald is five. I saw the captain of the ocean steamer letting the little lad steer the ship for a few moments. He chats with members of the crew and is also allowed into the engine room with them. On arrival in Boston the captain invites Ronald and his family to a harbour pub to which later, as a young man, Ronald often returns to meet up with the captain and his crew.

During Ronald's school years the family live near Boston as his father is employed by a shipping company. Later, when he finds employment with a railway company, the family move further westwards several times. Ronald has to go to school, but he would far rather spend his time in a circus. An elderly lady, a neighbour, has introduced him to an animal keeper and tamer to whom he takes packages of cake and other food she gives him. Perhaps he is her son. The keeper is dumb, and Ronald never dares ask the old woman about this.

When Ronald is 18 and his father has joined the administration of a railway company, the family moves house westwards with several horse-drawn wagons. The trek is attacked by Indians. Ronald's sister is killed by an arrow before the soldiers arrive to chase off the hostile Indians. The girl was a capable young violinist of whom her parents had had high expectations.

Ronald feels partly guilty of her death because he persuaded her to move with the family, which she had not wanted to do.

Although Ronald had planned a different career for himself, from now on he works only at music. He takes over his sister's violin and looks up her friends in Boston and New York. He finds an elderly and influential violin teacher who wants to train him as a virtuoso. For two or three years he enjoys his studies at the music school until one day, in the middle of a performance exam, he realizes in a flash that he is playing the wrong instrument. He immediately lays the violin down on a chair, excuses himself and, to the astonishment of his fellow students and the embarrassment of his teacher, disappears without more ado, never to set foot in that school again.

Instead he goes to a piano teacher whom he has got to know at a concert. The teacher takes him on and soon Ronald is his favourite pupil. The day of Ronald's solo concert arrives. He is probably playing Haydn sonatas but in this Imagination, although I could see his way of playing and therefore follow the music inwardly, I was not able to hear the music externally. This concert takes place somewhere around 1864. In the middle of playing Ronald feels a strange pain in his hands and his fingers get stiffer and stiffer until, to his despair, he has to interrupt the performance. His teacher excuses him to the astonished audience and announces a short interval. Instead of the interval coming to an end, however, it is the concert that ends, for the paralysis in Ronald's hands does not disappear, neither over the next few days nor over the coming weeks. The doctors are unable to help.

In his despair he takes his father's advice and seeks employment with the railway company which has lost many of its best employees to the army and death on account of the civil war that is still in full swing. Hitherto Ronald has taken various measures to stay out of the war. But now he sees no alternative but to help his father as a nightwatchman along the railway line. After several months the paralysis in his hands does disappear, but he now notices that his yearning to become a concert pianist has also left his soul. He decides to stay with his father. Over the next few years, by doing practical work, he finds his profession as a railway engineer. He becomes a map-maker and his work is connected with the route the rails are to follow, coupled with the necessary surveying of the terrain. Several years go by in a mood which he feels is morose rather than happy.

The only friends he makes are Quakers. Even in his days as a musician one of his friends, William, had been a Quaker. Having many friends amongst the Indians, William is now critical of much that Ronald does in connection with his railway work. Since the days of William Penn the Quakers in America have identified strongly with the cause of the native population. I saw Ronald conversing with William in the garden of his white-washed house. In community with the Quakers he is searching for the inner light that can be kindled by God in individual souls through communal silence.

William is engaged to a kindergarten teacher, Siwe. She is passionately opposed to the building of a railway through the reserve of the peaceful Lakota Indians outside her town. Through Ronald she tries to influence the management of the company, which includes Ronald's father, to choose a different route skirting round the reserve. She organizes a petition which, however, fails to make any impression at all on the gentlemen, who have made up their minds once and for all. Ronald wants to remain neutral and can therefore do nothing either for or against the matter. Then comes the tragedy. Siwe throws herself in front of a train, giving her life for the Indian cause. Ronald is personally acquainted with the train driver, Marcus. Everyone, especially Marcus, is deeply disturbed by this event. After the death of his beloved, William sinks into a deep depression from which he fails to emerge for the remainder of his life. He wants to stand up for the Indian cause but lacks the strength to do anything. Only inwardly can he continue to feel for the tragedy of the native population.

This is the time when Ronald is entrusted with the task of negotiating with the Lakota Indians about the railway line planned to cut across their buffalo prairie. On the day of the meeting he is standing at the spot the line has reached so far. A few hundred metres behind him, in the navvies' camp, the management are waiting to hear the outcome. Ronald has money in his pocket and in his hand he holds the map showing a new route that he has worked out as a compromise. A small group of Indians approaches slowly on horseback from the west. They halt in front of him but do not dismount. Ronald greets them and is greeted in return by the chief in the Indian's language. One of them translates into English. Ronald continues to speak in his own language, explaining the map and saying that in this case the white men are willing to pay a far higher sum than usual. The Indians have no interest in the white man's money, declares the chief. They want to continue living as they always have on this land. Gerasawak, the chief, makes a slight gesture with his hand towards the rifle slung over his shoulder. The interpreter explains that the chief's name signifies 'He who shoots with firearms'.

At this moment Ronald feels his heart being moved in a way quite unlike the feelings roused in him by music or the Quaker meetings. What is this? He looks at the Indians and sees their serious, melancholic faces and deep, dark eyes. He resolves: 'I want to give my life to these people. That is my life's task.' To the surprise of the Indians Ronald suddenly tears the map in two and throws the pieces on the ground, saying: 'I understand the difficult position you are in. Let us live in peace with one another. I shall cease working for the railway and become a champion of your cause instead.' The Indians believe him, dismount from their horses and sit on the ground to smoke a pipe of peace with Ronald. The men from the railway company soon realize what has happened and even his father cannot persuade him to change his mind.

Ronald now breaks free of his 'European' way of life and becomes intimately connected with the Indians. He is introduced to Gerasawak's tribe and finds many new friends there. He learns their language, and many other tribes also take note of his change of heart, wishing to gain his help as a negotiator as well.

Takatimas, a medicine man from another Lakota tribe, takes him on as an apprentice. One day he leads Ronald to a hill where he instructs him about the gods of the elements. Takatimas makes a fire and using an animal skin shapes the smoke into various signs. Ronald asks him about the message he is sending. 'I am proclaiming your name to the spirit of the moving air, I am announcing your name to the spirit who makes the weather. In our language your name is Ariloma, 'the peaceable.'

This conversation on the hill with Takatimas is a minor initiation for Ronald. He understands that soon his name will be taken up by ever more Indians and he finds that wherever he goes—even as far afield as California—people already know that he is on his way. He gains familiarity with a number of Indian nations, their various cultures and languages. He very much enjoys living with the Hopi, and he is also accepted by the Maidu and the Shasta-Achomawai in California.

Wherever he goes he takes small objects from the European world as presents for the Indians, things for the children, the women and the men. In one of the Hopi tribes a chief falls in love with his white hat. So Ronald/Ariloma swaps the hat for a lovely picture painted on an animal skin, depicting an ancient creation myth.

One member of this tribe lives alone in the wilderness. A strong friendship grows up between him and Ariloma. It turns out, however, that this man is a woman in disguise who lives alone trying to understand the books of the white man, an activity not permitted in the settlement. Ariloma begins to teach her English. But she desperately wants books from the land in the east beyond the great ocean. Thus arises the peculiar situation in which a former musician from Boston, born in Europe, sells Indian artefacts on the east coast of America so that he can give his friend in the wilderness books by, for example, Goethe, and read them to her.

Ariloma has arranged to meet Takatimas so that instruction for the full initiation into the work of the medicine man can continue. But an urgent message arrives from Gerasawak asking him to come immediately. He takes leave of Takatimas, promising to return as soon as the matter, whatever it is, has been settled. However, they never meet again because Ronald becomes involved in events that take a great deal of time, and Takatimas dies in the interim.

Gerasawak is once again up in arms about the white men. Years ago they have put down their railway lines across his buffalo prairie. Now they have begun shooting at buffalo from the trains, causing unrest and misery in the harmony of the natural order. What can Ariloma do for his brother? His real father is of course the chairman of the railway company. Ronald contacts him having not seen him for many years. His father is delighted to see his son again, but he is unable to prevent the cowboys from hunting in this fashion. Ronald rides to the district himself and tries to talk sense into the men on the train. One of them, whom he knows from earlier times, threatens to shoot him if he does not depart immediately.

Ronald/Ariloma rides away and from a hill watches what is going on. He sees the hunted buffalo, but near them he also suddenly sees a horse ridden by a small girl who, perhaps because of the dust, has not yet realized the danger she is in.

Ariloma whistles a warning to her, but she is too far away to hear him. Then the girl notices the approaching buffalo. She turns her horse so sharply that she falls off. She remains lying on the ground while the horse gallops off towards Gerasawak's settlement. Quickly but carefully Ariloma approaches the spot where the injured girl is lying. He thinks of all the things he has learnt about animals from the Indians; he remembers the many situations in which he has observed and painted birds in flight. He reins in his horse when he realizes that he cannot save the girl from the wild buffalo.

Ariloma gathers up all his consciousness of the divine world and directs his feelings towards the spot where the girl is lying. He sees the buffalo making a detour round her. He sees the hunters on the train shooting many of them. He sees a wounded buffalo lie down to die between the train and the girl as though to protect this small human being. He observes the herd of buffalo departing to the south, leaving the area in deathly silence except for the excited shouts of the hunters. Ariloma rides to the spot where the girl is lying. Lifting her up in his arms he realizes that she is Hawatha, the daughter and only child of Gerasawak. A buffalo hoof has struck her; she is dead.

With the body of seven-year-old Hawatha, Ariloma rides to Gerasawak. He has already been searching for his daughter since the return of her riderless horse. She had gone riding without permission. Gerasawak is seized by sorrow and rage. Now he will take revenge with his own hand. The tragedy unfolds when Gerasawak kills Ronald's father with a single shot. Ronald cannot prevent his dear friend from being sent to prison where he spends many years until his death.

After these terrible events Ronald Dixon, with his Indian name Ariloma 'the peaceable', discovers that his teacher Takatimas has also died. I have been unable to follow any more of his life's path in the Akashic Record. The impression I have is that he turned his back on the western world in which he had been born and grown up, obliterating his tracks to such an extent that even in the Akashic Record it will be difficult to find him. Perhaps he settled amongst the Hopi or the Achomawi-Shastan. But it seems more likely that he took an Indian wife and lived with her in the wilderness until he died—I rather believe in the early years of the twentieth century.

4

Further experiences

*[An initiate] would feel unfree if he could not fulfil
the tasks allotted to him by his former lives.*
Rudolf Steiner

A new life situation

In the crisis I experienced in 1995 I felt as though my life had
actually come to an end. I had no friends who kept in touch with
me or, as I saw it at the time, who had any interest in my difficult
situation. One year later, after the very profound experiences I
have described, I felt: My life really is at an end, but I am still
alive! I experienced myself as a being of light, a being of love. I
realized immediately that I could only very slowly bring my new
knowledge out into the open in my life with other people. There
were many things about which I would have to remain silent for a
long while.

I found that the enlightenment had changed my sense per-
ceptions. My hearing was more acute, my sight had changed. I
could be sitting in a bus looking in at shop windows, and I would
see the people at work right inside the inner offices behind the
shops and even learn something about their lives. Walking down
a street I could look along its whole length and experience every
single person rushing by. I perceived the way the chakras moved
in the people with whom I worked, which helped me to know
how I should behave towards them. I had entered a degree of
intensity of soul and spirit that gave me an idea of what it must be

like to be an angel. But I still had a physical body, indeed the same old physical body that I had had for 42 years.

From my earlier lives on earth I tried to deduce what my next task was to be. I related what I found out to what I knew of anthroposophical and general world evolution since the death of Rudolf Steiner. And I came to the conclusion: 'I want to find a way of making a new beginning with karma research based on spiritual science. I must get in touch with others who are making efforts along the same lines.' Since the turn of the year 1996/97 I have been consciously working in this direction. Unfortunately this decision led to my breaking off relations with my family at Järna and my other friends there. The pain that this has caused in souls on both sides has meant that this has now become a new motif in my destiny which I try to work at in my meditations and prayers.

The decision to embark on initiation

In a lecture I once gave I spoke about a feeling I got after spiritual experiences and Imaginations of my earlier lives on earth, a feeling of something special affecting my present life. When I followed this by saying that in some ways I had finished working on my karmic tasks, some people in the audience thought I meant by this that I had finished everything to do with all my incarnations. This is of course absolutely not the case. However, the feeling in question, a kind of karmic freedom, is so remarkable that it generates a need to undertake karma research if only in connection with one's immediate personal circle of friends. Later on I re-read the lecture by Rudolf Steiner from which the following quotation is taken. My experience was exactly what he was describing there.*

---

* *Karmic Relationships, Vol.I*, London: Rudolf Steiner Press 1972, lecture of 23 February 1924.

Most people believe that initiation science only has theoretical effects. No, its effects are realities in life, and among them is the one I have just indicated. Before a person has acquired initiation science, his reasons for finding one thing important and another unimportant are due to some obscure instinct. But having acquired it, you could think, he might as well sit down in a chair and let the world run its course, for it really does not matter whether this is done or that is left undone; after all, whatever happens will eventually be balanced out. However, initiation science has more to offer him, and that is the ability to look back into his former lives on earth. From his karma he can then learn of the task awaiting him in his present earthly life, which means that he can do consciously what those former lives have imposed upon him. He does not leave things undone out of a feeling that doing them would encroach on his freedom. He does them because, having found out what he has experienced in former lives, he also realizes what went on in his life between death and the next birth during which he reached the conclusion that the sensible thing to do will be to carry out the compensating actions. In fact, he would feel unfree if he could not fulfil the tasks allotted to him by his former lives.

This experience creates a 'turning of the time' in one's individual life, something which is expressed in the final lines of the *Foundation Stone Meditation*:

That what we found from our hearts
What we guide from our heads
Will be good.

It was in a situation like this—during the weeks at Moss in November 1996 about which I wrote in Chapter 2—that I decided to embark on a conscious collaboration with the spiritual world. If the spiritual world found me sufficiently mature I would put myself through the tests and exercises which belong to a modern initiation in Rudolf Steiner's sense.

I was living in my spiritual home, my 'hut', with 'Sigrid'. I did the research in her presence and she strengthened my being with supersensible powers during that time. One day, in the meditation, she and I both noticed that the room, which was normally almost circular with an ever-changing pillar of light in the middle, had been enlarged and now contained a space with a stage. Our angels led us on to that stage and placed us before an altar. I saw two figures, one clothed in blue, the other in red. The two individuals, whom I linked to the names of Christian Rosenkreutz and Rudolf Steiner, united the two of us in a special spiritual process.

In lectures Steiner gave at The Hague in 1913* he quoted examples of various changes that take place when a human being makes progress in the spiritual world through his inner schooling and search. He spoke of the Paradise Imagination and the Parsifal Imagination. After I had had the Imagination described above I knew what he had been talking about.

The initiation events continued in the next meditation. I had to unite myself inwardly with 'Sigrid' and sacrifice my being spiritually into her being. This procedure—almost a consecration—was so unusual that it is almost impossible to describe it further. On the Sunday morning I woke up and found that it was not I who got up. I was now right inside 'Sigrid' and she entirely filled and imbued my physical body. I found myself to be totally useless and was not able to carry out a meditation as usual and then prepare the coming week as planned. During the morning I, or rather 'Sigrid', went for a walk. It felt very strange to be inside my own body and at the same time experience myself as being carried by my spiritual bride as if she were a mother. Back at home 'I' was utterly exhausted and could not imagine how this would go on. 'I' was certainly not permitted to speak to anyone

---

* *The Effects of Esoteric Development*, New York: Anthroposophic Press 1997.

about it, and yet 'I' had to chat with my house-mates. When I went to bed that evening, however, 'I' had a sense of new hope as I sank into a profoundly deep sleep.

Very early on Monday morning I woke up in the midst of a continuation of my 'chymical wedding' Imagination. I experienced a spiritual birth, emerging by a kind of 'caesarean' from 'Sigrid's' womb. Over the next few days I lived my normal life as a teacher and painter, and 'Sigrid' remained with me. I had to care for her spiritually for some time because my unusual birth had left her with a 'wound'.

On the Sunday morning, when I had given up my normal self and was waiting to see what the future would bring, I had a Parsifal Imagination that was adapted for me personally. In it I was led to a third teacher of humanity whom I linked with the name of Mani. The reason why I linked that spiritual individual with Mani was that, by his presence during an encounter with the Guardian of the Threshold, he connected what happened in that encounter with what was shown to me later as a specifically Manichaean task. I mention Mani here because what I shall describe in the next section is connected with the consequences of my encounter with him.

The Greater Guardian

During this period I was given a number of Imaginations of which the Paradise Imagination can be mentioned by name. In my search for and effort to find the higher self, my archetypal self, these Imaginations led me to the higher archetypal name (mentioned at the beginning of Chapter 3) which had until that moment been unknown to me in my earthly consciousness. As with Opherus, who became Christopherus in the legend, the archetypal name each one of us possesses can be developed to become a Christ-name.

I was shown how long ago I was called from Paradise as Arjuna to my very first physical incarnation as a man in Lemurian times. The meaning of the name Arjuna was interpreted thus for me: 'Imagine you are waiting for someone who is approaching across earthly hills. In his hands he carries a vessel filled with something to drink. The only way you have of describing what he gives you is: "peace".'

Arjuna means: Bringer of Peace. When I received this archetypal name into my consciousness I underwent a complete transformation of my whole being; I experienced this as a kind of illumination which reached right down even into my physical body. It was in this situation that I first discovered the reality covered by the concept 'chakra' and realized what a healthy awakening and strengthening the kundalini power can encompass.

I was also shown how by combining the present incarnation name with a special kind of speech formation I might find other people's Christ-name which would encompass the archetypal name as well. Later, when I was working with several incarnations of a number of individuals for whom I had found historical names, I was able to use this method to check what I had discovered. For every genuine incarnation I found for a person I was able to hear the relevant Christ-name.

For me, the discovery of my archetypal name meant the ever-stronger approach of my archetypal self for incarnation in my present constitution. I was permitted to experience Christ, the representative of humanity—'Not I, but Christ in me'—as the culmination of my initiation.

The meditative situation I found myself in and the spiritual experiences that arose might be met by some readers with embarrassment and lack of understanding if I did not veil my descriptions somewhat. In what follows I shall therefore give only very brief accounts and concise hints. The experiences took place on the edge of the abyss, at the threshold to the spiritual world, where the Greater Guardian as the 'being of spirit love' in his Michaelic form shows the spirit pupil his still imperfect nature in Imaginations of 'spirit animal forms'. There were also experiences in spiritual regions beyond the threshold. On the edge of the abyss I was shown, in a series of Imaginations, my encounters and relationships with earthly animals of all kinds which I had had in earlier incarnations. (I have included these with my descriptions of the relevant incarnations.) I realized that those karmic encounters with animals had been brought about by my higher self.

The Greater Guardian instructed me how to do inner soul exercises in order to integrate those spirit-animals—which corresponded with my own life of thought, feeling and will—into my being as a whole. With my spirit-friend Shilbur—the lesser guardian—I collaborated in a way that enabled me to move backwards and forwards across the abyss in a spirit-boat which originated in my spiritual home. This crossing of the abyss, which meant working to transform the three spiritual animal figures, was also a dying of the personality in question. By special inner exercises I had to try and attain an experience of death in soul and spirit. I tried to develop special breathing exercises which I later found described in a similar way by Rudolf Steiner in the published parts of the so-called 'Esoteric School' of 1904–14. Only someone who has had similar experiences through karma or by means of exercises can possibly comprehend the inner pain, the utter loneliness and darkness that can be experienced.

After further experiences in the spiritual realms beyond the abyss I was put through a kind of examination by the Greater Guardian. I learnt in those realms that even the physical body can be included in a 'taking-hold-of-oneself' during certain sculptural processes of transformation which can be called 'Christotoli'—

the touching of Christ. This sequence of exercises and processes ended with a kind of 'Damascus experience'. I was also introduced more deeply to apocalyptic motifs. By this I mean that I was shown future possibilities for the development of humanity and received indications about a Manichaean challenge to evil. The Greater Guardian lovingly and seriously conducted these incredible happenings while not at all impinging on my inner freedom.

In his Book of Revelation in the Bible, John the Apocalyptist describes a figure of light having 'in his right hand seven stars; and out of his mouth went a sharp two-edged sword; and his countenance was as the sun shineth in his strength'.

What happened in this spiritual schooling went beyond any earthly fantasy or contrived invention. In my own being I felt Christ's love streaming out of my own mouth in order to touch through Christ's 'loving-logos-light' a being of the abyss who appeared to have entirely forgotten its own divine origins. By this transformation the ancient sexuality in my physical body became a servant of the Logos, a theme that I shall not enlarge on here, although in my opinion it is central to the modern mysteries. What eastern yoga describes as the kundalini was something I recognized in the Michaelic yoga in my whole being through 'breathing of primal self' as 'not I, but Christ in me'.

Before receiving the above-described experiences I practised in my soul what Rudolf Steiner described in *How to Know Higher Worlds* as the acquisition of the so-called four faculties: the ability 'to distinguish ... between truth and appearance, between what is true and what is simply opinion', the 'ability to value truth and reality rightly in relation to appearances', the 'application ... of control of thoughts, control of actions, perseverance, tolerance, faith and equanimity', and 'the love of inner freedom'. After I had proceeded through this series there came a shining of the lotus flowers accompanied by after-effects that lasted for weeks in some cases and for months in others. The description in John's Gospel of Mary Magdalene thinking the Risen One was the gardener is a pointer to this mystery. These spiritual events and christotolic measures resulted in nine months of various after-echoes in the consciousness soul which prepared and strengthened me for further great trials in my life.

Animal and human being

In my former incarnations there had been many encounters and relationships with animals. This helped me understand why in my youth I had wanted to become a vet. One of those instances—which is a custom Roman historians also mention—was connected with Antonia *minor* who had a pond in the garden of her summer house near Naples in which she kept large, dangerous fish which she decorated with jewellery.

The Guardian instructed me to follow up these animal situations beyond the threshold in order to find new insights into my own being. The upshot of this work refers to themes that are only sparsely described in anthroposophical esoteric literature, and I myself am also only able to give brief sketches in this connection.

On going once more to where Ramishanda was taming the leading she-elephant by sitting on her back, I discovered that from the moment when she had looked into the elephant's eye her own 'higher self' had been working in the animal. Ramishanda experienced this in the fact that when she was on the animal's back she sensed a divine power of gratitude rising up from the elephant. When I first had this Imagination I did not perceive this difference.

In the scene where Shida Dong and the other children saw the dragon rising up from the lake I found that the 'higher selves' of Shida and the others had taken part in creating the Imagination of the dragon. I was able to watch through the eyes of the dragon as the children fled along the shore, and had a strange sense of carrying out the task of a guardian. I have not tried to investigate whether the spiritual powers of the priests, who had been warned by guards of the forbidden presence of the children, also played a part in it.

These experiences while being trained by the Guardian led me to realize that the eastern idea of human beings incarnating in animals is a late echo of ancient mystery wisdom in which the 'higher self' of a human being could indeed incorporate itself in animals.

This and other knowledge I received prepared me for an encounter with my spiritual animals. The lesser guardian, my good helper Shilbur, appeared to me in a new shape. He had the head of a bull, the belly of a crocodile and the limbs of an elephant. He was even equipped with a trunk. The one-sided development of my life of thought, feeling and will since the time of Shamu'radhin had increasingly imprisoned him spiritually in that shape. Now I was able to try and set him free by taming those spiritual animal forms through special inner exercises, so that they could be integrated in my higher self. If I were able to carry this through consciously he would be permitted to continue assisting me every time I passed across the abyss.

The light emanating from the individual

There is an expression coined by Rudolf Steiner that is sometimes used in anthroposophical circles without being put into its proper context. This is the technical term 'Lord of Karma'. In the lectures *From Jesus to Christ* Steiner described the background to this expression. It is the term for a position in the spiritual world which was once also occupied, among others, by the individual known outwardly by the name of Moses. As the spiritual world progresses in our time, however, Christ is taking over this spiritual office of judgment which will raise the connection between human karma and spiritual guidance on to a new level. The relevant description in a lecture Steiner gave on 7 October 1911 will serve as the point of departure to which I shall then add an experience of my own:

> Just as on the physical plane, at the beginning of our era, the event of Palestine took place, so in our time the office of Karmic Judge is passing over to Christ Jesus in the higher world next to our own. This event works into the physical world, on the physical plane, in such a way that human beings will develop towards it the feeling that by all their actions they will be causing something for which they will be accountable to the judgment of Christ. This feeling, now appearing quite naturally in the course of human development, will be transformed in a way that makes it imbue the soul with a light which little by little will emanate from the individual himself, and will illumine the Form of Christ in the etheric world. The more this feeling develops—a feeling that will have stronger significance than the abstract conscience—the more will the etheric Form of Christ be visible in the coming centuries.

Since my profound experiences in the supersensible world I have had many new meetings with people, encounters which gave me the feeling of being bathed in an unusual quality of soul light. The special intimacy of such an encounter is such that it is difficult to find the right words to describe it. I shall now recount one such encounter which had these noticeable new qualities and which also then led to a specific deepening of karma that became fruitful for a larger circle of people.

I was giving some lectures on understanding karma. After one of the lectures a young student approached me who was enthusiastic about what she had heard but who also asked whether I would be prepared to have a talk with her about her own personal questions concerning life. I agreed, and we arranged a time that suited us both.

After the first conversation, several more followed over the next two weeks. I learnt a lot about her biography and present life situation. She told me about her friends and a failed relationship with her boyfriend whom she still loved very much. I noticed that she appeared almost as though paralysed from her neck down to her feet. The way she dressed and moved made it look as though she did not want to identify at all with her lower body. In the way she thought and spoke, however, and in artistic activities, she was wide awake and participated fully.

A soul space of trust developed out of the exchange between us, but within this our conversations triggered a crisis situation which brought her unconscious fears to the surface. She showed me her diaries. They were full of lovely poems and small coloured drawings, but in every case the subject was sadness, fear and pain. Many of the pictures showed a human figure, often with its back turned and blood pouring from large wounds.

I was deeply moved by her situation and developed a soul-love for her which, turning to Christ, I took into my meditations. I carried out the four-day karma exercise but there were no Imaginations of the kind I was used to. Instead I had very remarkable dreams which presumably showed karmic situations belonging to her.

In one dream something happened near the sea shore. A great wooden boat, like a Viking ship, is approaching. It has a crew of several men who are rowing fast in order to escape enemies chasing them in another boat. Some of the men in the first boat throw themselves into the water which is full of reeds here at the water's edge. The others reach the shore and hide in the woods. One of the men trying to hide in the reeds has a sack with him. It contains important documents and treasures of a holy place which must not fall into enemy hands. When the men in the other boat arrive and beat down the reeds with their oars to find anyone who might be hiding, the man with the sack ducks under the water with it and remains under the cold water for a long time without making any waves or blowing any bubbles. When he cannot wait any longer for air he finds that the enemies are still very close by. But the evening twilight is approaching and the guardian of the treasure finds a better way of hiding under a tuft of beaten-down reeds. He stays still in the water for hours on end, but the sack gradually gets too heavy for him. In the end he drowns, still clinging to it, and his final thought is that perhaps the enemies will discover the treasures when he is gone.

Another dream showed the following situation: A group of men looking like Spanish conquistadores sit in a room chatting merrily. One of them, the leader of the group in fact, will be having to appear in court. During one of their raids in a nearby town he has offended a high-ranking citizen by his rude ways. The group discuss the possibility of standing by their leader and all going to court together for, they argue, they all took part in what he did. Then one member of the group speaks out against this, saying that he has always tried to persuade the leader to behave better. 'If you don't want to be one of us,' says the leader angrily, 'you can go.' The man hesitates but then picks up his things and turns towards the door. The leader jumps up and throws his dagger at his friend. It stabs him in the back. Before he can turn round all the others also throw their daggers at him. None of them can be called to account for his death so the whole group is condemned to death by hanging.

On waking up after these dreams I had a feeling that those dramatic death scenes had been experienced by the young student in earlier lives. After thinking the matter over carefully I recounted the dreams to her and also, with her permission, to others among her circle of friends. Although she was capable of taking in the dramatic content, her awareness of it caused her to become more fearful than ever. I called up all the powers of soul I possessed that have anything to do with wounding, sympathy and conscience in order to create an envelope of light around her. There were some remarkable moments when her own intuition made her begin to scream the fear out of herself. After more conversations during the ensuing days it became clear that she needed medical help. One of her teachers made the necessary arrangements.

This encounter with the young student led for me to a situation in which I had to practise a schooling of soul that was not abstract. It seemed to me that I had experienced a soul-light that was directly connected with the work of Christ. When you have this feeling of being able to share in the work with an invisible Lord of Karma it is not a matter of subjecting yourself to a power that will tell you what must be done. What you do is try to act, serve and care on the basis of nothing, on the basis of what you cannot yet do. Subsequently, if the light is still there in other life situations, you discover whether you have acted rightly or wrongly.

Lucifer and Ahriman

Rudolf Steiner's mystery plays* have shown me the manner in which the spiritual powers of opposition, Lucifer and Ahriman, can test, obstruct and seek to hinder a person who is treading a path of spiritual schooling.

With regard to social life I was for many years able to investigate the matter of spiritual opponents without having any direct Imaginations. After the Imaginations had begun this realm of the spiritual world also became visible to me as an object of soul-spiritual observation. I shall here describe briefly my early experiences in this field.

---

* Steiner wrote a series of four 'mystery plays'. See *Four Mystery Dramas*, London: Rudolf Steiner Press 1997.

Early in 1996, through a friend I had known for a long time, I met the woman who later brought me the Imagination about Willibald which I have already described. Our first encounter made no particular impression on either of us. When we met again in September we remarked on this. We were both visiting her friend, and now an almost unbearable atmosphere immediately arose between us. There was a strong attraction which, as I was later to discover, covered up a strong fear. We met several times during the autumn and the atmosphere between us remained. I felt more and more sympathetic towards her, whereas she had a feeling that told her to be careful. She was not able to reciprocate my feelings.

In this situation I decided to do the four-day karma exercise directed at her. On the fourth morning the Imagination arose. Afterwards I sat in my room and was aware that she lived over 50 kilometres further north and that she was there at that moment. I became certain in my self that my feeling for her did not emanate solely from me. I found that my feeling of love bore a kind of supersensible colouring that was streaming from a third being. This being, I decided, was Lucifer. After the Imagination my feelings for her or—put more precisely—the urgent need to love her, were gone. What remained was that other quality, which I called a 'colour'. I followed up this flood of colour in spirit and recognized a figure that had, as it were, been standing behind the woman.

I turned towards Christ but without being able to see him, and asked for his help. Was Lucifer permitted to seduce me in this manner? I even experienced an echo of the urge to desire the woman sexually. A figure of light appeared which I later recognized as my angel. The attitude adopted by this figure told me: Lucifer has every right to seduce you because you are karmically indebted to the woman. After the further Imagination, described in Chapter 3, showing the ambush in my medieval incarnation, I realized that there was something different and much older hidden in me, another fact from another life, which was now urging me to continue seeking contact with the woman.

As I continued to work I reached a survey of our mutual karmic relationships through many incarnations. I recognized her as the Quaker William, who knew so much about the Red Indians, and Elizabeth of Valois. In Rome I found her as the young athlete Amtherion, the friend of Antonia *minor* who had died fighting as a gladiator. In Greece she had been Deidera, Agamon's wife. In Egypt I experienced her as Chaembasa. In China she was the temple priest Ranga Jia and in India the high priest of the southern people, Brahmakatzar. Shamu'radhin made room in his gamamila for the widow of the hunter who had died, and Retana experienced the drowning of his first wife. In all these incarnations I recognized the woman with whom I had fallen in love in my present incarnation. I saw an individual who wants to draw other people's attention to the joy in life by means of the dramatic element.

When I tried to follow up the later years of Ray in Nubia to see what became of his relationship with Chaembasa, I discovered a dark shadow over some events on the Nile. Pursuing this black 'lid' I discovered, in the darkness which I could not yet penetrate, the 'pot' containing the cause of the special colour described above which I had found belonged to Lucifer. I then suddenly saw the creator of that spiritual darkness: it was the being Ahriman. I recognized him as a being who would not permit me today to know about my deeds in the past. He was trying to use in a legitimate way for his own purposes the powers that had arisen out of my karmic forgetting.

Once again I turned to Christ and found that this time he was able to help me. My angel mediated and told me that it was now my right as a spiritual being to know every karmic connection regarding what I had experienced or done by the Nile so long ago.

With the utmost inner effort within my self I entered Ahriman's shadow and noticed a light arising around me. The Imagination of Ray's escape with Chaembasa arose for the first time, and also of the subsequent events that led to her tragic death and his initiation at Dendera, which I have described in Chapter 3.

The Manichaean challenge to evil

At the end of this chapter I shall now bring forward some themes which I myself still find puzzling. I want to mention the following as a way of outlining a number of tasks that have to do with certain aspects of the coming Manichaean challenge to evil.*

For example there is the task of building 'spiritual prisons' for demons in the supersensible earth sphere. I once attempted to do this while travelling in an aeroplane. I built meditatively, as a model, a transparent double-walled hangar with a kind of 'mousetrap', locating it geographically in an Egyptian desert. I 'inspected' this spiritual 'prison for demons' and gave it a 'code name'. Then I asked Christ to show me a situation anywhere in the world where a criminal act was at that very moment being committed.

The following Imagination was the result: There is a street in a town which I cannot recognize. It is dark. Street-lights illumine the right-hand pavement. The point from which I am looking is a little above the middle of the right-hand side of the road. Up ahead are several parked cars. Further away, on the pavement, there is a typical red Swedish phone-box. I see two people, a man with his small daughter, walking past the phone-box making for the nearest car.

The man stops and points a revolver at a house further back,

---

* Mani was a spiritual teacher of the third century, the founder of Manichaeism. Steiner spoke of him in connection with the task of metamorphosing evil.

where electric light shines on to the pavement from a window. Now I understand the situation. I am filled with resolve and know what I have to do. In the soul of the man I see a dark spiritual being, an anti-social demon which has taken possession of him. The man stands still for a moment. I direct my higher self towards the demon and address it, saying that it is in the wrong place and that in future there will be other, more noble tasks for it to do. It will be given those tasks if it departs from this human being in Christ's name and in my name—which I breathe towards it out of my higher self.

I command it to go to the place where a new house has been built for it and its friends. I make this request three times, giving the codename of the 'demon prison' in 'Egypt', and then I see something like a dark comet going away from the street. With my inner eyes I watch the demon flying away across 'Europe' and landing in the hangar.

The man has loosened his grip on his daughter. I turn to him and tell him that Christ will help him find a solution different from the one he has thought up himself. I tell him to let his daughter return to her mother. I tell the girl not to be afraid, for Christ will help her and her parents find a good solution. I ask her to go home, and say that she will see her father again. I watch the girl walking back to the house. The man stands still and doesn't know what is happening to him. I tell him to turn his revolver on to the tyres of his car and watch him shoot three times. I 'hear' the bangs. I ask him to throw the revolver on the ground and to throw himself on to the pavement. I watch him do this. I tell him to wait until the police arrive and that he need not be afraid since Christ will protect him and help him in what is to come.

As time went on I experienced several more such 'crimes in Imagination'. One involving the disfigurement of corpses was so horrible and painful that it continued to affect me for a long time.

But I never found out through news bulletins or newspaper reports whether what I had experienced so realistically and helped to bring about in the soul and spirit realm had really happened in the physical world. However, these experiences gave me a clear idea of what we can expect of Manichaeans in the future. These Manichaean exercises showed me how our violent environment can be socially transformed for the good by spiritual measures which I see as involving 'white magic'.

In his final book, *The Battle for the Soul*, Bernard Lievegoed wrote about the coming incarnation of Mani-Parsifal. He stated that this individual would work together with many others who are now children or still waiting to incarnate, in order to bring about a world-wide movement that could be termed an 'action to save the souls of all humanity'. I believe the time has come for us to find new ways of relating to one another based entirely on love at all levels. By beginning to recognize karmic reality, by continuing along the road towards personal threshold experiences, by beginning to see through our own tendencies to form doubles, by talking with sisters and brothers who share our quest for the spirit and by helping each other in our spiritual trials, we begin to prepare the ground on which the coming Manichaeans can find their path. It is the path of the One who says of himself: 'I am the way, the truth and the life.'

The theme of the future Manichaeans touches on and dovetails with another one, which I shall mention only briefly here. It is what we are told will be the physical incarnation of the originator of all demonic power, Ahriman himself. It must be assumed that the coming incarnation of Mani and those who will want to find their way to him will be linked specifically with the once-only incarnation of Ahriman in an earthly body in the near future.

The best way of preparing for events which will of necessity take place is to study karma and seriously to want and support karma research. This is because Ahriman, and also the other spiritual opponents of humanity, have always tried and will continue to try and destroy the mystery of reincarnation and karma and separate the human self from the karmic treasures which belong to it. On 4 August 1924, only a few weeks before his final illness, Rudolf Steiner had the following to say on this matter (in *Karmic Relationships Vol.III*):

> I have told you about the return of those who are now finding their way to the things of the spirit and taking them in full earnestness and sincerity; this will come about at the end of the century. But that is the very time which the Ahrimanic spirits wish to use most strongly, because human beings are so completely wrapped up in the intelligence that has come over them. They have become so unbelievably clever. Even today we are quite nervous about the cleverness of the people we meet! In fact this anxiety dogs us nearly all the time, for nearly all of them are so clever. The truth of the matter is that the cleverness which is thus being cultivated is used by Ahriman. And when in addition human bodies are especially adapted to a possible dimming of consciousness, what happens is that Ahriman himself emerges, incorporated in human form.

An attitude that negates the spiritual schooling and research described in this book would make it all the easier for Ahrimanic beings to make contact with human souls. As Steiner said: 'To acquire the power of discrimination in this sphere is absolutely necessary, my dear friends.'

5

Karmic connections and consequences

In reverence I bow before the many souls
who ... shape again their human destinies.
Christian Morgenstern

The timing of my incarnations

In order to follow up various connections I have entered my
incarnations from China onwards on a parabola with the Mystery
of Golgotha in the year 33 at the central point (see over). By linking 747 BC and AD 1413 I get a line (dotted) running diagonally
up to the right. Roughly parallel with this is the line linking the
life as Ray with my present life. The life as Agamon can be linked
with that as Christian von Buch by a similarly almost parallel line.

Another line running down to the right links Shida Dong with
Mary Queen of Scots. A line (broken) roughly parallel with this
leads from Ray to the time of Charlemagne (approximately AD
750–850). I have found no incarnation of my own in this period
spanning the eighth and ninth centuries, but what I have found
are the incarnations of many individuals who did not accept
Christianity in the first century but who are karmically connected
with Antonia *minor*.

When I tried to follow Antonia's post-mortem transformations,
I discovered her in the spirit together with others who were dead,
sharing in the task of creating from the spiritual world the
Imaginations of the spiritual Grail temple necessary for Grail
seekers on earth.

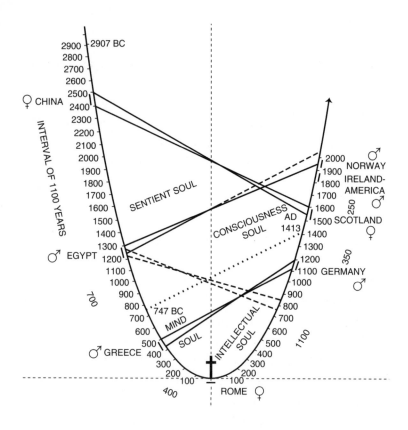

The temporal rhythm with ever shorter intervals between the four incarnations from Shida to Antonia corresponds with the same rhythm of incarnations from Christian von Buch to my present life. The long period between Antonia and Christian with the 'missing' incarnation at the time of Charlemagne corresponds with the interval between Ramishanda and Shida (the Persian cultural epoch) in which I also found no incarnation of my own. I do not yet know why this is so. Perhaps I shall still find these 'missing' incarnations. Or perhaps interesting karmic secrets lie hidden here.

Karmic connections

The research I did up to Easter 1997 provided many keys for an understanding of who the individuals with whom I had been connected thus far in my present life had been in former lives. I have found links between individuals in my karmic circles in various countries and almost all the men and women named in Chapter 3. It has been possible for me to follow these connections through several lives, which has helped me understand why one circumstance or another has arisen. To help the reader find the links leading from one life to the next and perhaps forestall speculation I want to lay bare the connections, as I see them, between myself and a few of the individuals concerned, in so far as they have died and now live in the spiritual world. As regards others, who are still here in their present incarnation, I shall reveal some links without bringing the connections up to the present time.

As I have already stated several times, I regard this publication as an aid to study and research for people seeking the spirit who want to help develop a modern form of karma research. All the spiritual experiences and karmic facts recounted are of such a personally serious nature that I request anyone wanting to work further with them to exercise great tact. The following descriptions will be very concise and it is left to the reader to fit them into the relevant incarnation as described in Chapter 3. In some of the examples I shall mention names that did not appear in the situations thus far described for a particular incarnation but which are relevant here.

In describing karmic links with individuals who have cropped up repeatedly in my incarnations, and in following some motifs right up to the present time, I have disguised certain things in such a way that those who might recognize themselves will not need to feel that their privacy has been invaded.

Unfortunately I cannot here retrace in detail the manner in which I have discovered these karmic links. In many instances I found the relevant incarnations in meditative Imaginations arising from memories I have of all these people in my life. By quoting a few characteristic examples I shall below briefly hint once more at the method of research which follows Rudolf Steiner's indications. In some Imaginations I found myself in spirit confronting persons whom I did not immediately recognize. In the normal thought processes of my daytime consciousness I then lived for some time with the question as to who they might be. Quite unexpectedly, in the midst of a conversation or after meeting a friend or colleague, I would suddenly have some intuitive insight into what the connection was. In other cases I occupied myself in thought for long periods until a karmic link manifested in my thinking or in an Imagination while meditating. Occasionally I woke up in the morning with the insight I had been seeking.

I have lived with the experiences here described for more than two years since finding them. And I have checked them by various methods, including comparison with what others have found.

The diamond

I see in Siwe in America—who was William's fiancée and who threw herself in front of a train, thus taking her own life—a kind of sister soul to William. When William was incarnated as Elizabeth of Valois I think the sister soul lived near her in Spain as Don Carlos.

In Imaginations about the Middle Ages I saw the knight Giorgio, a colleague and close friend of the knight Willibald. In the Greek life of Agamon and Deidera they had a son, Emterion. In Nubia it had been intended that Prince Gubomba should marry Chaembasa. In China, Shida Dong had a female relation, the musician Matunga. In India I think I found the same individual in the Shiva priest Tadgathiwan, and in Atlantis and Lemuria she was probably one of the two children mentioned.

It was said of Emterion that he lived in Athens where he sold the offerings made of cut and polished crystal by his father. About Don Carlos there is a report referring to when he was in prison and would not give up the idea of committing suicide. The Venetian ambassador Sigismondo Cavalli mentioned in a letter a new madness of the Infante of Spain: '...having heard that swallowing a diamond would kill a person, he swallowed one from the ring he wore on his finger. However, since it was a hard object and not pulverized, it reappeared several days later without having done him the slightest harm.' In trying to formulate in a single sentence the mission of this individual (a number of whose incarnations have not been mentioned here) Tadgathiwan-Matunga-Gubomba-Emterion-Giorgio-Don Carlos-Siwe, I have come up with the following characterization: This individual seeks to make the human being's youthful forces fruitful throughout the whole of life.

'He was well-spoken and highly educated'

In my view the individual who lived in the son of Mary Queen of Scots, James VI of Scotland and I of England, also lived in Rainald von Dassel. I recognize him in Roman times as Drusus, Antonia's husband, and in Greece as Haftoteles, Agamon's friend. In India I see him in Ramishanda's uncle Bugtamar, the potter and worker in basketry. In the Mercury Oracle he once bore the name of Tamu'thamas who taught Trinni'dadama in the Vulcan Oracle the new art of masonry.

The Italian chronicler Acerbus Morena, who met the German Chancellor Rainald von Dassel a number of times, described him around 1162 in the words quoted on p. 187. One can try to amalgamate the image projected by these medieval words with the image of the Mercury initiate teaching the new masonry technique using lively gestures and well-modulated song. And one can imagine the figure of the melancholy, highly educated King of England, James I, who writes subtle poetry and wants to support William Shakespeare. It goes without saying that in the twentieth century this individual could well be involved in some way with caring for Rudolf Steiner's impulse of the two Goetheanum buildings.

The Pythia

The Vulcan initiate Trinni'dadama can be found again, I believe, in Dithelia, the Pythia at Delphi, in the Emperor Caesar Augustus and in Eleanor of Aquitaine.

When I researched how the Pythia worked I found out the following: The priests brought her the questions asked by the petitioners who came from all over the Mediterranean region. Her specially developed ether body then enabled her to make inner contact with the various geographical locations. She thus became karmically linked in a special way with those locations, and this helped her in her next life as Caesar Augustus to oust Mark Antony's friends and win power over the whole Roman empire.

Trinni'dadama-Dithelia-Augustus-Eleanor is an individual who has the impulse to create an expansion of the social community through sacrificing the forces of will.

The dagger of damask steel

In Antonia's grandson Gaius Caligula I found a woman named Mirtelliam'gila who belonged to the 'moon periodicity workshop' in the Atlantean Mars Oracle. In India I found her again in the southern region and in China her name was Bami Dong. This was Shida's grandfather who was present at the birth of her first child.

In Egypt I found an administrator in Karnak called Mubital, and in the Acropolis there was a temple serving maid named Apalia. I recognize the same individual again in Barbarossa's son, King and Emperor Henry VI. It was Christian von Buch who helped him win the German crown.

In some of the lives of this individual there was much humour, but also drama and violence. In her novel *Apollonius von Tyana, Leben und Werk eines Eingeweihten* about the first-century philosopher and wandering preacher Apollonius of Tyana, Maria Schneider has described the circumstances around the assassination of Caligula and how Apollonius received news of it:

> When shortly thereafter the news of Caligula's assassination reached Ionia a Roman slave asked the way to the dwelling of Apollonius, and when he found himself standing before the sage presented him with a small dagger of damask steel. 'Marcus, the father of Julian, sends to Apollonius of Tyana the holy dagger that slew the tyrant,' he announced solemnly. 'My young master, Julian Marcus, perished once he had pierced the Emperor's heart. My young master commanded me, should he perish, to seek you out and give myself into your possession on all your journeys and in every danger. His father sends me to you. I and the dagger are yours.' ... Apollonius asked: 'Who rules in Rome now?' 'Gaius Caligula's uncle, the weakling Claudius, and with him Messallina, his infamous wife', replied the messenger gloomily and hopelessly. 'Many desired the Republic. But the soldiers dragged him from the palace where he was hiding and payed homage to him as Jupiter Imperator. All was accomplished too hastily, with too little preparation. Marcus too, my dead master's father, is deeply disappointed.' Apollonius sighed and stood there staring at the ground. Then, in a soft voice, he asked the slave: 'What is your name? What can you do?' 'My name is Paris, and I am a stenographer,' he replied. 'That will suit very well,' said Apollonius, 'You the stenographer and Melytos the calligrapher will come with me when I set off for the East.'

Three notions are mentioned in this quotation: dagger of damask steel, stenographer and calligrapher. They are well worth contemplating in conjunction with a miniature from the Heidelberg manuscript (*Codex Manesse*) depicting Henry VI as a minnesinger, for they might well put one in mind of an individual who seeks to transform rigid might into nimble, lively speech.

Little Red Riding Hood

I recognized the Emperor Frederick Barbarossa in Emperor Claudius, in Maathorneferure and in the sun initiate Tami'tame'sham. I also found him in my vicinity as Mantilasakam, Ramishanda's maternal grandfather, as Mengong Dong, one of Shida's sons, and as a woman in Athens called Clamydia whom Agamon got to know during theatre performances there.

The wolf has been an image in Rome from the beginning. Legend has it that Romulus, the founder of the city, and Remus his brother were suckled by a she-wolf. For this and other reasons the wolf came to be used in subsequent Roman history as a symbol linked to the leading position in society, that of the Roman Emperor.

We are told that Antonia *minor* one day went for a walk with her friends and servants amongst whom was an augur who could foretell events from observing birds and understanding the meaning of myths. While the adults chatted about goings-on in the empire the children and youngsters ran around playing. All of a sudden blood spattered on the white dresses of some of the girls. No one could understand where it came from until the augur pointed to the sky where an eagle was circling with a wolf-cub in its beak. As though rooted to the ground the company watched the dramatic flight.

Then the eagle dropped its prey and the wolf-cub hurtled towards the spot where they were standing. Everyone jumped aside except Claudius Drusus, Antonia's eldest son who was not only absent-minded but also lame. The cub fell right into his arms. Wide-eyed the augur stared at the young man, for this was a sign that could not be misinterpreted. Antonia realized that the gods had spoken and demanded that the augur tell her what he knew. But for the moment he remained silent. Later she took him aside and learnt the meaning.

Several decades later Claudius was chosen to be Emperor by the praetorians. Certain influential citizens of Rome who had heard of the story about his youth knew from it that the choice was the right one and therefore felt able to back it.

Emperor Claudius was a Roman who did not accept Christianity in that life but only later in an incarnation as a woman during the reign of Charlemagne. I found that the individual who had lived in Claudius was also incarnated in Emperor Frederick Barbarossa. Externally his position in both incarnations was similar, but in the medieval German lands the symbol of the ruler was no longer a wolf but a bear or a lion.

One version of the Kyffhäuser legend has it that Frederick Barbarossa did not die during the Third Crusade but is still alive and waiting inside the golden mountain above the town of Tilleda. He is sitting at a table of stone and letting his red beard grow as he waits for a new age in which the glory of the empire will be reborn, in connection with the return of Christ.

I have found this individual in the twentieth century in an incarnation as a woman. The biography she has made for herself has as though inscribed within it the tale of Little Red Riding Hood. In Atlantis this individual, as Tami'tame'sham, experienced the most radical transformation of the atmosphere through the fire temples. As Maathorneferure, the Hittite wife of Rameses II, she was living proof of the first peace treaty between two great powers in the history of the world. As the Emperor Claudius this individual drove the Jews and Christians into the catacombs and later banished them from Rome altogether. As Barbarossa he fought with cross and sword for the Christian cause. In the present time, in a modern-day catacomb situation in which she is forced to live, she is creating, through 'the bitterness in the stomach of the wolf', a transformation that by means of wonder, sympathy and conscience is bringing into being coloured vestments for the Representative of Humanity.

'Let from the East be kindled what from the West is formed'

In Henry the Lion I see Agrippina, the fourth wife of Emperor Claudius and mother of Lucius Domitius who is known by the name of Nero. I see the same individual in the Pharaoh Rameses II, and in Atlantis the Mars initiate Abtra'muthin who introduced Gamu'radhin to the animal wisdom of the cave paintings.

There is much that I could write about this individual and his path through the history of humanity, frequently in positions of public view, for he achieved so much. (There were also other incarnations as historically known persons which I shall not mention here.) Better than any recounting of deeds, the following words from Rudolf Steiner's *Foundation Stone Meditation* summarize this individual's overall endeavours in the service of culture and art throughout many incarnations: 'Let from the East be kindled what from the West is formed.'

The little donkey

I found Agrippina's mother, Agrippina *maior*, who was married to Germanicus, the son of Antonia, in the Middle Ages as the Abbot Wibald of Stavelot and Corvey. I also think I have seen this individual in the Red Indian chief Gerasawak. In the Mars Oracle his name was Magni'magisan who had sent Shamu'radhin on the assignment which led to his downfall. In Eleusis this individual was the person at the front on the right-hand side of the cart during Agamon's initiation.

In his present incarnation this individual had to live for many years in an environment that showed no understanding for his true life impulses. The story of the little donkey fits in with this life. As already mentioned, he was in Atlantis a representative of the Mars Oracle who had the task of getting the asses' skins ready for the Sun Oracle. He lost his position on account of certain circumstances which meant that he and one of his closest colleagues had to leave the oracle.

Shamu'radhin's father

Charlemagne's foremost counsellor was Alcuin, the Irish monk and later Abbot of Tours. In the first century I found this individual in Tamara, a young Christian living in the catacombs at the time when old Antonia received her baptism. I also recognize this individual in the world-renowned Greek dramatist Sophocles.

This individual was also, without doubt, Shamu'radhin's father Tadga'menerthin in Atlantean times. In India he was Margatudin, the prince consort of Ramishanda. As Ming Dong she gave birth to Shida, and in the Hathor Temple he was the high priest Maanthorthebin who oversaw Ray's initiation.

In the Middle Ages she was the wife and then widow of the knight Vincent von Schauenburg who served King Conrad III. In the nineteenth century as Marcus he drove the train that killed Siwe. Having already incarnated once in the twentieth century, he then came again and has the impulse, together with others who are also still children, to develop further in about 20 years' time whatever will have come about as a culmination of anthroposophy at the turn of the millennium.

The piano teacher

Tame'xan'dima, the mother of Tame'mani'sham, lived for a while in the Sun Oracle. She was reborn as King Gumatamar, father of

Ramishanda. In China, Shida had a friend, the woman Shivabei, who was sent to her from the Shinto Temple.

Her name was Enthramada when she was Ray's mother. In Epidaurus, Agamon met the priestess Elitania from the Temple of Aphaea. Antonia *minor* had a relative Trajanus, who was a major in Gaul. This individual was called Kander when he served Charlemagne, and as Disa von Medebach she was a nun in a convent near Mainz that belonged to the archbishopric of Christian von Buch.

Ronald Dixon encountered the same individual in his piano teacher.

The violin teacher

Bishop Udalrich II of Treffen, whom Emperor Frederick made Patriarch of Aquileia, was more than once a brother in arms to Archbishop Christian of Mainz. In him, I believe, lived Trusteri'gamon who, on account of Shamu'radhin's destiny, had once been prevented from finding the way back to the Sun Oracle.

She was also Queen Muritama, Ramishanda's mother, and served Shida Dong as the eunuch Barigong. As Muustragathichaem he was initiated into the Mysteries of Nut and then, under Rameses II became an architect in charge of the sculpture work. Agamon competed with the charioteer Trapestarion at Olympia and Sparta. The same individual is known historically as Messalina, the third wife of Claudius. The immoral life of many Roman men and women ended when they were punished by law for participating in the orgies she organized.

Ronald Dixon met her in his violin teacher whom he so bitterly disappointed by unexpectedly laying down his violin.

The dragon motif

I would be able to recite the karmic relationships for over a hundred other individuals through three or more incarnations.

Some people have been mentioned already in this book as having played a part in forming my life. Since they have been dead for seven years or more, and since I have already introduced them in conversations or lectures elsewhere, I want to include their karmic relationships here too. Turid Marianne Saether (1930–87), my dear mother and quiet companion on the way to anthroposophy, brought me the Imagination of her as Tragge'mitram, the man with the little compost heap in the Mercury Oracle.

I also found her later in Djingotan, Shida's husband, and as the actress Lysistrate at Eleusis. In Rome I recognize her as Agoria, who became a baker through Antonia. In Italy, Christian von Buch had a second knight, Giorgio, who was also a minnesinger. In the circus in Boston Ronald met the same individual again as the dumb animal keeper.

I had a memory that lives in me as a kind of confirmation. In my childhood home there was a photo of my mother as a little girl of two or three. She is wearing black oriental pyjamas and the jacket is decorated with a special motif in yellow and red: a dragon. As children we were occasionally allowed to take this suit out of its drawer and look at it. It is now kept safely by my sister.

The tentmaker

I found my much-loved handwork teacher, Åslaug Nysæther (1920–1980), who taught children with special needs, as an initiate in the Venus Oracle. She was also one of those who took forward the silk work at Dong'du. In the Hathor Temple of Dendera she was the high priestess who presided over the death ritual of Ray.

She came to Rome as the tentmaker Aquila. Antonia *minor*, whom he got to know through his wife Priscilla, the chamber maid, was prepared by him to join the Christian faith. In Italy the same individual was the historian Acerbus Morena. Christian von Buch liked to stay on his estates at Lodi.

The pillar of social impulse

In the Steiner Waldorf teacher Stig Pedersen I recognized the individual who lived in Bertha von Sulzbach, known as the Empress Irene of Byzantium, and also the Jewish-Christian teacher Hermas in Rome, who stemmed from Alexandria.

In my attempt in Chapter 2 to recount my experience with the deceased Stig Pedersen the motif of the 'pillar of social impulse' is mentioned. This is the best way of describing the concentrated strength and expansive gentleness of this individual.

Tumbling into the ordure

I have found the artist and teacher Kurt Wegner again in Ludwig III, Landgrave of Thuringia, son and successor of Ludwig the Hard. He received his education in France, probably also at Chartres, and was a brother of Hermann of Thuringia, who instigated the singers' contest in the Wartburg castle around 1206.

In a booklet about the Liudolfing dynasty, *Die Ludowinger, Aufsteig und Fall des ersten thüringischen Landgrafengeschlechts*, Hilmar Schwarz has recounted an old tale from Thuringia in which a quarrel between Landgrave Ludwig III and the citizens of Erfurt took an unexpected turn:

> In 1184 an all too horrible misfortune occurred at Erfurt. The Emperor had sent his son Henry to the town to mediate between the parties. They met with all their followers and a good many Thuringian nobles in the provost's office. When they were all gathered and the burden of the argument weighed too heavily, the floor gave way and many of those present plunged into the depths. Over 60 men are said to have perished, among them five counts. They drowned miserably in ordure many metres deep that had

accumulated underneath the building. Henry of Schwarzburg and Burchard of the Wartburg were among the dead. King Henry and the Landgrave escaped with no more than a fright. The arbitration had not been intended to take such a turn, but in the event it was not without effect. For a while at least there were no more reports of any further quarrel between the wranglers.

In the court case against the Swedish pharmaceutical and toiletry firm Weleda in the mid-1970s, Kurt Wegner argued courageously and shrewdly in defence of anthroposophical views against the accusations brought by representatives of traditional medicine. Something of Ludwig III became visible once again. Although he was known as 'the Kind' or 'the Pious' he was also redoubtable and strong. Wegner contributed energetically to enabling anthroposophical medicine to continue in Sweden and thus in the whole of Scandinavia, and indeed to unfold on a new and firmer footing.

Experiencing oneself as the prodigal son

Hans Glaser (1903–90) taught children with special needs, inspired the introduction of biodynamic agriculture to Sweden and was a man with a practical turn of mind. In him I recognized the individual who had been Duke Welf VI of Bavaria who, after the death of his son Welf VII, became one of the greatest monastic benefactors, both financial and otherwise, of the twelfth century. Chronicles confirm that, for example, the young poet Walther von der Vogelweide attended festivities at his court in Gunzenlee.

Many interesting stories are told in connection with Welf VI, and an especially humorous one appears in Karl Jordan's biography of Henry the Lion (*Heinrich der Löwe, Eine Biographie*). In his younger years Welf was in constant dispute with King Conrad III. In the summer of 1140 he lost a battle beside the fortress of Weinsberg near Heilbronn, so that the city finally had to capitulate:

The story of the 'faithful wives' of Weinsberg refers to its capture by the king who, so it is said, permitted the women to leave the fortress taking with them only what they could carry on their shoulders. Out came the women in a long procession bearing their husbands on their backs to save them from captivity. Conrad, though surprised by Welf's trick, declared that he would not break his word.

In November 1961 Hans Glaser wrote in his diary: 'Does my soul live between fear and hope? Yes, it does. Without such an inner instability I would not be a human being. Only when I experience myself as the prodigal son will I be inclined to seek Christ.' In July 1957 he wrote: 'I complain about the tyrants who are outside me. Have I not more reason to complain about the tyrants who reign inside my body?'

How can karmic motifs be detected today?

The above descriptions hint at many karmic motifs that follow on from earlier times. Let me now give a few examples of the very concrete manner in which themes from old karma appear to interfere with present events. I shall either take something from one of the incarnations I have described and show how it manifests today, or I shall first describe something belonging to the present and then look for the explanation in an earlier life.

Apart from the methods described above, there are also deeper hints which Rudolf Steiner gave as to his methods of karma research. In the earlier karma lectures he described concrete examples of how some 'suggestive pointer' in the life of an individual could lead to true Imaginations about former incarnations. He also referred to 'significant characteristics', 'occult effects in the body' or 'strong clues'. Rather than repeat Steiner's examples here, I shall give some of my own.

It has been my experience that Steiner's methods are well worth applying, and there have been many occasions when what he would have called an 'unimportant motif' has led me to karmic connections. I have either used such pointers in a person's present life as the starting position for my meditative research or, in an Imagination of an earlier incarnation, I have found hints that point to the correct individual in the present.

The following examples relate to connections between the present time and a number of my former incarnations and refer to individuals whom I have known or still know today. Some of them died many years ago, while the descriptions of others are slightly disguised to avoid immediate recognition. I give these examples to encourage the reader who is interested in doing his own research into karma to take account of this aspect of karma research as well.

Atlantis and the present day

By juxtaposing my present biography with that of Shamu'radhin/ Gamu'radhin I find aspects that mirror one another. My child-hood and youth in the Sunndal valley point to experiences Gamu'radhin had in the great valley of the Sun Oracle. My years in Sweden as an artist correspond with Gamu'radhin's years doing cave painting and building the Fafagatimir town. My experiences after 1996 mirror Shamu'radhin's life as a gamamila helmsman. My initiation story points imaginatively to events in general both then and now, although it is expressed in images that interpret my present life.

I have found that in many present encounters between people there are ancient threads waiting to be brought into the light of day. Old magical faculties and links with the elemental world that had of necessity to reach a culmination in the Atlantean incar-nation, or else that were lost through misuse, can be re-awakened today in a metamorphosed form through conscious schooling. Here are some examples by way of a description.

I knew a young woman whose parents were worried about her because she wanted to study astrology instead of a more normal subject such as psychology. I followed this individual back to Atlantean times where I found an initiate in the Sun Oracle belonging to the workshop in which incarnating souls were drawn down towards the earth. To help her in her search in this present life I gave her the address of an anthroposophical astrosophist. Since then she has been able to remain true to herself while her parents have come to understand her unusual bent.

In another woman who was seeking to use eurythmy in a social or healing way, but who had begun to doubt whether she was doing the right thing, I found a midwife in the Venus Oracle, a so-called 'mamiugama' around whom the other initiates had the task of inwardly testing relatives in order to find suitable parents for the souls descending to the Sun Oracle.

A third woman had suffered from insomnia for over 20 years without ever finding a doctor who could relieve her condition. Only long periods spent in South Africa helped her gain a little strength. I found her as an initiate in the Venus Oracle. There it was her task to use the forces of her own enlarged ether body during the spring festivals to induce a lethargic sleep in couples who had been brought together to become parents.

In a mother and her autistic daughter I found an unfavourable mixture of initiations in the Mercury and Venus Oracles which had led to an unpermitted birth outside the normal annual rhythm. These two had made contact with other initiates who had been excluded, which only served to complete their own exclusion.

Then there was a man who had spent all his life searching in vain for evidence to prove that he was a child of the German occupying forces in Norway during the Second World War. In Atlantis I again found a child born outside the annual rhythm, the son of a captain. He had been excluded from his tribe as a result, and when he later returned but was refused re-entry, he destroyed the settlement and caused a landslide, bringing about the deaths of many people.

I could quote many similar examples and complete each one by precise karmic, biographical and symptomatological explanations. But I hope these few cases have shown up a pattern in the karmic laws connected with Atlantis.

Rudolf Steiner gave important indications regarding the way our culture mirrors that of ancient Egypt. I believe there is a similar karmic link between present-day and Atlantean initiation motifs. Atlantis appears to have risen up karmically in our midst out of the 'Akashic ocean'. We can either deny that spiritual continent from the primeval past and continue to bear the consequences of incarnations then as nothing more than present constraints and suffering. Or we can recognize the karma deriving from it as one that can be metamorphosed into forces for the future.

Any research into Atlantis by means of a spiritual science that is in harmony with Rudolf Steiner's impulses must first of all involve exploring the connections by means of many examples and descriptions. At the same time the individuals concerned must be helped to build the future out of their present life situations in the light of these perspectives.

The elephants

I have developed a form of conversation in which I try to inspire my conversation partner to embark on a meditation in my presence in which the 'building of a hut' can be practised. Taking my departure in soul and spirit from Christ's words, 'When two or three are gathered together in my name...', I am able, in this kind of 'karma session', to help and accompany the other person to achieve a 'spirit-remembering'. This is a method of regression which I have established with reference to the School of Spiritual Science founded by Rudolf Steiner and which I practise on my own responsibility. I call this assistance in karmic research 'accompanied remembering'.

In the case of the woman with the autistic problems mentioned above among the Atlantean examples, I have tried to help her in her present life through biography work, encouragement to meditate, gratitude exercises and 'accompanied remembering'. In one of her karma sessions she received Imaginations from various lives, in one of which she saw herself in an Indian village where strangers on elephants were breaking in and trampling down the huts. With shock and despair she re-lived the experience of seeing many members of her family killed. She saw herself fleeing with a son along a river to another village where she hid in the dwelling of a relative.

Her description of this Imagination was rich in detail and corresponded with my own experiences at that time, but now from the point of view of the other tribe, for Ramishanda and Gangatami (as I had to admit to myself) were two of the elephant riders dressed in beautifully coloured garments. I had earlier already discovered Gangatami in a woman with whom I had a karmic connection and who was the sister of the woman I was now trying to help. In her Imagination she recognized her present sister and myself in the two elephant riders.

The royal altar of Wang

Two years ago I visited a friend whom I had recognized as King Wang. Now aged over 70, he took me up some steps and into his workshop in a loft to see the results of his most recent hobby. What I saw before me filled me with astonishment:

The whole large attic was full of numerous small and larger

pieces of furniture and carvings. Enthusiastically he showed me a large cupboard with delicate carvings round the doors. It looked like an ancient wooden altar! He had done all this work over the previous winter. The situation was rather special and gave me the opportunity to have a good conversation with him and his wife about karmic relationships.

The question of a successor

When I was researching the life of the scribe Ray and discovered his unauthorized sale of the papyrus document, I found in this the karmic background to an event in my life which I could not forget for many years and which continued to haunt me for a long time because of its painful consequences.

I had for several years shared in the running of a course on the theory of colours which took place annually. Now I and another colleague were asked to take over responsibility for that course, but then, for the reasons I shall explain, the responsibility was not handed to me after all. The course, which was very comprehensive and involved lectures, experiments and painting exercises, was usually carried out by five teachers. But in 1992 I had to run it with a single colleague because the other three had cancelled at the last minute for various reasons. Although another responsible colleague, who had sat in on the course every day, spoke up on my behalf, it was subsequently hinted that I had run the course very badly and not carried it out in the intended way.

Before the karmic background of Ray's failure to become the new vizier, which was now casting its shadow into my present life, I learnt to see the situation in my present life in a new light even though no suitable objective solution was found on account of the inexplicable misunderstandings. This taught me that in ordinary life the almost unbearable feelings which are inevitably generated by situations of bullying in the workplace can be borne and transformed by karmic insight.

Cutting up apples

In my next example I shall repeat some things mentioned earlier about my teacher at school, who has since died. From the fourth to the sixth class he always taught us by using apples in various ways to demonstrate what he was saying. For arithmetic he used to divide up the apples with a penknife. When he had finished his demonstration and set us sums to do on our own, he sat at his table cutting the apples into even smaller pieces before eating them. At the same time he picked his ears with the same little knife. Many years later, after he had died, I heard that as a small boy he had been given a penknife by his grandfather which he subsequently lost. He had then gone to a lot of trouble to find and acquire a similar knife.

When I was researching the childhood years of Christian von Buch I came across the miller Wulf and saw young Christian cutting the miller's back as he tried to rape his cousin Johanna. The hint given by my schoolteacher's peculiar use of his penknife helped me recognize the miller in him.

Scolding

Having more than once in my life worked as a teacher, painter and colour designer in anthroposophical establishments for people with learning difficulties, I wanted to try and follow up karmically some relationships between the carers and those they cared for. I shall here recount one of the many interesting examples that led me to the Middle Ages.

An adult woman with a number of problems came from another establishment to the one where I was working. Initially it was impossible to go near her during lunch, let alone touch her, for she never stopped scolding. You could hear her shrill voice from afar, swearing like a trooper but not directed at anyone personally.

One of the carers managed to help her more than the others and restrain her from scolding quite so much at least while they were at work, for example with the cows in the byre.

I found the woman in a male incarnation in the Middle Ages. I saw the conditions that arose as Christianity, helped by violent means, spread eastwards towards what had formerly been Slav regions. The period is probably that of the Second Crusade around 1148. Several Slav lords have banded together to win back the lands taken by the nearest bishop, Wickmann of Zeitz. They fight unsuccessfully against the church prince who has set up his court on one of their former lands.

Several times they send in a cunning peasant to steal cattle, which he manages to do successfully for quite a time, to the satisfaction of his employers. Then one night he is caught by the bishop's men and hauled up in court before the bishop himself.

The bishop embarks on a long tirade with examples from history of how thieves used to be punished. Several times the peasant tries to justify himself, but is always interrupted by the bishop's hard voice, scolding loudly and saying that he knows all about his misdeeds. Unable to get a word in edgeways the peasant remains silent while he listens to the punishment to be meted out to him and while it is painfully administered as well. With his own hand the bishop whips him, and other nasty punishments follow, as was the custom in those days. The peasant escapes with his life but from that day forth remains far away from the bishop's lands. He returned as the scolding woman, and the bishop as her closest carer.

The kleptomaniac

In a social therapy establishment where I was doing some lazure painting work I was able to investigate a situation in connection with the life of Ronald Dixon.

There were two adults and their carer, and the two men had

rather contrasting problems. One of them, a good-natured man, was dumb but able to understand whatever was said to him. He liked working out of doors in the fresh air, while the other disliked outside work and preferred to stay indoors watching television or chatting with people. He always carried several coins in his pockets which he juggled between his fingers very skilfully.

The three men set off on their weekly trip to town where they went to a café and did some shopping. Meanwhile, having finished one coat of paint, I went to my guestroom for a little rest. There I discovered that my purse, which had been lying on the table, had been emptied out. I immediately realized that the second man was a kleptomaniac. After a phone call to the carer the matter was sorted out satisfactorily.

What had happened enabled me to investigate the situation karmically. The carer, I discovered, had been the captain of the Atlantic steamer who liked visiting a particular pub in Boston. Then I saw that the kleptomaniac had been the owner of the pub, who had always sat in the shadows behind the counter. She always wore black and had hardened her soul in order to survive in the male world of the seaport while carrying on her business. Sometimes she had to fight off drunken seamen with her fists. There was also a waiter in the pub, a Mexican singer who played his mandolin for her and sang Spanish songs. He no longer enjoyed his work and wanted to set off for Europe in the company of the captain. But the owner wanted him to stay and did everything in her power to persuade him to continue working in the pub because his singing attracted many customers. I recognized the Mexican in the dumb man.

Reincarnation and karma as a metamorphosis

The reader of course understands that I consider the incarnations retold in Chapter 3 to be segments of my own journey on earth.

But quite apart from this personal recognition it is also possible to look at the sequence objectively as a unit in order to trace certain themes that point to developments brought about through karma.

Several such ongoing themes are evident in these lives and they can be followed up in the light of a number of viewpoints, such as continuity, compensation or consistency. In the life of Shamu'radhin the foundations are laid for a variety of themes that are taken up again and again in subsequent lives. These themes undergo development, they shrink or even disappear for a time, then remain in the background before returning to the front of the stage in a new form in a later life. The many incarnations might be regarded as a great 'plant', or the various themes might be seen as many different plants that weave together in a manifold living construction. Goethe's idea of metamorphosis, the law of transformation of living forms which Rudolf Steiner took up and developed further, fits very well into this context.

The mercurial element, which has to do with handing on, creating contact, speaking more than one language, interpreting for others, diplomacy and writing letters, appears as a theme in several of the lives described. All these are variations on a continuing theme which reaches a kind of culmination in Christian von Buch in the Middle Ages. Another aspect of continuity shows in the way several of the incarnations happened in periods of great political or cultural change. Connected with this is the fact that several incarnations involved an initiation (Shamu'radhin, Areldingun, Ramishanda, Ray and Agamon). Here, again, continuity plays a part. There is also continuity in the way several of the incarnations involved direct service to the political system of the time.

In each of the lives there are themes that have karmic consequences in subsequent lives, but I can only give a few examples here.

The guilt towards the animal world which Shamu'radhin took on himself reached across to the next life but one as Areldingun, who had to try and catch bulls in Crete in order to tame them. He failed, and the consequence of this failure in Atlantean times reached over to Ramishanda who first succeeded in fulfilling this karma in connection with the Shiva mysteries. Out of this arose a positive relationship with animals which became a continuous theme that unfolded in all the lives, right up to the present time.

Then we have the compensation between action and inaction. We see it in Tanamira, who developed the telling of stories through spending the first third of her life with paralysed legs. The moral lapse in the use of magic by the helmsman from the Mercury Oracle has the effect of causing Tanamira's fall from the cliff. Shida Dong had to compensate for the violence committed against the southern people by entering the service of the Shinto Temple. Another kind of compensation, this time for being parted from someone, is seen in the way the death of Chaembasa in Ray's life is followed by Agamon finding the same individual as his life's partner in the next. There was also a compensation for the non-completion of Ray's initiation in the way Ariloma/Ronald received tuition from Takatimas. However, a full initiation was not vouchsafed him in the Red Indian setting, so in this respect compensation from what did not happen in Egypt has had to wait until the present incarnation.

An interesting metamorphosis of the Atlantean 'Magi Thagawan', the shamanic power of the hands, appears in Areldingun in his ability to master the signs of the elements through the language of the Druids, which is a language exercised by certain gestures of the arms and hands. Later, Shida Dong acquired skills on the one hand in handling silken materials and on the other in the art of carving wood to make vessels for the temple. In Ray this living-in-the-hands was taken up in being a scribe, while in the years of her imprisonment Mary Queen of Scots worked away at many different kinds of embroidery and sewing.

Music also recurs again and again. Shamu'radhin made and developed wind instruments which he played himself. Tanamira performed her stories in a kind of sing-song. There were a number of musicians connected with both Ramishanda and Shida Dong. Ray learned the secrets of the sistrum and rattle in Egypt. There were a number of minnesingers in the circles of Christian von Buch, and Mary Stuart played stringed instruments and loved dancing.

Two other themes also recur again and again in the incarnations. Firstly there are boats and ships either as a means of transport or in connection with temple events or initiations. In the very early times of human culture Retana was a boatbuilder. For Shamu'radhin, the gamamila was the main focus of his work, which means: of his destiny. Tanamira lived for many years with a seafaring people on the western coast of the Atlantean continent, until an opportunity arose for her to cross the sea herself. Areldingun was familiar with the sea. The theme almost disappears in Ramishanda's life, but reappears for Shida Dong in one of her husband's professions. Living by the Nile meant that Ray had to use river boats for many of his journeys. Even his travels with the help of a carrying chair represented a transformation of the same theme. In the Hathor temple at Dendera the ship for the gods was one of the main features of temple festivals.

For Agamon, Antonia and Christian von Buch the theme disappeared almost entirely into the background, although for Christian permission to use the Venetian fleet made it possible for him to win a battle against Ancona, one of the hostile seaports. Two sea voyages were of the greatest importance for Mary Queen of Scots: firstly her departure from Scotland as a child, and secondly her return to her kingdom as a widow. During the second voyage she was so indignant about the plight of the rowing slaves that she had them unchained. To his great delight, little Ronald Dixon was once allowed to steer the great Atlantic steamer all by himself, and during the years he spent amongst the Indians he much enjoyed the fun of paddling his canoe on the lake.

The second of the two themes is that of having both a public and a withdrawn lifestyle within one incarnation. The two tendencies belong together and keep reappearing in varying metamorphoses and interrelationships. For Shamu'radhin there was the polarity of his travels on the one hand and the creation of a gamamila on the other. It is interesting to note, by the way, that old gamamilas which could no longer be used or steered, were abandoned at the spot where they ceased to function and left to dry out. These spots came to be regarded as holy places where special initiations were carried out.

In Tanamira there was the polarity between outwardly having to travel great distances and inwardly being able to receive Imaginations; and in Areldingun the polarity between working for the people in Ireland and the trials with the wild cattle in Crete. Virtually the whole of Ramishanda's youth was given over to her training as a tamer, while her life as an adult elephant rider was devoted entirely to serving her people. Apart from certain dramatic happenings in her Chinese environment, Shida Dong led a rather harmonious life cultivating religion and faithfully carrying out her craft. Ray's life moved on the one hand between reading ancient papyri and doing practical artistic work, and on the other between political tasks at widely-separated locations and the temple service at Dendera. After many years of service in sport and diplomacy, Agamon spent his final years in creative retreat at Eleusis where he devoted his time to the study of Greek mythology.

For Antonia the breach between worldliness and retirement took another form. In the years of caesarean madness in Rome she made a life for herself in Greece that was strictly incognito. Christian von Buch had to spend a year in prison towards the end of his life; many long years after his youth in the monastery, this lent him the peace and quiet necessary for a return to cultivating his inner life.

Mary Stuart had to endure 18 years of imprisonment; Antonia/ Ioana spent a similar period as a clandestine Christian in the first century. Ronald Dixon withdrew entirely from the world in his final years, so much so that it was difficult for me to find those years in the Akashic Record.

The present task is to create a healthy relationship and harmonious dynamic between the two tendencies. The 'staff of Mercury' provides a helpful image with which to practise meditating in this respect.

There is a further detail in the life of Ronald Dixon which it is easy to leave on one side unnoticed: his encounter with the Quakers. It seems to me that this involves both an ending and a new beginning. His experiences in those quiet meetings, when it was not unusual to sit together for an hour or more without anyone saying a word, enabled him to find an entry to the life and ways of the Red Indians. At the same time, unnoticed by him, there was in his being an echo that had to do with his Atlantean past. The silence and contemplative repose of Ronald Dixon the Quaker was a complete metamorphosis of the Mercurial liveliness and Martian strength of the same individual which led him to his encounter and work with the Indians. Externally this integrated the past into the present of the nineteenth century. Internally it created the karma that was to lead the individual to the anthroposophy of the twentieth century.

The present karma of my betrayal of the Mysteries in Egypt

Right up to the final days of writing this book I kept asking myself why I have experienced so many karmic and spiritual facts. Since 1996 I have met many people who have told me their own spiritual experiences, but none was able to tell me the whole sequence of his or her incarnations, nor had any of them had such varied spiritual encounters as those I have recounted here. Am I therefore merely an abnormal example of the phenomena that are supposed to manifest at the end of the twentieth century? What am I to think of myself in being so 'abnormal' in this matter? Many students of Rudolf Steiner, including some who have known me for many years, doubt the authenticity of my experiences. Some think they are nothing more than fantasies, and maintain that I am cracking up psychologically. They very much want to help me and protect me from having any more such 'fantasies'.

I have often despaired during the course of the last two years; I could not and did not want to believe what I experienced. But the facts and observations of my Imaginations spoke their own language. So I tried to follow and investigate further, and this book is intended to be the first comprehensive documentation of this self-examination.

The individual in the Red Indian medicine man Takatimas, it turned out, was the same as in Kamitirida, mother of Chaembasa. I also saw that Ray's Hathor initiation was actually a success, but that he had not abandoned his egoistic longing to find his dead lover. In the midst of his spiritual visions Ray realized that because of this his initiation was in some respects forced, and he saw that he would not be allowed to live with this insight. Therefore in that incarnation he was not granted the fruits of that initiation. However, because the leaders of Dendera had not seen through him in advance, they had made themselves guilty towards him. In later times, too, even in Greece, he was unable to benefit from the positive karma of his initiation. The Egyptian mysteries at the time of Ray were still directly connected with the spiritual world from which the oracle wisdom of Atlantean times also stemmed. But this was no longer the case in Eleusis at the time of Agamon. So Agamon's initiation at Eleusis must be interpreted as belonging to a different karmic context.

Not until his encounter with Takatimas was Ronald once again offered an opportunity to receive an initiation that had maintained a direct line back to the Atlantean mysteries. But he did not immediately seize this chance because for moral reasons he first wanted to help his friend Gerasawak, and meanwhile Takatimas died. So even in that incarnation there was no chance of taking up the initiation karma of Egyptian times.

By laying the foundations for new mysteries, Rudolf Steiner's anthroposophy has the potential of subsuming all ancient mystery possibilities, and because of this a new opportunity emerged for me to harvest the fruits of my Egyptian karma. I have lived my life in accordance with anthroposophy, and have conducted anthroposophical studies, meditations and karma exercises to the best of my ability as a part of my practical artistic activities. It was on this path that my first spiritual experiences arose. I must ascribe the actual initiation described in this book to the special circumstances of my Egyptian karma.

By means of consciously seeking knowledge of karma, anyone can find dormant destiny themes that carry within them fruits for the present and the future, regardless of whether initiation was received in earlier lives or not. One might say that those who were once initiates now have the karma of renewing their initiation individually or in collaboration with their sisters and brothers who also seek initiation. Not to do this would mean to omit a part of the tasks awaiting us at the turning point to the new millennium.

6

Methods and reflections

...in an instant there really lies before one,
with time transformed into space,
the whole of one's earthly life in mighty pictures.
Rudolf Steiner

Correcting errors

As already stated earlier, this book was not intended to be a scientific discourse. Nevertheless, I want to mention a few points here to show the reader why I consider the work I do to be scientific research. Work is scientific firstly when one comes to grips with the findings of other researchers and shows one's position in relation to them; and, secondly, when one constantly checks and re-checks one's own findings and conclusions, revises them where necessary, and shows the process by which one has arrived at the revision. I would like to enlarge on this here before mentioning a topical case in point.

It was not my purpose with this book to compare my findings with those of others or to get others to check them. Although less likely in the case of the themes and questions pertaining to Atlantis, it would certainly have been possible, and also with regard to many aspects of the twelfth century. But I decided initially to confine myself merely to reporting. We shall see whether it becomes possible in the future to write scientific theses on these many historical themes.

My intention was to give sufficient examples of how, by using

Rudolf Steiner's exercises and starting points, I linked my work with a method derived from anthroposophy and spiritual science which has led to the results described. In order to practise, for example, the so-called 'four-day exercise' I had to come to grips with Rudolf Steiner's own description of it, which is in fact quite generalized. When my own method of practice led to results I then dared to formulate a new description of the exercise in 13 steps. In lectures, seminars and conversations I have passed this interpretation on to many people, a number of whom have meanwhile achieved results of their own. This means to say that something which has proved successful for me has been taken up by others and practised in the same way up to the point where specific karmic results have emerged, which were then reported back to me. The formulation of a practical way of proceeding which others can follow is, to my mind, one of the first criteria for scientific work.

For example my descriptions of 'building a hut' have now been confirmed by many individuals, either because they had already had similar experiences of their own or because they took up my suggestions which they have now confirmed through many new and individual experiences which they have reported to me and in which they have permitted me to accompany them. The profusion of karma research and spiritual seeking that is going on today and of which I have become aware through my work would easily fill another book. It would have to include descriptions of controversial findings that have occurred when, for example, different karmic backgrounds for the same person have emerged.

There is an aspect of my work that has led me to develop my ability to form judgements. It can happen that episodes in an Imagination are only fragmentary. If I have been unable to place or interpret these I have initially left them on one side. Some of them have reappeared in a wider context in subsequent research; others I have retained as questions living in me which will find their place later or else be discarded as false or visionary inter-ference in my endeavours in Imagination. That this kind of inner picture can also emerge taught me to treat supersensible experiences with scepticism and not be too hasty in drawing conclusions until more material has accrued. As time has gone on I have learnt to observe and to some extent control my own life of inner pictures which often wants to rush into action too quickly.

I have checked to my satisfaction the examples made public in this book by very thorough methods and in different modes of consciousness and have pondered them in my thoughts before deciding whether it is suitable to hand them over to others. The rules I applied are those I used to use as an artist in deciding whether pictures were suitable for exhibition. All those which were not finished or which only depicted personal steps along the way had to remain in the studio-pictures, in other words, on which the paint 'had not yet dried'. I now regard this book with its many examples from Imagination to be 'dry' enough for publication.

In the years prior to my first Imaginations, when I was still using normal study in my investigations about the twelfth cen-tury, I privately made a number of claims concerning my rein-carnations between then and now. But some of those claims had to be revised in the light of later results reached through Imagi-nation, and those results have since stood up to being thought through very thoroughly in ways that have underpinned the meditative findings.

In the case of Hildegard of Bingen, for example, I made a connection between her and a person today who is deeply reli-gious and does impressive good works. I even thought I saw several links between that person's present circle and people who were near Hildegard. However, these assertions later proved to be erroneous when I recognized another individual, working in a similar way and living geographically not very far away from the first, as the re-born Hildegard of Bingen. What decided me was not the person's present occupation with medicinal plants, which I had found as a theme that linked both incarnations, but the very intimate friendship I discovered this person had with someone whom I recognized as the re-incarnated Conrad of Wittelsbach. Conrad was Archbishop of Mainz from 1160 to 1165 and had been able in Hildegard's later years to counter to a considerable extent the negative opinions people held about her.

Another phenomenon that has caused me to be mistaken more than once is the way indications about a person's name in the present incarnation come into Imaginations about that person's past incarnation. For example when Mary Stuart met John Knox on the steps I clearly heard his first name in my inner hearing. Still in the meditation I immediately connected the name with a relative of mine with whom I am quite good friends. Several months passed before this idea was proved false. I was giving a lecture in a town where I have met several people with whom I am karmically connected. After the lecture I had a talk with a person who had the same forename as my relative. In his positive stance towards me I recognized the negative attitude John Knox had shown to Mary Stuart. His recognition of my present activities, which suddenly flashed up like lightning out of a brief remark, ignited in me an intuitive understanding of certain far-reaching karmic secrets. I grasped a feeling of inner forgiveness which rose up in me, and this bridged the centuries in a single instant, creating possibilities for a positive will towards future collaboration.

Right up to the final revision of this book I was convinced that I had recognized certain karmic connections of Henry Stewart, Lord Darnley, Mary Stuart's second husband (murdered on 10 February 1567), and also of James Hepburn, Earl of Bothwell, her third husband. I had linked them with two individuals whom I know in my present life.

The interpretation I had put on certain aspects of my own Imaginations had made this error even more credible. A tragic event a few years earlier connected with a woman I knew had caused me to be even more convinced about her being the re-incarnation of Darnley. She was divorced from her husband but still lived close by and thus kept in touch with his work. He had bought a motor-boat together with his partner with the intention of expanding their business, but one day both men were killed by an explosion on board. I thought these must be the two men who had caused the explosion in Scotland in the sixteenth century before going on to suffocate Darnley.

Quite other events connected with other people subsequently showed me a different karmic route both to Darnley and Bothwell, as well as to some of their contemporaries in Scotland and England, thus disproving my earlier assumptions. What enabled me to begin new investigations were the controversies that erupted when I began to go public with my karma research. Those disputes brought with them karmic knowledge about many people connected with those times, knowledge that now calls for a great deal of patience and composure owing to the very complicated inter-relationships that still have to be endured.

I want to make a point here of calling this mistake of mine an 'exemplary error' because it involved jumping to conclusions too quickly both in how I observed the Imaginations and in how I drew conclusions from the physical events which I thought were connected with what the Imaginations had shown me. It illus-trates the heavy responsibility you embark on by telling others about your research results. I am also fully aware of the significance in the occult sense of the responsibility involved.

Nowadays I try to be much more careful and circumspect about what I do with my knowledge about karma than I was in the early months of bringing my work out into the open. As a rule the discovery of karmic connections provides entirely new keys with which to unlock an understanding of past and present motivations. In the case of Mary Stuart many complications are still waiting to be unravelled which have led to all kinds of difficulties in subsequent lives including my present life both with regard to the research itself and also in relation to the scale of what will need to be dealt with day by day. For example, I think I have discovered that one's birth horoscope showing the position of the planets in the zodiac corresponds with the fundamental character of former incarnations. In my case Saturn is in Scorpio, which would certainly fit in with Mary Stuart's biography. My interpretation is that, in her life, death was constantly present and also lived through in tangled and complicated intrigues such as the murders of her Italian secretary David Riccio on 7 March 1566 and of her husband Darnley a year later, as well as in various matters during her period of imprisonment which led to the execution of many individuals. I shall have to do more research into all this if I want to find specific karmic threads.

Since the spiritual situation involving the forces of Saturn in Scorpio is visible to the eye of the spirit in its purest form, embarking today on researching the karmic relationships around Mary Queen of Scots will be hampered by tangled present-day life circumstances. If I am to get to the bottom of these things I shall need inner strength for developing freedom by overcoming certain death forces in my own being. The 'exemplary error' described above has clarified certain things for me, but that does not mean that I have by any means finished with following up all the karmic threads that seem important for recognizing old moral guilt brought about by myself or by others. (Researching and describing the role of guilt in karmic development is one of the most complicated themes in this area, which is why I shall not go into it more deeply here, apart from the matters connected with guilt which have already been described in earlier chapters.)

The self

All my life one of my main concerns has been the search for and understanding of the self as the soul centre of one's consciousness. By reading the written works of Rudolf Steiner, which I did already in my youth, I initially gained a philosophical understanding of the human self. Studying Hermann Poppelbaum's *Man and Animal* on the one hand and a whole range of other literature on the other provided further knowledge that helped me verify my ideas and inner pictures in this matter.

In the autumn of 1978, when I was quite new to creative artistic work, Urban Forsén at the Robygge bookshop asked me whether I would write short blurbs on some of Rudolf Steiner's books and lecture series for use in a mail-order catalogue. I spent many an autumn evening working on these texts, and this gave me a further opportunity to examine Steiner's basic books. I re-read once again many chapters in *The Theory of Knowledge*, *Truth and Science*, *The Philosophy of Freedom*, *Christianity as Mystical Fact*, as well as other works by him, and then endeavoured to write short sentences formulating his concerns comprehensibly in my own words. This gave me my first insights into the creative possibilities of the human self in the life of thought.

In March 1979 I read Steiner's *Anthroposophy and the Inner Life*, and in a discussion group at the Järna Seminar gave a short talk about questions raised in the first lecture, which had appealed to me. I was asking myself at that time how the self relates to the consciousness soul and to the activity of remembering.

Some years later, when I was writing my essays about 'the battle against the self' for the journal *Antropos*, I delved into Steiner's *Leading Thoughts* and found Carl Unger's essay on the language of the consciousness soul a great help in trying to school my thinking further. I carried on these efforts to understand what it means to school the thinking side by side with my artistic activities, which helped me work at schooling my feelings. At the same time, all the practical craft work connected with the exhibitions, the carpentry work and all the other things that needed doing, provided a very varied schooling of the will life which unfolded during all those years of social interaction with artist friends and colleagues.

The various studies I carried out with the focus on writing those essays in 1982 led me to conclude that the self of which we are aware in our normal consciousness appears to be merely a fragment of a far greater being. In the years that followed, the search for that more comprehensive being of self became a deep inner concern for me.

I am emphasizing this undercurrent in my life yet again because I want to make it clear that I spared myself no effort in observing the self in all its manifestations, both in myself and in other people. I delved into Rudolf Steiner's image of the human being with the help of living examples shown to me during my time working with people with special needs and during a series of important lectures on the senses given by Hans Glaser, also in 1982.

During the 1980s the philosophical concept of the self remained for me a central concern which I felt I must constantly work with and develop. In 1996 this concept was challenged when I received the first Imaginations. Would I now have to jettison the concept I had worked out thus far, or could it help me in this situation of an entirely new kind of consciousness? I found that in the consciousness of Imagination there was no need to jettison my former experience of thinking as an activity of the self, for I was able to transform it. With hindsight I saw that the concept of the self in thinking had been a seed that in the con- sciousness of Imagination now developed into a plant. The self availed itself of thinking, absorbed thinking, and then let think- ing shine out as light with which it surrounded itself; this light caused the self to appear as a living, expanding being. This is my endeavour to describe the process in my own imperfect words. In Steiner's works there are many and much better descriptions of how consciousness of the self is maintained in the world of Imagination.

This section is included here to explain how important it was to me in the autumn of 1996 to carry on developing and supporting the self within me when I was plucking up courage to continue with my work in Imagination which was soon to put me to the test spiritually and psychologically in many ways. In addition to carrying out the meditative work it was also mandatory for me to re-read some of Steiner's writings and lectures yet again because I continued to have doubts about my experiences.

The schooling of thinking and the life tableau

The following descriptions of two schooling themes I have worked with are included here to demonstrate the part that thinking plays in the kind of meditation I practise. Over a number of years people have criticized me repeatedly by finding the way I school my thinking unsatisfactory. I want to show that spiritual research as Rudolf Steiner inaugurated it, and as I now practise it, cannot attain a suitably high degree as a science of the spirit if thinking itself is not schooled. Which of course does not mean to say that I myself have been adequately successful in schooling my own thinking.

My path of spiritual research encompasses two themes that have progressed side by side. On the one hand there is my artistic work and practice through the medium of painting, and on the other there are the karma exercises in which for me it has always been important to include thinking when viewing internal and external processes. The schooling of thinking has never constituted the main issue for me, since my path has tended to involve the will more strongly, but once I began to have super-sensible experiences it came to the fore in my work because of the fact that I wanted to express these experiences in language. I want to be able to give information in a manner comprehensible to anyone. Therefore I have to continue with schooling my thinking, on the one hand so that I can follow up my experiences consciously, and on the other so that I can enable others to tread the same path. When I described experiences with elemental beings I gave an example showing why it is essential to school the thinking in connection with anthroposophical spiritual research. It will be easier to understand what I shall now state if those interested will first read the lectures by Rudolf Steiner which I shall mention.

On the one hand I want to point to the schooling of thinking through wonder, through reverence for the foundations of the cosmos, through wisdom-filled harmony with cosmic evolution, and through devotion to cosmic processes. These themes are treated in lectures Steiner gave in Hanover on 27 and 28 December 1911.* On the other hand there is the matter of viewing the life tableau about which Steiner spoke in Basle on 9 April 1923.†

I practised the four 'steps in schooling one's thinking' in different ways. One simple, preparatory method is to go more deeply into the thoughts or statements people make which one finds strange. The more difficult part is to transform these steps into soul moods and bring them into the whole process of meditation. I practised this kind of preparatory work in the schooling of thought when I was examining the biographies of

---

* *The World of the Senses and the World of the Spirit*, N. Vancouver: Steiner Book Centre 1979.

† *Was wollte das Goetheanum und was soll die Anthroposophie*, Dornach: Rudolf Steiner Verlag 1986.

people like Munch, van Gogh, Ibsen, Strindberg, Steiner and Walter Ljungquist. I tried to understand the way the artist or author in question thought, and then go as far as I could towards finding my own concepts for this thinking.

In an unpublished article on Ljungquist, for example, I concerned myself with one of his novels in which the protagonist describes a life crisis from two different standpoints of awareness. First he describes the crisis in his diary. Then, several years later, he re-reads the diary and from this new standpoint corrects what he remembers and reaches a new interpretation of the crisis. For me the novel was also a fictionalized description of a life crisis undergone by the author himself. I myself was not in any crisis at the time, but I endeavoured to conceptualize the various levels of a psychological crisis situation such as that laid open for me in those literary studies. I saw a crisis as a state that arises in the human soul when it is abandoned and feels it has reached the end of the road. The only way of carrying on is to make a free decision to do so and possibly to ask others for help.

When one begins to experience the elemental world one has to withhold one's thinking from the truth of the world thoughts in which the elemental beings live and work. When I encountered elemental beings I found that my normal thinking, connected with the intellect and thought pictures, could not gain access to them. My reflective thoughts were, you could say, mirrored back into my own soul, and I was expected to show them another kind of thinking, a kind of thinking which did not reflect back. Instead I was to let my thinking flow into their stream of thinking which in my normal way of thinking I could not grasp. A reversal of consciousness was required.

Let me use an image taken from painting to illustrate this kind of living thinking. When you paint with watercolours you have several pots of liquid paint in different colours and you use a brush to apply these to the paper in various shapes and forms.

The finished picture is rather dry and dull when compared on the one hand with the lively movement of the hand as it makes the brushstrokes and on the other with the vibrant purity of the colours in the paint-pots. I discovered that the thinking to be placed at the disposal of the elemental beings had to be as pure and as fluid as the colours in the paint-pots. I was not welcome in the elemental world with the finished picture of my dry concepts, and were I to force my way in without having schooled my thinking I would only cause damage which would harm the elemental beings.

During my meditations my spiritual guides gave me certain exercises which I needed if I wanted to remain strong enough to cope with the impressions coming from the elemental world. They were among what have been termed the 'subsidiary exercises'.

At this stage I now also had the experience described by Rudolf Steiner in the lecture on 9 April 1923 mentioned above:

> Now that one has passed through this portal of knowing, and on into the spiritual world, the first experience one has is a review, like a tableau, of one's whole life on earth up to that point. It is scarcely too stark to say that in an instant there really lies before one, with time transformed into space, the whole of one's earthly life in mighty pictures. Yet these pictures are quite distinct from anything one might gain about this life by sitting down and trying to call up into memory everything from it, going back in a continuous sequence almost to the moment of birth.

It is not surprising that the biographical karma exercise is a good preparation for an experience of this spiritual fact. In the life-tableau, which is a kind of Imagination, one can discover the principal theme running through one's life. This theme arises in accordance with karmic laws we receive in an Imagination before birth which gives us a preview of our coming incarnation.

Metamorphosed into images of life in general it resembles a folk-tale. I even discovered that the motifs in my own karma fit the story in an existing folk-tale.

With these brief hints I wanted to show that if thinking is not schooled sufficiently before spiritual experiences begin, then it certainly must be schooled thereafter. As he treads his path, a spiritual pupil will come up against experiences and trials which require clear and sober thinking, and this appears to me to be more important than the fruits of school-ing the feeling and will. Nevertheless I want to stress in this connection that there is also as yet too little understanding of another prerequisite for success in spiritual research, and that is working and practising in art, and looking at art, in the way Rudolf Steiner and many of his heirs have shown us over the past century.

The new art of eurythmy is foremost for those who want to make progress in the spiritual world. This art is a source out of which a schooling of all three soul powers can always be practised and developed in a manner that accords with the consciousness soul. Eurythmy cannot arise without thinking, feeling and will in the human being's quest for the spirit. Conversely, where eurythmy is worked at, the soul's threefold nature is developed in a way that can bring about genuine contact with the spiritual world, and for this contact to become clair-voyant only a small step is then needed to find a vantage point in the self that enables one to see oneself critically.

The faculty of Imagination as a light-soul-process

To help the reader understand what an Imagination is and what it means to activate the faculty of Imagination I shall here explain an important concept brought forward by Rudolf Steiner in a lecture on 30 November 1919: 'The Ancient Yoga Culture and the New Yoga Will.'*

In this lecture Steiner described how the constitution of the human soul gradually changed throughout the post-Atlantean cultural epochs. He distinguished the way the soul relates to itself and to the world in what he called the pre-Christian 'air-soul-process' and the post-Christian 'light-soul-process'. This is best clarified by quoting Steiner directly:

> There was a time before the Mystery of Golgotha when the earth possessed an atmosphere filled with soul that was part of the human soul; but that atmosphere has become empty of soul, of the soul element shared by human beings; for the element of soul that formerly lived in the air has taken up its habitation in the light which surrounds us during the daylight hours. It was Christ's uniting himself with the earth that made this possible. Thus both air and light have undergone a soul-spiritual change in the course of the evolution of the earth.

Steiner was speaking in this lecture about the historical fact that human beings lost their awareness of the pre-existence of their souls to the degree that their breathing processes ceased to be filled with soul. He maintained that the last remnants of a primeval culture have disappeared during the course of recent centuries in which scientific, intellectual thinking has gained ground. But now human beings can reach a new understanding of the Mystery of Golgotha and thus gain the ability to find the spirit in matter. The following quotations about this step which modern human beings can take in their meditative life are from the lecture mentioned above.

> But once we are again endowed with ensouled sense perceptions, a crossing-point will be re-established, and in that intersection we

---

* *The Archangel Michael. His Mission and Ours*, op.cit.

will all take hold of the human will that streams up out of the third level of consciousness which I have been describing these past several days. At the same time, this will provide us with the subjective-objective element that Goethe so longed for ... Cosmic thoughts enter us from without, the human will works outward from within, and that will and the cosmic thoughts meet and overlap at a crossing point, just as once upon a time an objective element met and crossed a subjective element in the breathing process. We must learn to feel how our will works through our eyes, and how true it is that the activity of the senses delicately mingles with the passivity, whereby cosmic thoughts and human will meet. Indeed, we must develop a new yoga-will.

In further clarifying this kind of future Michaelic culture of the will, Steiner gave a number of examples. First there is the example of the flame in connection with which he described the process Goethe employed to open the subject of his theory of colours—the fading after-images of the physiological colours:

But it is not just a subjective process; it is an objective process. You have the possibility of recognizing how something that takes place within you is simultaneously a subtle cosmic process...

Then Steiner gave another example:

If I say to a person that somebody told me something or other (it doesn't matter whether it is true or not), that constitutes a judgement, a moral or intellectual act, performed inside me. That too, fades away like the image of the flame. It is an objective process in the universe. When you think a good thought about someone, and it then fades away, it exists in the cosmic ether as an objective process. And when you have a bad thought, it too is an objective process that fades away.

The following statements can stand as a summary for our time of what Steiner had been saying. They characterize my individual karmic and spiritual experiences:

To imbue ourselves with such an awareness is to open the door to the Michael culture. If we take light as generally representing sense perception, we must go forward to an understanding of light as ensouled, just as it was wholly a matter of course for people of the second and third pre-Christian millennia to conceive of the air as ensouled ... Broadly speaking we may say: air-soul-process, light-soul-process. This is what we can observe in the evolution of the earth, and midway between these two processes, bringing about the transition from one to the other, the Mystery of Golgotha occurs.

In my lifetime I have in various ways cultivated a relationship with this light-soul-process. Firstly for two decades I carried out all kinds of exercises, experiments and observations in the field of art and in connection with Goethe's theory of colours. There is no doubt that living in the way I did with external colour phenomena and images enabled me to practise certain inner faculties which later helped me awaken in my soul the faculty of Imagination.

I have also endeavoured to deepen my awareness of the seasons of the year, which I have never found easy even though I have lived most of my life in rural areas. Working with the themes of Rudolf Steiner's *Soul Calendar* and also with the *Foundation Stone Meditation*, as well as my efforts in special needs and adult education, have led to ongoing concern for the relationship between nature, the world and the human being.

In connection with a specific life-situation, for example, I was travelling by train one day when I found myself able to allow echoes of certain meditative attitudes to enter into my soul with regard to that specific situation. I was on my way to visit one of my friends, and I was examining my inner mood by means of various deepening and widening soul processes. The train was travelling through a beautiful spring landscape. I watched the setting sun sending bright beams northwards and southwards through little gaps in the thick clouds. A spectacle of lights unfolded which I experienced as though it were a stage setting for my personal destiny situation at that moment. As the train approached my destination the play of lights sought out new openings in the clouds, which in my imagination I saw as God's sense organs. Finally a heart of ruby red shone out, together with a tiny star sparkling in purple, announcing that the evening twilight had arrived. The ensuing meeting was accompanied by these images of the sunlight in a way that made it seem as though each self wanted to manifest as a sun penetrating the clouds.

There will be many such situations in any biography, situations in which a person can experience soul and nature mirroring one another. If we cultivate such situations or other experiences or encounters through remembering them we will not find it hard to take a further step towards artistic, social or meditative exercises.

Some of the karma exercises suggested by Rudolf Steiner which I found helpful actually involve precisely this: to work consciously with memories of this kind, either quite recent ones or those that stem from earlier periods of one's life, even as far back as childhood.

I will now give a more detailed description of the four-day karma exercise discussed in the lecture of 9 May 1924, linking it with themes from Steiner's *Foundation Stone Meditation*.

The four-day karma exercise

When I began talking about my experiences in courses and lectures, I tried to depict my way of carrying out the four-day exercise in the form of an illustration. The result was a sequence of 13 steps, which can also be helpful in linking this exercise with the *Foundation Stone Meditation*.

The following table shows the steps in relation to the transformation—through the various members right down to the physical body—undergone by the memory picture made by the self of a specific encounter, in keeping with the description in Steiner's lecture. Some of the main themes from the *Foundation Stone Meditation* are shown on the right as belonging to specific steps.

Step 1	Day 1	Encounter	SELF
Step 2		1st Evening meditation	'Spirit-remembering'
Step 3	Night 1	Sleep	ASTRAL BODY
Step 4	Day 2	Waking up	'Spirit-considering'
Step 5		Everyday life/work	
Step 6		2nd Evening meditation	
Step 7	Night 2	Sleep	ETHER BODY
Step 8	Day 3	Waking up	'Spirit-beholding'
Step 9		Everyday life/work	
Step 10		3rd Evening meditation	
Step 11	Night 3	Sleep	PHYSICAL BODY
Step 12	Day 4	Waking up/Morning meditation	
Step 13		Possible Imagination	'Christ-Sun'

While working with the *Foundation Stone Meditation* I discovered that it describes a cosmic karma exercise. I reached an understanding similar to that of Athys Floride in his beautiful book *Stufen der Meditation* (Stages of Meditation). This meditation not only provides protection for karma research, as he rightly describes. It is also a source of such research if it is incorporated into the four-day exercise. In fact, the importance of the *Foundation Stone Meditation* for all future spiritual research cannot be overestimated. It is a key, fitting for our time, with which to unlock knowledge of higher worlds.

For many years the text of the *Foundation Stone Meditation* lay on my bedside table for reading in the evening. I had lived with the relevant daily rhythms and tried to include them in a meditative process. At the time I failed in this. Not until I had been successful with the four-day exercise was I able to recognize many connections and themes in those verses.

7

Esoteric questions

Each day holds the chance for a new beginning.

Hans Glaser

This chapter is directed primarily to students of Rudolf Steiner, whom I want to address specifically regarding certain questions.

I am aware that this book represents a new departure within the realm of anthroposophy, out of which it has arisen. I am breaking with a tradition that Rudolf Steiner regarded as valid, namely that it is not done to speak or write about one's own former lives. Some people maintain, and endeavour to prove, that Steiner spoke indirectly in lectures for members of the Anthroposophical Society, e.g. during the Christmas Conference at Dornach in 1923–24, about his own incarnations and those of some members of his audience, without expressly linking this with his current individuality or those of the others. Walter Johannes Stein, one of Steiner's pupils, is said to have mentioned an earlier incarnation of his own in an essay in a journal, but this is one of the exceptions in anthroposophical history.

On the other hand there is, as far as I know, no new rule stating that we must now publicize our incarnations. I have nevertheless decided to publish the results of my research as a contribution to karma research in the sense Rudolf Steiner intended. I reached my results by applying the research methods suggested by him. I also regard this book as an encouragement to other karma researchers. So the honest thing to do is introduce myself before publishing karmic connections concerning other individuals.

Joseph Beuys, and the way in which he put himself into his art, serves me as an example for this project, which should be seen as an artistic one. My hope is that anthroposophical karma research will come to be formed by the forces of the individual self, where individuals gain the courage to link something concrete from the karmic past with the present-day anthroposophical situation in which they find themselves as karma researchers.

I believe that we as anthroposophists have so far not placed Rudolf Steiner's karma research sufficiently at the centre of our work. He gave his first karma lecture on 16 February 1924, the very day on which he also gave the first class lesson within the School of Spiritual Science. Over 70 years later there has, as far as I know, been very little concrete research involving the means of spiritual science which he described in those lectures and in that School. The School of Spiritual Science, in which karma research ought to be given absolute priority, has to date had only one spiritual researcher, Rudolf Steiner himself, who died 75 years ago. As compared with the world at large, which has hitherto taken very little notice of anthroposophy, this is an anachronism. In view of this fact we anthroposophists should try to learn what it means to feel ashamed. I find this situation shaming. Rudolf Steiner would surely not be glad to find that there had been no further spiritual researchers after him. I believe he wanted there to be many who carried on his work.

As I see it, the greatest problem in anthroposophy today is that it has become too much a matter of belonging to a group. For many anthroposophists it functions as a kind of group code of morals. The 'ethical individualism' which Steiner proclaimed in his book *The Philosophy of Freedom* as a free, individual and infinitely variable model for action cannot be said to have become a social reality yet. So karmic forces and disturbances still have exactly the same effect in anthroposophical circles and life partnerships as they do everywhere else in modern society. In my opinion there is very little knowledge of karma or karma research as an impulse for social change in the sense intended by Steiner. If we read the descriptions in the karma lectures that refer prophetically to the present time and try to glean from them a characteristic picture of this age, we are forced to conclude that an entirely different karma consciousness ought to have developed by now. We have, in my opinion, reached a very tragic dead end, and in order to extricate ourselves from this a radical step appears to be called for: I have learned certain karmic facts which I do not want to keep to myself; I cannot dress them up in a guise that might render them acceptable in polite society; all I can do is try to make them comprehensible by publishing them in their entirety.

With this karmic autobiography I am thus breaking free of previous constraints because I believe that this is a way of contributing to a transformation that is necessary for our time. A pupil or master in what have been called the 'new mysteries' is, in the sense of *The Philosophy of Freedom*, permitted to 'go public' if he so wishes provided he does this with the intention of doing something that is for the good of others. Something regarded as being esoteric is thus forced out into the cold light of day and must be able to withstand the sternest glare of publicity. The intimacies of former incarnations are certainly esoteric in the truest sense. But I think it is possible and indeed necessary today to make such intimacies public so long as the individual himself shoulders the responsibility for acting in this way. Meanwhile one must trust that the spiritual world will safeguard the mystery nature of what one has done. For such action may, after all, turn out with hindsight to have been a social gaffe.

As Josef Beuys and others after him have pointed out, initiation into the new mysteries could take place in the middle of a railway station or in any other public place. When something like that happens the question is: How can such a person describe his experiences in a way that shows him to be a legitimate initiate and yet avoids his being embraced by a crowd of luciferic devotees or rejected and mocked by ahrimanic opponents? I hope that the manner in which this book is written will help to mitigate these tendencies, which I have unfortunately already experienced a number of times during or after lectures or courses I have been involved in. I am convinced that the spiritual world, or rather the michaelic guides of our age who share responsibility for the evolution of humanity, do now give incarnated individuals who feel able to be responsible on earth for the Michael School the freedom to look after their own karmic realizations and even publish them. Since 1996 I have been speaking publicly about myself, and the spiritual world has so far not withdrawn from me. Indeed, I have continued to feel inspired by its presence, and have been furnished with many new encounters that have confirmed my research and the way I have gone about things. What I understand to be collaboration with spiritual beings is illustrated in this book by many examples.

In the 1970s and 80s I entertained certain expectations for the future as I entered hopefully into what Rudolf Steiner had prophesied for the end of the twentieth century as a new level of anthroposophical contribution to general culture arising from the expected *rapprochement* of Platonic and Aristotelian souls. In the 1990s these expectations were fulfilled in an entirely unexpected way when I suddenly realized that I myself was one of those who could contribute to these events. Between 1994 and 1997, first by study and then through higher consciousness, I discovered the karmic background to the twelfth century events described and my own involvement in them. It then became clear to me that I could try to contribute to contemporary events by making this knowledge known. I decided to do so, and since 1997 I have been devoting all my time to karma research, having virtually set aside my earlier work as an artist and art teacher.

My experiences in meditative work, combined with the critical spiritual situation and psychological and health needs of humanity in the 1990s, showed me that knowledge about karma will have to enter much more clearly into consciousness if anthroposophical contributions to general culture are to become more influential. I told myself that it is now imperative to make the transition from general questions affecting humanity to considerations of what is real for the individual. Nevertheless, this imperative which the needs of our time have shown to me must not be asserted as something compulsory. It is up to individuals to decide in freedom where they want to go or what they want to accept by way of ideas, thoughts and suggestions. In this sense I have described only the motifs I myself have researched, and these can be critically and freely accepted or rejected. As I have already said, however, I maintain that they are not private but belong to the general culture of the long-awaited 1990s. It is in this sense that I publish them out of an inner sense of duty towards the spiritual world and towards any fellow men and women who find themselves following the same quest.

Hence the three directions in which this book's dedication is directed: firstly to a friend who has died and thus represents connections with the spiritual world, secondly to my contemporaries and friends who have stood and will continue to stand shoulder to shoulder with me in wrestling for the new, and thirdly to my children as an expression of the next generation who can base their steps into the new century on karmic forces if we prepare the ground well for them.

To help the reader understand me in my decision to act in a manner different from that chosen by Steiner, I shall now mention a few more of the considerations I have mulled over in the last few years. The idea of writing a karmic autobiography took shape during the autumn of 1996 when work with a number of Rudolf Steiner's karma exercises had led to numerous experiences in Imagination which showed me many of my own earlier incarnations as well as those of other people with whom I am connected. Further meditative work then led to an abundance of spiritual encounters with the dead, with elementals and with higher spiritual beings both evil and good, as well as spiritual experiences which, in view of Steiner's descriptions, I feel I can call initiation experiences.

After using my faculty of thinking to begin checking these results of spiritual research I started telling members of Anthroposophical Society branches about them in lectures, seminars, conversations and consultations in Sweden and Norway. It occurred to me that this was the right way to communicate spiritual experiences. I re-read many of Steiner's lectures and books and found statements which I had previously not noticed but which I now saw as confirmation of what I was doing. In one of his earliest karma lectures he even stressed that the best way of speaking about karmic discoveries was to tell them in the form of a story, since this might be the only way of passing on such intimate matters in view of our age being so strongly marked by intellectualism.

Initially I therefore hesitated to report on my experiences in writing. Then in December 1996 I made the experiment of giving a number of friends in the School of Spiritual Science in Sweden amongst whom I felt at home a first short report of my experiences in the form of a private publication. This did not lead to any further collaboration with those friends in the field of karma research, something I had been endeavouring to set in motion for some time.

When I told another friend who was familiar with my earlier artistic and literary efforts about my karmic Imaginations, he suggested I might write novels. I did not want to do this because I felt that it would fail to do justice to a contemporary inner need I thought I had perceived. Amongst the people around me I had met many who longed to hear directly about personal spiritual and karmic experiences. In meditation I asked the spiritual world whether that world would help me if I passed on my knowledge publicly. How I experienced an answer has been described at the appropriate point in this book.

When Nothart Rohlfs then invited me to write on karma questions for the journal *Die Drei* I did not find it difficult to comply. In this way, side by side with rather more traditional essays by other authors on the same theme, appeared my first, very abbreviated but in anthroposophical circles rather unusual essay about my research into karma. In it I described my twelfth-century incarnation as Christian von Buch. The issue of the journal appeared as a contribution to a Goetheanum conference on reincarnation and karma at Easter of that year in Berlin, in which I also participated as the leader of a conversation group.

Although the essay drew no comment from anthroposophical publications I found that individuals appreciated my oral descriptions and requested further written ones, so I felt it was my task to try and publish more of my research. I wanted to begin by writing something about Atlantis both because this was a subject close to my heart and also because I thought that it would find broader acceptance than, for example, descriptions of the Middle Ages. However, nothing was published immediately, despite some promising negotiations and an interview—not published—with the journal *Das Goetheanum* with which I had made contact in Berlin.

So in August 1997, in the town in Norway where I was born, I began to write the first draft of this book because I wanted to give other people an overview of my experiences and research. My initial plan was to recount the incarnations I had found as individual stories standing alone. Of my present life I only intended to say as much as would provide a basis for understanding the path of exercises I had followed. I was only going to give a few examples and hints regarding my intimate encounters with elementals, with the dead and with higher beings, and I wanted to give only the briefest hints about the intimately personal initiation experiences I had been having since November 1996.

Then, in March 1998, the three essays about Atlantean oracles finally appeared in *Was in der Anthroposophischen Gesellschaft vorgeht*, the journal for members of the Society, but not in the public section of the weekly *Das Goetheanum* as I had hoped. I had complied with the editors' wishes and told the experiences in story form without any in-depth comments. This led to a great deal of confusion amongst readers regarding my schooling path and my method of research, and consequently many questions were asked and allegations made. My original hope of making contact with other anthroposophists took a turn that I had not envisaged.

Throughout 1998 I had many interesting and fruitful meetings in a number of European countries with people I had not known before. They, too, had had spiritual and karmic experiences, or were undergoing crises as the result of threshold situations. These meetings showed me how important it is to tell others about your spiritual experiences, as well as listening to one another and giving meditative help, not least because you gain direct assistance in your own efforts too. I thought the time had come to have such conversations in public. When I began to go public with my discoveries I met with criticism, reservations and even considerable fear and rejection from many anthroposophists—interestingly enough frequently from those who held positions of responsibility within the Anthroposophical Society. Initially I found this very surprising. But then I noticed that in what I was describing I had not shown sufficiently clearly, in a way that others might follow, what steps I had taken both in my method and in the way I thought through my experiences. The criticism thus helped me to improve the way I was explaining things orally as well as to strive for objective clarity in my essays. But I also investigated the antagonism spiritually and realized that it was possible, too, to understand those negative attitudes both on the basis of karmic causes and of spiritual influences.

My own experiences of the Guardian and of the Threshold, and not solely Rudolf Steiner's descriptions, gave me various insights into the way the spiritual forces of opposition function. Through this I learnt that it is possible to place oneself—with all the soul faculties one has gained through working with karma—within the spiritual situation of the present time. I therefore changed my plans for the way I had intended to write this book and decided to describe a good many of my most intimate spiritual experiences quite openly.

I have written this karmic autobiography out of an awareness that it should be an answer to a spiritual question put to me during meditation. It is intended to be an attempt to link up, in association with the spirit of the age, with the reality of the new mysteries founded by Rudolf Steiner in which one endeavours to make former incarnations of one's own into the starting point for karma research in keeping with spiritual science. I wanted to make this attempt through love for the Being Anthroposophia so that Rudolf Steiner's karma research can be re-founded and further developed.

It is, it seems to me, our task today to unite with the impulse Rudolf Steiner launched at the beginning of the twentieth century not only by studying and thinking about the knowledge but also through thinking and feeling in meditative deeds. If my research is widely rejected or misunderstood—as it has already been on a small scale by a number of prominent anthroposophists—then others will have to search for other ways. This touches on the earnestness with which every sentence in this book has been written.

My hope is that with this book, written in greatest inner honesty, I shall touch the hearts of readers without impinging on their individual freedom, so that at the threshold of a new millennium I can share a little in the creation of a genuine modern spirituality which can arise between human heart and human heart out of love for the truth.

Barbro Karlén

For the past year or two there has been a case that has led to argument about reincarnation as a phenomenon and been discussed a good deal also in anthroposophical circles. I refer to the fact that Barbro Karlén, a Swede, has presented herself publicly as a reincarnation of Anne Frank.* At the stage these discussions have reached up to now I do not really want to take up a position regarding her statements. However, as I have several times been asked to comment on this case during public meetings I do feel obliged to give some sort of open statement as to my attitude towards her.

I have not yet met Barbro Karlén, and the written descriptions and observations by third parties that have so far appeared have not provided me with a genuine point at which I would want to begin examining this phenomenon through spiritual research. Impartially both I and many readers who have not met her have gained a positive picture of what she says, but this does not in itself prove that this case of presumed reincarnation is necessarily true.

---

* B. Karlén *And the Wolves Howled. Fragments of Two Lifetimes*, London: Clairview Books 2000.

In my opinion the important thing is not whether Barbro Karlén was Anne Frank or not, but the fact that she has put herself forward and stated that she was. Those who know or have met her should ask themselves what this might have to do with them. Does it touch a chord in their heart or not? If it does, then they should try and find what karmic path leads them to this person. If it does not, then they should perhaps rather concern themselves with other, more pressing matters of the present time. Actually I think that the way Barbro Karlén has brought her statement into the public domain tells us something about a profound wish in people today to learn about destiny. Conversely, the way anthroposophists have been either critical or euphoric about it points clearly to a lack in their own circles, namely that karma research and knowledge in Rudolf Steiner's sense has not yet been sufficiently taken up there. If it had been, perhaps they would have been able to meet Barbro Karlén in a more brotherly (or sisterly) fashion. It seems to me that for lack of examples amongst themselves, anthroposophists have found in her someone who can soothe the bad conscience they have before the world.

This brings me to some difficult questions which I want to bring up in connection with the way Rudolf Steiner proceeded. Of course we do not know what Steiner did in the soul and spirit realm to help the further development of such individuals as the American President Woodrow Wilson, about whom he spoke to anthroposophists in connection with his karma research (interestingly, in 1924, the year Wilson died). Did Steiner not perhaps take on some responsibility for that individual, which may even have had karmic consequences for him, when he worked at coming to grips with his outlandish ideas, of which we are still seeing the direct consequences today, e.g. in the recent Balkan wars? To take this thought further: Surely anyone who is not able to check on such things through spiritual research should be sparing with opinions about Barbro Karlén so as to maintain a 'human bridge' towards her? If it is thought that a good deal of what she has to say about Anne Frank's life cannot be correct, then this must of course be taken seriously. But should one not refrain from making an absolute judgement, or at least regard such a judgement as tentative? Genuine research should leave the door open for new insights, which might even show why a person has arrived at what turn out to be misinterpretations.

With these remarks about Barbro Karlén—which are of course not intended as comments on her as an individual—I wanted to express that my own case, too, would be best researched and tested through direct confrontation between individuals. A number of persons have passed comments about me which I have heard of through third parties. Whether these are positive or negative, the point is that they are entirely foreign to anthroposophy as such because they lack any soul element relating one heart to another in a way that could build a bridge between us which might lead on into the future. In matters of supersensible experience we should be far more aware of the difference between forming a judgement and entertaining a prejudice.

Knowledge of karma helps bring about an attitude of will that focuses on reality and life and discovers how anthroposophy becomes the living content in human souls. When you begin to recognize yourself and others karmically, the tendency to have negative feelings towards people gradually dwindles and then ceases. But if you do still entertain such feelings you have a much stronger sense of 'evil' spirits working in *yourself* and *not* in the other person. So you then endeavour to find a further path of self-knowledge and spiritual schooling which is individual even while you share it with others. Individual esoteric work becomes social esoteric work. It is in this sense that karma research is in high measure a social impulse. It provides Rudolf Steiner's idea about a threefolded social organism with a new, common ground on which it can grow as a workable ideal in the hearts and minds of all human beings. This is because we discover that without becoming integrated with others we cannot go on living; nor indeed could we have lived in the past without such integration.

'The aim of the anthroposophical movement...'

In several of the lectures he gave on karmic relationships in 1924, Rudolf Steiner spoke about the collaboration between Platonists and Aristotelians which he expected by the end of the century. For example on 18 July 1924 he said:*

> Thus—let me put it this way—in the Anthroposophical Society we have Aristotelianism working on, but in a spiritualized form, and awaiting its further spiritualization. Then, at the end of the twentieth century, many of those who are here today will return, but they will be united, then, with those who were the teachers in the School of Chartres. The aim of the anthroposophical movement is to unite the two elements.

At the end of the same lecture he carved the same attitude of expectation even more clearly into the spiritual sculpture of the souls who were present. Whether they were incarnated in physical bodies at that moment, or whether they heard the words through the mediation of Michael—they would not be able to miss that goal if they were karmically linked with either of those two streams:

> By this I want only to indicate how spiritual movements reach into the immediate present. But what today shines in as it were through tiny windows must in the future become a unity through that connection between the leaders of the School of Chartres and the leading spirits of Scholasticism, when the spiritual revival whereby

---

* *Karmic Relationships Vol.VI*, op. cit.

intellectualism itself is lifted to the spirit, sets in at the end of the twentieth century. To make this possible, let human beings of the twentieth century not throw away their opportunities!

What is the situation regarding missed opportunities now, at the beginning of the twenty-first century? Have we missed finding our task—many thousands of us who were alive in the twentieth century, having been karmically prepared in the best possible way to recognize our own karmic background in order to know where to find the others? Now that the twentieth century has finally reached its end, I think we should pull ourselves together and look back and see in how far we have succeeded or failed to create the expected unity.

It has been my hope to show by this book how, as a representative of the search for that task, I have wrestled and made efforts to tread a path, knowing that the opportunity must not be missed. By awakening our realization that each one of us is placed within this question we can surely, from one moment to the next, banish much pessimism and exhaustion and change them for the good.

Epilogue

To write this book I have had to live and move amongst invisible people and spiritual beings. In writing it I have been able to bring more clarity into some parts and correct certain details as well. Much has had to be omitted either because it could not be fitted into the context or because more research was needed. Other aspects cannot be included because publication would impinge on the freedom of persons close to me or on whose behalf I have done the research.

There is now not much more for me to write. Peace encompasses my tired soul. My fingers are stiff but, thank goodness, not paralysed from all those hours of keyboarding. They are glad they will no longer have to spend day after day tapping away at the small Macintosh lent me by a Swedish friend for this work.

Outside my window mist is descending on the gentle hills of the Saarland, Germany, once cultivated by the Romans. There is much political unrest in the world. If I have understood the news on the radio correctly, more American strikes against Baghdad are expected. Love and trust towards unknown people is not yet a reality in world politics. What would be the consequences for the world at large if the leaders of commerce, politics and culture were to recognize karma as the practical consequence of more than one life on earth? What if they developed the will to seek and find their own former lives? Also: why do so few anthroposophists embark on the relevant exercises which would help them find their own karma?

I look around my small study, lazured in yellow. Before me on my desk is a reproduction of Rembrandt's painting of Matthew the Evangelist. The old man holds a pen in his hand while a young angel whispers into his ear. Do I always know which being is whispering into *my* ear? A propped-up postcard shows the sculpture of the Maitreya of Mirokoku-Bosatsu from the Koryuji Temple in Japan. Are there any bodhisattvas in the world just now, and if so, where? To seek them would be a lofty task. Another postcard shows the head of Nofretete. Is she, perhaps, somewhere on the earth in a new physical form? On piles of letters, essays and proof sheets lies a book on the Hopi Indians, a biography of Mary Queen of Scots, another of Frederick Barbarossa, a novel by Robert Graves about Claudius, and a map of the Atlantic ocean floor. There are still many journeys I want to make in this life to see what specific places are like now.

A small elephant given me by my wife Constanze stands on the printer. On the bookshelves are photos of my children in Sweden whom I do not visit often enough. Beside these is a postcard showing the mosaic in the Angel Chapel on the Odilienberg in the Vosges, a picture of the so-called Agamemnon mask from the Mycene acropolis, and three watercolours of dramatic scenes which I painted in 1989. There is a small pile of photos, including one of Sigrid Mørch-Reiersen taken in 1912, sent to me recently by her daughter. In another pile are *Oedipus Rex* by Sophocles, a small illustrated volume on elephants, a paperback on Rameses II, and the Wartburg document on the Liudolfingers.

Sitting on the shelf are the collected works of Plato, waiting to be read; also several lecture cycles by Rudolf Steiner; a few books on elemental beings; a book on courtly manners; a volume of the *National Geographic Magazine*, and other journals. Another bookcase holds my small history library. It would not be too difficult to assume that all the tales I have told here are nothing but extracts from all this reading matter, with fanciful embellishments added. If this were really the case, well, perhaps the result would still be a saleable story...

All my other books, paintings and artefacts have remained

behind in Järna. On floor and coffee-table lie piles of papers, notes, letters from friends in several countries telling me of their meditative activities. I have replied to many, but others still wait to hear from me. On the radiator is a reproduction of Raphael's *Transfiguration*. I turn over the pages of a book of diary entries by the Czech-Swedish teacher of special needs children, Hans Glaser, *Der Mensch als Gestalter seines eigenen Schicksals*.* In 1954, the year of my birth, he wrote words with which I would like to close this karmic autobiography.

I revive within myself the thought:
Each day holds the chance for a new beginning.

I place all my thoughts and actions
into a space of renunciation:
That space becomes a space of freedom.

In it dwell neither haste nor sloth,
neither fear nor expectation:
Hopefulness, love and humility abide there.

---

* Dornach: Verlag am Goetheanum 1998.

Clairview *publishes books by individuals who are writing out of their own spiritual perception. Bypassing dogma, sectarianism and fixed teaching, each Clairview book is an individual testimony to the reality of life beyond the physical dimension.*

www.clairviewbooks.com

AND THE WOLVES HOWLED
Fragments of two lifetimes
Barbro Karlén
ISBN 1 902636 18 X

LIGHT BEYOND THE DARKNESS
How I healed my suicide son after his death
Doré Deverell
ISBN 1 902636 19 8

A MESSAGE FOR HUMANITY
The Call of God's Angels at a Time of Global Crisis
K. Martin-Kuri
ISBN 1 902636 27 9

MY DESCENT INTO DEATH
and the message of love which brought me back
Howard Storm
ISBN 1 902636 16 3

PSYCHIC WARRIOR
The true story of the CIA's paranormal espionage programme
David Morehouse
ISBN 1 902636 20 1

SEVEN STEPS TO ETERNITY
The true story of one man's journey into the afterlife
as told to 'psychic surgeon' Stephen Turoff
ISBN 1 902636 17 1

WHEN THE STORM COMES
and A MOMENT IN THE BLOSSOM KINGDOM
Barbro Karlén
ISBN 1 902636 23 6

www.clairviewbooks.com